MW01155105

Post Roads & Iron Horses

A Driftless Connecticut Series Book

This book is a 2011 selection in the DRIFTLESS CONNECTICUT SERIES, *for an outstanding book in any field on a Connecticut topic or written by a Connecticut author.*

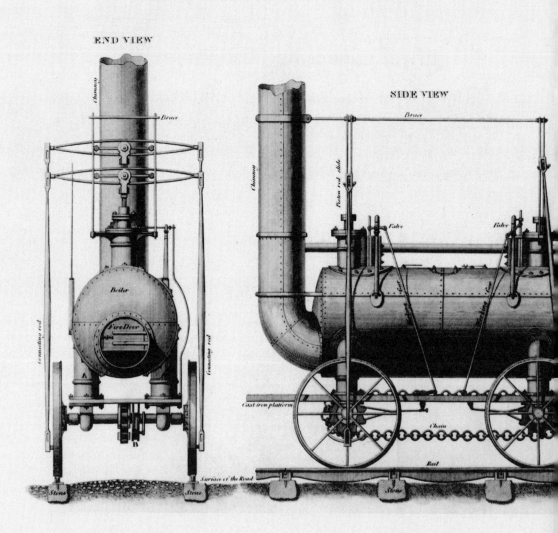

Transportation in
Connecticut from
Colonial Times to
the Age of Steam

Richard DeLuca

Post Roads & Iron Horses

WESLEYAN UNIVERSITY PRESS

Middletown, Connecticut

Wesleyan University Press
Middletown CT 06459
www.wesleyan.edu/wespress
© 2011 Richard DeLuca
All rights reserved
Manufactured in the United States of America
Typeset in Charter and Clarendon by
Keystone Typesetting, Inc.

The Driftless Connecticut Series is funded by the
Beatrice Fox Auerbach Foundation Fund
at the Hartford Foundation for Public Giving.

Library of Congress Cataloging-in-Publication Data
DeLuca, Richard.
Post roads & iron horses : transportation in
Connecticut from colonial times to the age of steam
/ Richard DeLuca.
    p. cm. — (Garnet books) (Driftless Connecticut
    series)
Includes bibliographical references and index.
ISBN 978-0-8195-6856-4 (cloth : alk. paper)
ISBN 978-0-8195-7173-1 (e-book)
1. Transportation—Connecticut—History. I. Title.
II. Title: Post roads and iron horses.
HE213.C6D45 2011
388.09746'0903—dc23
2011019301

5 4 3 2 1

For my mother and father

Olympia Nappi DeLuca

Nicola DeLuca

Contents

ituated on the northern shore of Long Island Sound, Connecticut has always been the gateway to New England, and the land between the major commercial ports of New York and Boston. This book is the first to look in detail at the evolution of the transportation systems that helped to define the history of the state and the region, and to explore how these technological innovations transformed Connecticut from an agricultural colonial settlement to a nineteenth-century industrial powerhouse.

Evidence of Connecticut's multimodal transportation past can be found on road signs around the state: Canal Street in Plainville, Aircraft Road in Southington, Plank Road in Waterbury, Long Wharf Drive in New Haven, Railroad Avenue in Cheshire, Toll Gate Road in Berlin, Old Stagecoach Road in Weston, Trolley Place in Norwalk, and Rope Ferry Street in Niantic. These names (and dozens more like them) reflect specific moments in a long and complex history that spans four centuries and includes different modes of transport. In that time, Connecticut people, including its many inventors, were active participants in the economic and transportation developments occurring in New England and the nation. Thus, the story of Connecticut transportation is central to our understanding of a broader regional and national history.

Transportation history is defined by three major themes: the land, and how it is used; the technology of transport and its evolution; and the law, and how it relates to the financing, construction, and regulation of transportation improvements. While each chapter in this book stands alone as a portrait of a particular time or mode of transport, the importance of the story's three major themes—land, technology, and law—builds from chapter to chapter across the centuries through turnpike, steamboat, canal, railroad, and street railway developments of the nineteenth century to the fall of the New York, New Haven & Hartford Railroad's transportation monopoly on the eve of World War I. The result is a story dominated by private enterprise and the technology of the external combustion steam engine yet complete with a wide range of human actions and emotions: creativity and competition, arrogance and greed, errors in judgment and good intentions gone awry. The result is a unique vision of Connecticut history that emphasizes the importance of transportation to the history of the state as a whole, while providing a new lens through which to evaluate that history. A second book that continues the story of Connecticut transportation in the twentieth century will be forthcoming.

———

Tackling a project of this scope required a lot of help, and I was fortunate to receive more than my fair share from all quarters: from mentors and colleagues, from librarians and research staff, and from the writers of history named in the bibliography whose hard work explored portions of this topic before me. This book could not have been completed without them.

In particular, the author extends heartfelt thanks to the following persons and institutions: Robert Asher, the Association for the Study of Connecticut History, Peter Benes and the Dublin Seminar, the Collections Research Center at Mystic Seaport, Central Connecticut State University, Kit Collier, the Connecticut Department of Transportation, the Connecticut Historical Society Museum, the Connecticut River Museum, the Connecticut State Library, Abbott Cummings, Faith Davison, the Dodd Research Center at the University of Connecticut, the Law Library at Quinnipiac University, the public libraries of Cheshire, Hamden, Wallingford, and Waterbury, David Martineau, Brenda Milkofsky, the New Haven Museum and Historical Society, Cece Saunders, the Shoreline Trolley Museum, Patty and Bruce Stark, Amy Trout, Matt Warshauser, Walt Woodward, Guocun Yang; and to Suzanna Taminen and Parker Smathers at Wesleyan University Press for their patient support of this project. To those whose names have slipped my mind, a heartfelt apology.

Lastly, I would like to acknowledge those for whom no amount of thanks is ever enough: my parents, who provided the moral compass and educational opportunities that continue to give my life meaning; and my wife, Phyllis, whose love makes all things possible.

Transportation is the vital link between a people and the land they inhabit; the means we choose to move ourselves, the resources we require, the goods we produce. By overcoming the limitation of distance, transportation makes possible the myriad of economic and social interactions that allow a community, a people, or an entire culture to thrive. Regardless of the mode considered—whether foot or horseback, ship or rail, automobile or airplane—the land between remains the common denominator of all transportation. It is appropriate, then, that the story of transportation in Connecticut begins with a look at the evolution of the state's physical landscape, for the composition and arrangement of the state's physical features—its valleys and uplands, harbors and river systems—as well as its location in the region impact that story in important ways by influencing the pattern of settlement on the land, the uses to which the land has been put, and the location of major transportation corridors.

The Connecticut Landscape

The physical landscape of Connecticut has been an ever-present influence on the story of the state's transportation developments.

Connecticut is positioned at the southern edge of New England, bound by the states of New York on the west, Massachusetts on the north, Rhode Island on the east, and on the south by the waters of Long Island Sound. As Connecticut has a land area of only five thousand square miles, extending approximately one hundred miles west to east and fifty miles south to north, travel within this state has always been quite manageable, even on foot.

The state's surface features can be divided into six geomorphic regions: a central valley bisected by an extended north-south ridge of exposed trap

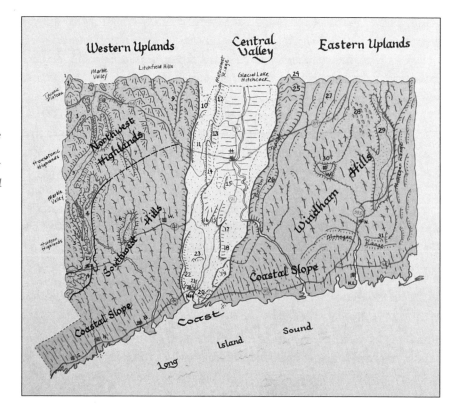

rock; a western uplands region that can be further divided into a region of southwest hills and northwest highlands; a single eastern uplands region called the Windham Hills; and along the state's border with Long Island Sound, a coastal slope that extends west and east of the central valley. Parallel north-south river systems drain the interior of each region: the Housatonic and Naugatuck rivers in the western uplands, the Connecticut River in the central valley, and the Thames, Shetucket, and Quinebaug rivers in the eastern uplands. All these rivers are navigable in their lower reaches.[1]

In contour, this landscape is neither too timid nor too bold in its variations. Within twenty miles of the coast, the land rises to an elevation of five hundred feet and then slopes gently upward from southeast to northwest, reaching heights of one thousand feet in the eastern uplands and two thousand feet in the western uplands. The highest elevation in the state is found at Bear Mountain in Salisbury, at 2,380 feet above sea level.

The natural landscape we see today—its bedrock geology as well as its surface features—is the result of hundreds of millions of years of geologic change that has occurred in three phases: the collision and separation of continents associated with the drifting of the Earth's tectonic plates; the erosion of an ancient mountain range formed as a result of these tectonic collisions; and most recently, a recurring cycle of glaciation associated with a cooling of the Earth's climate. Over the eons these world-shaping geologic processes of continental drift, surface erosion, and repeated glaciation have each contributed to Connecticut's topography. The following overview highlights the influence these processes have had on the settlement of Connecticut and its transportation history.

Some five hundred million years ago, the configuration of Earth's landmasses was quite different than it is today. North America straddled the equator and had a tropical climate, as did portions of what became the European continent. Further south, in the position of Antarctica today, lay the western portion of the African continent. In between was a chain of large islands called Avalonia, in an ancient ocean that geologists have named Iapetos.

Driven by the convection heating of the Earth's inner core, the dozen or so tectonic plates that comprise the Earth's crust and on which continents and ocean floors rest, began to shift position, drifting atop this molten center toward one another. Over the next 250 million years, all of Earth's landmasses drifted together to form one supercontinent called Pangaea. In this collision of tectonic plates, as the land masses of Europe and Africa began closing in on North America, the islands of Avalonia and the crust of the intervening ocean floor were squeezed together and welded to the eastern edge of the North American plate, forming the land mass that is now southern New England. Under the pressure of this collision, exerted inch by inch over 250 million years, the sediment of the Iapetos Ocean was metamorphosed into the hard bedrock that underlies much of Connecticut's western and eastern upland regions. The force of this collision was so great that it raised a range of ancient Appalachian mountains from today's southern United States to Newfoundland that rivaled in height the current Himalayan range.

About two hundred million years ago, the drifting plates changed direction and began to move apart from one another. As Europe and Africa drifted away from North America, a series of rift valleys appeared along the eastern boundary of the North American plate. The easternmost rift became the continental edge along which the Atlantic Ocean opened, while to the west, a second, smaller rift widened to form the Connecticut River valley, New England's central lowland.

As this valley opened, the ongoing erosion of the ancient Appalachian range filled the lowland with sediment, and the evolution of the Connecticut landscape entered its second phase. Over the millennia, this eroded sediment compressed under its own weight to form the soft brownstone rock that underlies Connecticut's central valley. The reddish-brown hue of the rock, a color typically associated with tropical regions, is evidence of the seasonally wet monsoon climate that prevailed in Connecticut at the time. So complete was the erosion that it leveled the ancient five-mile-high mountains. During this period of erosion, lava flows from volcanic fissures on the eastern edge of the valley deposited layers of magma within the sediment. Under compression, this magma was transformed into basaltic trap rock interspersed within the more prevalent sandstone.

Some sixty-five million years ago, a series of gradual uplifts caused surface streams to flow more quickly and to carve their way into the hard bedrock of both the western and eastern uplands. The rivers that formed as a result of this region-wide uplift generally flowed from north to south, creating an undulating terrain of north-south river valleys separated by east-west hills that from the beginning of human occupation made north-south travel in Connecticut easier than transverse travel across the state. Likewise, the hardness of the bedrock in the eastern and western uplands produced narrow, faster flowing rivers that later provided water power for Connecticut's early ironworks and textile mills.

Meanwhile, along the course of the Connecticut River, as sedimentary layers yielded to erosion, a broad central valley was created, divided by a north-south ridge of erosion-resistant trap rock that can be seen today as prominent outcrops above the valley floor. The location of the settlements of Hartford and New Haven on opposite sides of this trap rock ridge made overland travel between these rival capitals of Connecticut particularly difficult until the arrival of the steam locomotive in the nineteenth century.

Most recently, the Connecticut landscape was shaped by the repeated glaciation associated with a cooling of the Earth's climate over the past three million years. In that time, Connecticut was covered by glacial ice at least twice, as ice sheets thousands of feet thick—high enough to bury the highest hills—moved down from Canada to cover all of New England. While such glacial action did not alter the arrangement of Connecticut's geomorphic regions, the force of advancing ice scoured the landscape, shaping hills into elongated drumlins—the sites of future hilltop farming towns—and replacing existing soil with a layer of glacial till, a mixture of clay, sand and broken

Connecticut's geologic history is evident in the many rock cuts visible along the state's highways. Top photo is an example of the metamorphic rock that underlies much of the state's upland regions; bottom photo is an example of the softer sedimentary sandstone in the central valley. (Top photo by Michael Bell and Sidney Quarrier. Courtesy of the Connecticut Department of Environmental Protection; bottom photo by the author.

rock carried beneath the ice. The rock litter left behind by receding glaciers was later gathered into thousands of miles of stone walls by Connecticut's colonial farmers as they cleared the land for planting.

Glacial debris impacted the landscape in other ways as well. In the vicinity of Rocky Hill, glacial material formed a dam that blocked the flow of the Connecticut River for thousands of years. Behind this dam formed a large body of water known as Lake Hitchcock, extending 150 miles from south to north and 20 miles from west to east. The silt and clay sediments deposited in Lake Hitchcock over the millennia helped to create the rich soils of the central valley so coveted by Ninnimissinuwock and European farmers. By contrast, the thin layer of glacial till deposited over the state's uplands made those areas difficult to farm. Not surprisingly, these uplands were the last regions of Connecticut to be settled.

At the western edge of the central valley, glacial debris also blocked the southerly course of the Farmington River, diverting it instead to the north and east and into the Connecticut River at Windsor. An attempt by New Haven businessmen in the 1820s to correct this accident of natural history by building an inland canal through the Farmington valley to the Connecticut River at Northampton, Massachusetts, resulted in one of the most imaginative and competitive efforts in all of Connecticut's transportation history.

Lastly, as the most recent ice sheet melted, the rising level of the sea drowned the state's coastline, creating numerous harbors and inlets, including Connecticut's best natural harbor, the lower Thames basin. At the same time, a large sandbar that marked the southernmost limit of the region's last glacier remained behind to form the landmass of Long Island, which sheltered the Connecticut shore from the heavy weather of the open seas. This drowned coastline ensured that the state's maritime trade would be dispersed among many small ports—as opposed to one or two prominent centers of maritime commerce—while the lack of ready access to the Atlantic contributed to Connecticut's reliance on the ports of New York and Boston for much of its overseas and coastwise trade.[2]

It was into this natural landscape, as the region's most recent glaciers began their retreat, that Connecticut's first human inhabitants migrated some eleven thousand years ago.

Connecticut's First Inhabitants

Southern New England was inhabited for thousands of years by Native American people whose way of life had its own transportation needs.

Evidence suggests that paleo-Indians first entered New England from the west at the end of the last ice age, as nomadic hunters crossed the cold tundra and glacial landscape in search of bison, caribou, woolly mammoth, mastodon, and smaller game animals. The oldest paleo-Indian site uncovered in Connecticut lies on the banks of the Shepaug River in the town of Washington, and has been dated to ten thousand years before the present. Artifacts at the site include a large quantity of stone tools used in hunting, hide-working, processing of plants, and manufacture of ceremonial objects. Samples of deciduous woods found at the site suggest that ground cover and animal species were already becoming more diverse and more modern as the region's climate moderated and the landscape evolved from glacial tundra to mixed-growth forest.[3]

With the changing landscape, native people began living in small tribal groups, each within its own territory, as the roaming lifestyle of the paleo-hunter evolved into that of the localized hunter-gatherer. By around the year 1000, these groups of hunter-gatherers had settled into three distinct ecosystems of the new landscape: the coastal ecosystem, where small bands of Native Americans lived along the region's coastline, relying heavily on the gathering of shellfish and the trapping of all types of larger fish; the riverine ecosystem, where tribal groups inhabited village sites along the region's many inland rivers, combining fishing with the more traditional hunting-gathering lifestyle; and the woodland ecosystem, where more mobile groups in upland areas relied for their sustenance on the hunting of deer, elk, and other game, supplemented by the gathering of seeds, nuts, and berries.[4]

Around 1300, the groups living in the riverine ecosystems of southern New England began to practice horticulture, clearing fields and cultivating plants such as maize, squash, beans, and tobacco as a supplement to their hunting, fishing, and seed-gathering. The practice of horticulture later spread to coastal communities as well, where it was utilized to a lesser extent. As food production increased, so did the population of native people, from about 25,000 paleo-hunters in all of New England to perhaps 120,000 hunter-gatherer-horticulturalists by the onset of the historic period. Eighty percent of this population likely lived in southern New England, with the densest concentrations along the coastal portions of Connecticut, Rhode Island, and Massachusetts.[5]

The larger tribal groups of southern New England were the Pokanoket and Pawtucket of eastern Massachusetts, the Narragansett of western Rhode Island, and the Mohegan and Pequot of southeastern Connecticut. Other groups included the Neepmuck of central Massachusetts and northwestern Connecticut, the Wampanoag of eastern Rhode Island, the Pocumtuck of Agawam, the Podunk and Sequin of Hartford, the Hammonosett of the lower Connecticut River, the Quinnipiac of New Haven, and the Paugussett of southwestern Connecticut. These groups all shared a linguistic and cultural heritage that we call Algonkian. The name they used to refer to themselves was Ninnimissinuwock, which meant simply: "the people."[6]

As in all cultures, transportation played an important role in the day-to-day life of the Ninnimissinuwock—first, as part of a lifestyle that required tribal groups to move among several sites within their territory as the seasonal resources they required became available. As salmon spawned, huckleberry bushes bloomed, and deer foraged, native people moved to the vicinity of the resource rather than transporting the harvest to a central village site. In addition, travel to and from the territories of nearby groups was customary for purposes of trade, and for ritual meetings between tribal sachems, whose reciprocal visits and kinship intermarriages helped maintain the social order among tribal groups.

Overland travel occurred along a network of well-worn footpaths, many no wider than a single person. Foot travel was eased considerably by the native custom of burning away the forest underbrush each year to increase the production of edible plants and seeds. Travel over open ground was also aided by the wearing of moccasins made of animal hide, and along snow-covered trails in winter by snowshoes made from the upper branches of saplings.[7]

The meandering character and the narrowness of Ninnimissinuwock trails made them of little long-term use to European colonists. However, many native footpaths delineated travel corridors that are important to this day, including the Bay Path, from Hartford to Boston via Springfield, Massachusetts; the Connecticut Path, from Hartford to Boston via Manchester and Woodstock; and the Shore Path, from New York to Boston along the northern edge of Long Island Sound. Likewise, the Paugussett Path from Norwalk to Canaan in the west, the Quinnipiac Trail from New Haven to Farmington

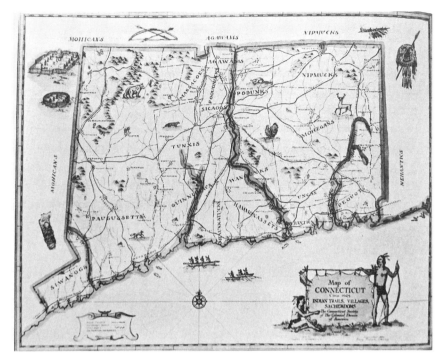

Indian trails, c. 1625. (Map Collection, Connecticut State Library)

in central Connecticut, and the Mohegan Trail from Montville to Woodstock in the east all still define important north-south transportation routes.[8]

For travel on rivers and through coastal waters, the dugout canoe was the primary mode of transportation. Typically twenty feet in length and made of pine, oak, or chestnut, a dugout canoe was crafted by burning the center of a fallen tree trunk and hollowing out the charcoal using clam shell tools and stone adzes. Coastal tribes used larger dugout canoes for fishing on Long Island Sound, where Ninnimissinuwock men used harpoons and hooks to catch deepwater fish. Such large canoes were up to forty feet in length and carried a dozen men or more. Smaller canoes made of birch or elm bark sewn together and sealed with pine pitch were also used, though these were seldom seen south of Massachusetts Bay. The Ninnimissinuwock also constructed timber rafts, which they used to cross larger rivers and coastal bays.[9]

Intertribal trade took place along the region's water and trail network in leapfrog fashion, with each tribal group trading only with its nearest neighbors. In this way, copper from the Great Lakes, shells from the mid-Atlantic coast, and stone tools from the Susquehanna region found their way to riverine villages on the lower Connecticut River. Likewise, wampum beads—a valued luxury made of certain shellfish found only in the coastal areas of southern New England—made their way to tribes in northern Maine. It is likely that the Ninnimissinuwock's knowledge of horticulture originated among the Native Americans of the Mississippi Valley and traveled east to southern New England via just such a trading network.[10]

In sum, at the onset of the historic period, the Ninnimissinuwock fully inhabited the land we now know as southern New England and had done so for thousands of years, living through the cycle of the seasons in a loose affiliation of small tribal groups whose means of transportation reflected the lifestyle they lived and the landscape on which they relied for their existence.

European Contact

Contact with European traders and settlers in the seventeenth century extinguished Native American culture throughout New England through the spread of disease and warfare.

In the first years of the sixteenth century, as their more traditional fishing grounds were depleted, European fishermen arrived in the New World to fish the waters near Newfoundland, Labrador, and Nova Scotia. Initially, contact with native inhabitants was minimal, but when the fishermen realized that they could augment their fishing profits by trading with Native Americans for furs, contact spread inland along the Saint Lawrence River and south along the coast of Maine. By the century's end, trading for the furs of seals, otters, beavers, foxes, martens, raccoons, and minks had become a major activity for European sailors, and a rivalry among England, France, and Holland over fur trading in the New World had developed into a source of conflict that continued into the colonial period.

Through their intermingling in the fur trade, Europeans introduced several diseases into the indigenous population for which Ninnimissinuwock people had no in-bred resistance, including measles, smallpox, typhus, and perhaps syphilis. As a result, illness spread rapidly in epidemic proportion among the groups that became infected, with a mortality rate of 80 percent or more not uncommon. Those Ninnimissinuwock who fled inland often took the contagion with them, further spreading the disease.[11]

In 1616, an especially virulent outbreak killed thousands of indigenous people living along the coast of New England, from the Penobscot River in Maine south to Cape Cod, drastically reducing the population in that area.

Within two years, news of the epidemic reached the English Puritans, who set sail for the New World with plans to establish a settlement at Plymouth Plantation "where there is a great deale of Land cleared, and hath beene planted with Corne three or foure yeares agoe."[12] As English colonization proceeded, as many as fifty New England towns were founded on the sites of Ninnimissinuwock villages that had been abandoned due to epidemic illness.

The death of large numbers of native inhabitants through the spread of disease not only provided colonists with land already cleared for settlement; it minimized the threat of native resistance. To the settlers, the effect of various contagions on the Ninnimissinuwock people served to sanction the divine mission of the English, as the governor of Massachusetts Bay, John Winthrop, made clear: "in sweeping away great multitudes of the natives . . . that he might make room for us there . . . God hath thereby cleared our title to this place."[13] From the viewpoint of the native people, however, the impact of such contact diseases was nothing less than a human tragedy that threatened their very survival as a culture. The extraordinarily high death toll made it impossible for survivors to maintain their accustomed lifestyle, which in turn upset the social order within individual tribal groups, as well as the balance of power among groups throughout the coastal region of Massachusetts.

In the European settlement of Connecticut, circumstances were similar. In 1614, the Dutch explorer Adriaen Block made first contact with the Ninnimissinuwock along the Connecticut River, after which Dutch traders from New Amsterdam (New York) established trading posts at Saybrook Point (1620) and Hartford (1633). This Dutch incursion was challenged by the English of Plymouth Plantation, who then established their own trading house at Windsor (1633). The following winter, several Dutch traders from Hartford attempted to outmaneuver their English rivals for the upriver fur trade by visiting a large tribe of Ninnimissinuwock living along the Connecticut River somewhere north of Windsor. William Bradford, governor of Plymouth colony, described the tragic results:

3. or 4. Dutch men went up in ye beginning of winter to live with them, to gett their trade, and prevent them for bringing it to ye English, or to fall into amitie with them; but at spring to bring all downe to their place. But their enterprise failed, for it pleased God to visite these Indeans with a great sicknes, and such a mortalitie that of a 1000. above 900. and a halfe of them dyed, and many of them did rott above ground for want of

buriall, and ye Dutch men allmost starved before they could gett away, for ise and snow.[14]

Reaching the English settlement at Windsor, the Dutch traders were fed and sheltered until they regained their health, after which they were allowed to return to their own trading post at Hartford. That spring, an outbreak of smallpox occurred among the Ninnimissinuwock who lived in the vicinity of Windsor. Bradford describes the ferocity of the disease in detail:

> those Indeans that lived aboute their trading house there fell sick of ye small poxe, and dyed most miserably; for a sorer disease cannot befall them; they fear it more than ye plague; for usualy they that have this disease have them in abundance, and for want of bedding & lining and other helps, they fall into a lamentable condition, as they lye on their hard matts, ye pox breaking and mattering, and runing one into another, their skin cleaving (by reason thereof) to the matts they lye on; when they turne them, a whole side will flea of at once, (as it were,) and they will be all of a gore blood, most fearfull to behold; and then being very sore, what with could and other distempers, they dye like rotten sheep.[15]

The year after this pox epidemic, English colonists traveled overland from Massachusetts to establish the first permanent European settlements in the Connecticut River valley at Windsor, Hartford, and Wethersfield. Evidence suggests that Connecticut's first settlers traveled from Massachusetts via the Bay Path, heading west from Boston to the Connecticut River near Springfield, Massachusetts, and then south on the east side of the river to Windsor, where they likely crossed the river on a raft. Within a few years, these three settlements totaled eight hundred persons, a formidable presence when compared to the number of surviving Ninnimissinuwock in the area.[16]

Additional English settlements followed along the shore of Long Island Sound at Saybrook (1635), New Haven (1638), Guilford (1639), Milford (1639), New London (1645), and Stonington (1649). By the time the Great Migration of Puritan emigrants to the New World had come to an end, two thousand English men, women, and children had been transplanted to Connecticut. From these initial settlements came the founders of English towns at Fairfield and Stratford (1639), Farmington (1640), Middletown (1651), Norwich (1659), Lyme (1665), and Wallingford (1670).

In 1662, the land containing these settlements was chartered by Charles II as a self-governing body corporate and politic, separate from the Massachusetts colony, and known as the English Colony of Connecticut in New England. Unable to obtain a separate charter, New Haven and its offshoot towns, which were founded as a separate colony by Englishmen with more mercantile interests, chose to merge with the Connecticut colony as a means of securing the right to their lands under English law. The merger was a reluctant one on the part of the New Haven colony and marked the beginning of a long rivalry between New Haven and Hartford, which remained dual seats of government for the colony and state of Connecticut for more than two centuries.

The influx of English settlers led to the withdrawal of the Dutch from Connecticut, and eventually to armed resistance from the Ninnimissinuwock people, beginning with the Pequot, who were defeated by the colonists in the Pequot War of 1637. Later, native groups near Springfield, Massachusetts, led by the sachem Metacomet (King Philip), were defeated in King Philip's War of 1675. By that time, disease and warfare had reduced the total number of Ninnimissinuwock in southern New England to 10 percent of their precontact population, and the threat of reprisals to English settlements in Connecticut had been all but eliminated.

A New Culture on the Land

In using the land's natural resources to provide for an increasing population, Native American and European cultures differed radically in their worldviews.

The European settlement of Connecticut brought with it a culture radically different from that of its first inhabitants. In place of the seminomadic lifestyle of the hunter-gatherer-horticulturalist, the English transplanted to America a sedentary lifestyle of family agriculture, supplemented by the raising of domesticated farm animals. As a result, the landscape was altered dramatically, as first-growth forests were cleared for timber, cleared fields were fenced in and put to the plow, and cattle, pigs, and other nonindigenous animals were set to graze in open pastures. The plants and animals imported from Europe, and the methods used to cultivate them, quickly overran the native landscape, altering not only its appearance but centuries-old biotic relationships as well. The European settlement of Connecticut was an ecological as well as a cultural event.

The ultimate concern of the Ninnimissinuwock and the transplanted English people were one and the same: to feed and shelter a growing population using the resources at hand. The methods used by each culture to accomplish that goal, however, could not have been more different. As early as 1642, the Narragansett sachem Miantonomo expressed his disbelief toward the English way of living on the land, and his words suggest the mighty divide between the Native American and European views of the natural world:

> You know, our fathers had plenty of deer and skins, our plains were full of deer, as also our woods, and of turkies, and our coves full of fish and fowl. But these English having gotten our land, they with scythes cut down the grass, and with axes fell the trees; their cows and horses eat the grass, and their hogs spoil our clam banks, and we shall all be starved.[17]

The English, too, were aware of the difference. Some men, such as John Winthrop, recognized the natural right of the Ninnimissinuwock to the land. But to the English mind, such natural rights were superseded by the right of individual ownership that had accompanied the rise of farming and agriculture in Europe. "As for the Natives in New England," Winthrop wrote, "they inclose noe Land, neither have they any setled habytation, nor any tame Cattle to improve the Land by, and soe have noe other but a Naturall Right to those Countries."[18] To English eyes, a landscape that appeared to be largely unoccupied and vastly underutilized was available for the taking. As the Puritan minister John Cotton proclaimed: "In a vacant soyle, hee that taketh possession of it, and bestoweth culture and husbandry upon it, his Right it is."[19] With a psychological divide between the two cultures as wide as the ocean that had once separated them, the possibility that the surviving Ninnimissinuwock could maintain their traditional way of life alongside the new European culture all but vanished.

The true impact of the European colonization of Connecticut proved to be ongoing and far greater than either Native Americans or English colonists could have imagined at the time, with cultural and ecological ramifications that haunt us to this day. The roothold of the dozens of English farming communities in Connecticut was only the first of many tidal waves of change to wash over the landscape as the centuries unfolded. From agricultural colony to industrial state, rural village to company town, urban city to sprawling suburb, each new wave of change altered the Connecticut landscape beyond the beliefs of generations past. Meanwhile, the forces of European technology and culture, and the ever-increasing number of people they helped to sustain, played themselves out on the land. The story that follows relates the four centuries of change that have flowed thus far from those first English settlements, as it is reflected in the evolution of Connecticut's transportation modes, policy, and industry.

Chapter One Colonial Connecticut

With the growth of the Connecticut colony in the seventeenth century, a network of local, intertown, and intercolony roads developed, poor though they were, and the first ferry and bridge crossings appeared. Since most towns did not set land aside for roads, the laying out of roads was a troublesome process. Likewise, since these early agricultural communities were largely self-sufficient, intertown roads were often reluctantly built and poorly maintained. With the establishment of the Post Road from New York to Boston in the 1690s, communication improved along three post routes through Connecticut, which together became the backbone of intertown transportation in and through the colony. The eighteenth century brought increased travel, and the construction of additional roads, ferries, and bridges, as Connecticut moved away from its Puritan roots and toward a secular society in which small-scale manufacturing and market capitalism were on the rise.

Settlement of the Connecticut Colony

The pattern of settlement and the process of town founding, along with the colony's geographic position in southern New England, were strong influences on the evolution of transportation in colonial Connecticut.

During the first 140 years of English colonization, the land was brought under English control and governance in three phases. Settlers and their offspring moved first into the fertile lands of the central valley and coastal slopes, then inland across the eastern highlands and southwestern hills, and lastly into the colony's northwest hills, until all the land within the bounds of Connecticut was in English hands. Given the importance of agriculture to the early colonists, the first regions settled contained the colony's best farmland, while subsequent phases of settlement corresponded to geomorphic regions of decreasing agricultural productivity.

The first phase of settlement began in the 1630s and extended to the conclusion of King Philip's War in 1675. In this phase, towns were established throughout the central valley, along the coast of Long Island Sound west and east of New Haven, and within the lower reaches of the Connecticut, Housatonic, and Thames river valleys. A total of twenty-five towns were founded in this period, each containing some of the most arable farmland within the colony. So thorough was the search for good farmland that colonists in this first phase discovered and settled the secluded Pomperaug Valley of Woodbury, an area within the southwest hills whose soil, by geologic happenstance, was as productive as that of the Connecticut River valley. By 1680, Connecticut colonists reported to their superiors in England: "Most land that is fit for planting is taken up. What remains must be subdued, and gained out of the fire as it were by hard blows and for small recompense."[1]

Because travel by ship was the principal means of transportation for the early colonists, most of these first settlements were readily accessible by water. Indeed, the original settlement of river towns such as Hartford and New London included land on both sides of the Connecticut and Thames rivers respectively, thereby incorporating the waterway directly into the community.

The second phase of settlement lasted from 1686 to 1734, during which time twenty-eight new towns were founded. Here, colonists moved into the Windham Hills of the eastern uplands and, to a lesser degree, the southwest hills of the western uplands, with all but seven of the new towns being founded east of the Connecticut River. The defeat of the Ninnimissinuwocks in King Phillip's War allowed settlers to occupy these two upland regions without fear of reprisal.

During the third phase of settlement, from 1737 to 1761, the northwest hills—where topsoil was thinnest—were settled, with the founding of fifteen new towns. The established towns of Suffield, Enfield, Somers, and Woodstock, which had been settled as part of Massachusetts, were placed under Connecticut jurisdiction, thereby rounding out the colony's borders. From this point forward, all new towns in the colony (and state) of Connecticut would be carved from the landholdings of these seventy-two original English settlements.[2]

The impetus behind the founding of new towns was population growth. Following the arrival of the first settlers during the Great Migration of 1630–42, Connecticut's population grew almost exclusively through natural in

Phases of Settlement

Phase One: 1635–75		Phase Two: 1686–1734		Phase Three: 1737–61	
Town	*Incorporated*	*Town*	*Incorporated*	*Town*	*Incorporated*
Windsor	1635	Waterbury	1686	Harwinton	1737
Hartford	1635	Danbury	1687	New Hartford	1738
Saybrook	1635	Preston	1687	Goshen	1739
Wethersfield	1636	Windham	1692	Canaan	1739
New Haven	1638	Glastonbury	1693	Kent	1739
Guilford	1639	Colchester	1698	Sharon	1739
Milford	1639	Plainfield	1699	Torrington	1740
Stratford	1639	Lebanon	1700	Cornwall	1740
Fairfield	1639	Mansfield	1702	New Fairfield	1740
Greenwich	1640	Canterbury	1703	Salisbury	1741
Stamford	1641	Durham	1704	Woodstock	1749*
Farmington	1645	Groton	1705	Somers	1749*
New London	1646	Ridgefield	1708	Enfield	1749*
Stonington	1649	Hebron	1708	Suffield	1749*
Middletown	1651	Killingly	1708	Norfolk	1758
Norwalk	1651	Newtown	1711	Hartland	1761
Branford	1653	New Milford	1712	Winchester	**
Norwich	1659	Coventry	1712	Barkhamsted	**
Lyme	1667	Pomfret	1713	Colebrook	**
Killingworth	1667	Ashford	1714		
Haddam	1668	Tolland	1715		
Simsbury	1670	Litchfield	1719		
Wallingford	1673	Stafford	1719		
Woodbury	1673	Bolton	1720		
Derby	1675	Voluntown	1721		
		Willington	1727		
		East Haddam	1734		
		Union	1734		

* Originally settled as part of Massachusetts.
** Settled by 1761 but not incorporated until later.
Source: Bruce C. Daniels, *The Connecticut Town: Growth and Development 1635–1790* (Middletown, Conn.: Wesleyan University Press, 1979).

crease. Growth was rapid, and large family size was the norm, with families of eight or more children not uncommon. What was a fledgling colony of four thousand English souls in 1650 reached a population of twenty-six thousand by 1700. By the time the third phase of settlement came to a close, the population of the Connecticut colony exceeded 150,000 persons.[3]

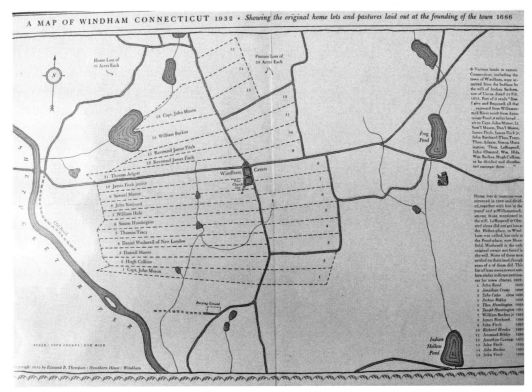

A MAP OF WINDHAM CONNECTICUT 1932 · *Showing the original home lots and pastures laid out at the founding of the town 1686*

Windham town plan, 1686. The original layout of many colonial towns made local roads difficult to construct, especially once outlying areas became populated. (Map Collection, Connecticut State Library)

Under its charter of 1662, the governance of Connecticut was directed by a General Court (later called General Assembly) that consisted of the colony's governor, a governor's council of twelve magistrates, and two deputy representatives from each town. Any action of the General Court, from town founding and tax collection to the establishment of roads and ferries, required the majority approval of both the magistrates and the deputies. A Court of Assistants (later called the Superior Court) composed of the governor or deputy governor and four designated magistrates, conducted the judicial business of the colony, since Connecticut's colonial charter did not provide for a separation of powers.

Following the merger of the New Haven and Connecticut colonies, the General Court created Connecticut's first four counties in 1666, with county seats in Hartford, New Haven, Fairfield, and New London. Each county had its own court, where certain judicial matters, including road-building disputes, were handled at an intermediate level. As settlement spread to the eastern and western hills, additional counties were established at Windham (1726), Litchfield (1751), Tolland (1785), and Middlesex (1785).

Rounding out a trilevel system of colonial government was a variety of locally elected officials who ran the affairs of each town. These officials included a board of selectmen who managed town affairs; a lister, to compile a record of the taxable property in each town; one or more constables to collect the taxes, and monitor mischief; and one or more surveyors to oversee the construction and maintenance of roads and bridges within each town.

While the general and county courts provided a combination of executive, legislative, and judicial guidance for the colony—from authorizing the incorporation of new towns to passing the laws of the colony and adjudicating disputes between towns—it was the individual towns, and the men who ran them, who were charged with executing and financing the responsibilities passed on to them by the general and county courts. Guiding each level of colonial governance in its various functions was the tradition of English law that the settlers brought with them from their old world to the new.[4]

With regard to transportation matters, the General Court's policy of town founding strongly influenced the colony's transportation infrastructure. The establishment of separate towns, each with its own civil authority, was a natural response to the demand for new lands to settle, but the result was a patchwork of numerous communities, of more or less equal size, spread out over the landscape, with most town centers having no more than eight miles between them.[5] This pattern of multiple population centers required a larger network of intertown roads relative to the land area of the colony than might otherwise have been the case. Together with the colony's surface topography, this pattern of multiple population centers, imposed on the land by the General Court, remained an important influence on the development of transportation routes within Connecticut throughout the colonial period.

Early Roads, Ferries, and Bridges

By 1700, a crude yet adequate network of roads, ferries, and bridges had appeared in the Connecticut colony.

TOWN WAYS AND COUNTRY ROADS

There were two main types of roadways in the Connecticut colony: town ways, or roads that led to various locations within a given town, and country ways, or roads that connected each town to neighboring settlements. Town ways were further subdivided into two kinds: public town ways that were of benefit to the entire community, such as the road to the local gristmill or sawmill; and private town ways that were of benefit to an individual land-owner, such as a road to a farmer's pasture or woodland. Since early Connecticut towns were founded with little consideration for growth, and with no land set aside for roadways of any type, the laying out of early colonial roads was often a cumbersome process.

A request for the construction of a public town way was typically discussed in an open town meeting. If the town's selectmen decided that the road petitioned for was necessary, a committee was appointed to lay out its route, after which compensation was set for those whose land would be taken, with the understanding that the affected landowners could appeal the damage payment to the county court if they thought it unjust. If the request for a public town way was denied, the petitioner could appeal the decision to the county court, and ultimately to the General Court of the colony.[6]

Providing for private town ways, which were numerous in an agricultural community, was more troublesome. Most early towns were founded as Puritan villages, with a central green and church and a wide main street, along which were situated home lots for the community's founding members. Beyond this residential core were farmlands, grazing pastures, and woodlands, portions of which were assigned to every household. Within this configuration, private town ways were laid out under the direction of the town selectmen so as to allow each family access to their outlands while causing minimal impact to the property of other inhabitants.

As a town's population increased and home lots for new residents were established farther from the center of town, providing convenient access for these newer residents to their outlands, which were often some distance away, became increasingly difficult. In 1678, when a number of Guilford farmers found their fields landlocked by the property of others, the town appointed a committee to resolve the problem by mapping out an improved road system for the entire town. In many communities, however, the resolution of a private town way problem was often not as harmonious, with petitions and counterpetitions being debated for months.[7]

By the early eighteenth century, as land speculators began to exert an influence over the founding of new communities, the layout of new towns began to change. Eager for a quick return on their investment, speculators laid out an entire town at one time, incorporating two or more public town ways within their design. The size of home lots was also increased to ten acres or more, thereby bringing pasture and woodland within the boundaries of each home property. The result was a more dispersed community of family farms that eliminated many of the difficulties associated with the laying out of private town ways in earlier communities. This new concept of land division continued into the third phase of settlement.[8]

For most of the colonial period, the private town way problem remained a local issue, with a town's board of selectmen being the final arbiters of the peace. In 1773, however, the laws of the colony were amended to allow dissatisfied petitioners to appeal a town's decision concerning a private way to the county court, which then had the power to reverse that decision, lay out the road as it saw fit, and allocate the expense of construction to the individual who was to benefit from the road. The petitioner could then pay the assigned cost in either money or land.[9]

The construction of country ways between towns was particularly problematic. Because Connecticut towns were to a great extent self-sufficient, providing adequate roads from town to town was of little interest to many communities. When a need became apparent for a country way between an inland town and a coastal port, for example, intervening towns usually resented the clearing and maintaining of a road through their community for which they might have little need. As a result, the clearing of intertown roads was frequently accomplished only after an order from the General Court. As with other roads, the laying out of country ways was originally a town responsibility, but as neglect and a lack of cooperation between towns became the norm, in 1702 the job of laying out country roads was given to the county court. The General Court decided the location of country ways that crossed from one county into another.[10]

The first country way to be mentioned in the records of the Connecticut colony was a road between Hartford and Windsor that the General Court ordered built in 1638. Through the early years of the colony, other country ways were initiated by the General Court between Hartford and New Haven; Hartford and Waterbury via Farmington; Hartford and Simsbury; Woodbury and Stratford; and Norwich and New London. In this way, despite the difficulties involved, a network of crude highways connecting newer towns with more established communities evolved, slowly but surely, as the colony expanded.[11]

Road building in the colony was accomplished through the English system of statute labor, under which every man aged sixteen to sixty and his team of horses or oxen were required to labor one day each year on the roads in his town. Within each town, roadwork was supervised by one or more town-appointed surveyors, who were responsible for the participation of the men in their district. The work was compulsory; neither laborer nor overseer was paid for his efforts, and both were subject to a fine for failing to perform their duties. Likewise, the General Court could fine any town that neglected its road-building obligations.

The use of statute labor first appeared in the laws of Connecticut in 1643, and was revised periodically thereafter to require additional days of service under increasing penalties for noncompliance. As time went on, exemptions from roadwork were given to magistrates, selectmen, ministers, physicians, and others. To replenish the labor supply, the law was revised in 1750 to include Native Americans, mulattoes, and slaves among those subject to compulsory road service. Men who were able to buy their way out of their service by paying the appropriate fines did so, and the money was used to hire other workers in their place. Despite the efforts of the General Court to require adequate road-building in the colony, most men saw compulsory road work as a burden most of the time, and this attitude was reflected in the poor quality of the work performed. Still, compulsory statute labor remained the backbone of Connecticut road-building and maintenance throughout the colonial period.[12]

Given the limitations of manual labor and homemade tools, the alignment of many roadways was chosen so as to avoid physical obstacles where possible, as the following remark in the town records of Cheshire indicates: "all difficulties about rocks, swamps and other impediments the surveyors and sizers shall have power to regulate by turning the highways a little out of a straight course as convenient."[13] Road construction usually amounted to little more than clear cutting a right-of-way of moderate width through forest and brush. If a marshy section proved too big to avoid, whole logs might be laid perpendicular to the direction of travel, with sand spread beneath and on top of the logs to create a travel surface through the muck. Such travelways were termed corduroy roads for their resemblance to the ribbed fabric, and not only made for a bumpy wagon ride but also presented a serious hazard to horses from the shifting of the logs.[14]

Once a road was established, maintenance was never-ending, and involved the repeated repair of ruts and mires caused by rain and ice, the twin enemies of all New England roadways. Given these facts of colonial road

Corduroy road, Fairfield. Archeological evidence suggests that this timber road, built about 1750, provided access from the center of Fairfield to a gristmill located at the mouth of Ash Creek. (Cece Saunders. Courtesy of the Connecticut Historical Commission)

building, it should be no surprise that travel by sleigh after a heavy winter snowfall often provided colonists with the best travel conditions of the year.

FERRIES AND BRIDGES

Ferries have existed in Connecticut from the earliest days of the colony, many rivers and streams being too wide to cross by any other means. Ferries were also utilized at crossings where bridges, though feasible, were too costly to construct. Unlike the construction of a bridge, whose capital cost was a drain on a town's treasury, a ferry was a low-cost alternative whose revenue income became an asset to the community. With Connecticut's drowned coastline and multiple river systems, ferry crossings became a fact of life for the colonial traveler, especially in the southern and eastern portions of the colony.

One of the earliest ferries in Connecticut was authorized by the General Court in 1641 to cross the Connecticut River at Windsor. Known as Bissell's ferry for the family that ran it, it may not have come into operation until as late as 1648. The crossing connected the two halves of the town of Windsor. On the east side, the ferry landed at East Windsor Hill, where it met the Bay Path for travel north to Springfield, Massachusetts. A second ferry was authorized by the General Court of the New Haven colony in June 1645 to cross New Haven's East (Quinnipiac) River. In addition to collecting a toll from each passenger—the amount of which decreased as the number of passengers carried per crossing increased—the operator of this ferry was also given several acres of land in a nearby oyster shell field for providing the service.[15]

As settlement continued, additional ferries appeared. By 1700, there were nine major ferry crossings in the colony: on the Connecticut River at Windsor, Hartford, Wethersfield, Haddam, and Saybrook; on the Housatonic River at Stratford; on the Quinnipiac River at New Haven; and on the Thames River at New London and Norwich. Ferries were also established across the Saugatuck and Niantic rivers; these crossings were considered among the more hazardous in the colony.[16]

The technology utilized by early Connecticut ferries varied from crossing to crossing. Most were scow-type, flat-bottomed boats that were either poled, rowed, or sailed across the water, or in the case of the Niantic ferry, pulled across using a rope line that spanned the river. The most ingenious crossing was at Windsor. Here a scow was attached to a cable-pulley system that was stretched across the river and firmly anchored to each shore, with the cable running through a pulley on the side of the ferry scow. After shoving off, the ferryman turned the boat at an angle to the current of the river, whose force moved the boat along the cable line much the way a sailboat tacks into the wind. On the return crossing, the angle of the boat to the flow of the water was simply reversed. Cadwell's Ferry in Hartford, when first established, also made use of a cable and pulley system.[17]

The right to operate a given ferry was granted by the General Court (or the town) as an exclusive privilege, which carried with it the responsibility to provide the service for a specified length of time, usually seven or ten years. In return, the operator was assured that no other ferry would be allowed in the vicinity of his crossing. As late as 1755, the court denied a petition for a ferry across the Connecticut River above Windsor because of its proximity to the existing Bissell ferry.[18] The granting of such exclusive privilege was considered necessary to entice a ferryman to assume the cost and

Bissell's Ferry, c. 1900, from George E. Wright, Crossing the Connecticut *(1908).*

responsibility of providing what was a public service. Exclusive privilege remained a legal principle utilized by the General Court throughout the colonial period.

The fare schedule for each ferry was set by the General Court when the ferry was first established, and toll rates depended on the nature of the crossing. Tolls were highest across the colony's two widest crossings, the Thames River at New London and the Connecticut River at Saybrook—where a further surcharge was allowed for a winter crossing. In 1702, the court issued its first general law concerning ferries, which required all ferrymen to provide "good tight boats sufficient both for largeness, strength, and steadiness for the safe transportation of travelers and their horses and supplied with oars and other implements and men who are discreet, strong and skilled in rowing." The statute was revised periodically during the eighteenth century.[19]

One of Connecticut's earliest bridges was authorized by the General Court in 1640, when it ordered "a strong sufficient cartt Bridge" to be built over the Little River in Hartford. The structure was to be "twelve footte wide bettwene the Rayles with Turned Ballesters over the Top." The next year the General Court of the New Haven colony ordered two cart bridges to be built "as speedly as may bee" over the West and Mill rivers in New Haven. Other bridges built during the early years of the colony included a cart bridge twelve feet in width over the East River in Guilford (1648); a bridge along the country road from Hartford to Farmington (1648); a great bridge in Hartford raised by statute labor (1651); two bridges in Hockanum also built by statute labor (1663); a horse bridge over the Norwalk River built by Norwalk residents on order of the General Court (1680); a bridge over the Manucketesuck River on the road from Saybrook to Killingworth built by the inhabitants of the towns through which the river flowed (1680); and a cart bridge between Wallingford and New Haven, the cost to be shared by the two towns in proportion to their grand lists (1692).[20]

Most early bridges were built using a simple timber structure known as a king post truss, first developed in medieval Europe. With stone abutments set against each shoreline, two hewn logs were placed across the span as stringers, and then a floor of planks was set atop the stringers parallel to the river. Each stringer was kept from sagging under its load by placing a center post at midspan. A diagonal member was then attached to each end of the bridge. For stability, a timber was sometimes also erected over the roadway to connect the center posts on either side of the bridge. Since the king post truss was similar to the truss work used in a house or barn roof, this basic bridge design was familiar to most village carpenters. For longer spans, a rectangular center section was inserted between the two diagonals of a king post design, thereby creating a queen post truss. King and queen post designs could be applied to spans of up to forty feet, which together with their ease of construction made them popular for bridges over small rivers and streams.[21]

THE KING'S BEST HIGHWAY

From the first years of settlement, travel between the English colonies in North America was prompted by the need for the sharing of information among government officials. As early as May 1638, the English colonies of New England petitioned King Charles I for the authority to establish a postal service in the new world, but their request was denied. By 1659, however, correspondence between Governor John Winthrop of Connecticut and officials in Massachusetts indicated that a makeshift postal service existed at that time that relied on trusted emissaries who were willing to "adventure through the wilderness" on the weeklong, one-way journey. But it was not until after the restoration of King Charles II in 1660 and the fall of New Amsterdam (New York) to the English in 1664 that the new governor of New York, Francis Lovelace, was instructed by Charles II to improve communication among the English colonies, in particular between New York and the colonies of New England. To this end, Lovelace and Governor Winthrop agreed to establish a regular post service between New York and Boston via New Haven and Hartford, "consonant to the commands of His sacred Majestie, who strictly injoins all his American subjects to enter into a close correspondency with each other."

Lovelace dispatched the first post rider to Hartford in December 1672 with a letter outlining details of the new post service:

> This person that has undertaken the imployment I conceaved most proper, being both active, stout and indefatigable. He is sworne as to his fidelity. I have affixt an annuall sallery on him, which, together with the advantage of his letters and other small portable packes, may afford him a handsome livelyhood. Hartford is the first stage I have designed him to change his horse, where constantly I expect he should have a fresh one lye. All the letters outward shall be delivered gratis . . . and reciprocally, we expect all to us free. Each first Monday of the month he sets out from New York, and is to return within the month from Boston to us againe. The mail has divers baggs, according to the townes the letters are designed to, which are all sealed up till their arrivement, with the seale of the Secretarie's Office, whose care it is on Saturday night to seale them up. Only by-letters are in the open bag, to dispense by the wayes. . . . I shall only beg of you . . . to afford him directions where and to whom to make his application to upon his arrival in Boston; as likewise to afford him what letters you can to establish him in that imployment there. It would be much advantagious to our designe, if in the intervall you discoursed with some of the most able woodmen, to make out the best and most fascile way for a Post, which in process of tyme would be the King's best highway.[22]

Service began in earnest when the next post rider left New York on January 22, 1673, laden with "two port-mantles crammed with letters, sundry goods, and bags." The rider traveled first to New Haven and Hartford, then along the Bay Path to Springfield, Brookfield, and Worcester in Massachusetts, and on to Boston, where he arrived two weeks later having covered a distance of 250 miles.[23]

The first postal service in the colonies had no sooner been established than it was interrupted by the Dutch takeover of New York in July 1673, and the violence of King Philip's War in 1675, in which several towns along the post route in Massachusetts were destroyed. During this period of disruption, the General Court of Connecticut acted to expand postal service within the colony in 1674 by setting postal rates between Hartford and two dozen other Connecticut towns. Post riders in Connecticut were allowed free ferriage, along with an allotment for room and board on overnight runs, to be paid from the colony's general fund.[24]

In 1685, mail service was reestablished by Massachusetts Governor Edmund Andros, who was charged with uniting the New England colonies under one governorship. Although Andros's attempt at unification failed, postal service was resumed under his administration along the upper post road from Boston to Springfield, Massachusetts, Hartford, and New Haven, and along the coast to Fairfield. The renewed service was later extended into New York.[25]

A royal charter in 1691 revitalized postal service throughout the English colonies in North America along a route that extended from Baltimore, Maryland, to Portsmouth, Maine. This time, service through Connecticut passed along the shoreline from New Haven to Saybrook and on to Providence, Rhode Island, thereby establishing a major travel route across lower Connecticut from New York to Boston. The stops for this service included Baltimore, Philadelphia, New York, Saybrook, and Boston, with a different post rider assigned to each leg of the route. Service through Connecticut left New York once each week in summer (every other week in winter) and followed the shoreline route to Saybrook, where the New York rider swapped mailbags with the rider who had come down from Boston via Providence.[26]

By the turn of the century, with the settlement of the eastern uplands under way, a third postal route from New York to Boston appeared across central Connecticut. This middle route veered east from Hartford and continued diagonally across the Windham Hills to Bolton, Coventry, Tolland, and Woodstock. The exact path of this middle post road is debated, but its existence is attested to by Benjamin Wadsworth, who traveled the route on a trip from Albany to Boston via Hartford in 1694. Leaving Hartford one August morning, Wadsworth and six fellow travelers encountered a road that was "very rocky, bushy, in many places miry: we were not troubled with many mountains and hills; but tho our road was bad and long, being counted about 50 miles, yet we came to Woodstock about 8 of ye clock" in the evening.[27]

As postal service through the colony became more regular, demands were placed on towns along the three post routes to keep the King's Highway in their town in good repair, including bridge and ferry crossings. To accomplish this, the General Court of the Connecticut colony required an extra day (or two) of statute labor from men living in those towns. But some of the towns refused to require such extra work time of their residents, resulting in complaints to the General Court about travel conditions along certain portions of the King's Highway.

The court reasserted its mandate in 1698, ordering towns along the three post roads to keep cleared "convenient highways as may be for the advantage of posts . . . with sufficient causeis and bridges as need shall require . . . with marks erected for direction of travailers where ways part." The court also singled out the county of New London and the town of Stonington, where "difficultie doth arise either for want of stated highways or for want of clearing and repairing highways where stated, and erecting and maintaining sufficient bridges." So recalcitrant was the county that the court empowered a committee of three men to force road construction or repair as was required "by all lawfull ways and means, and at the charge of the town in which the highway lies."[28]

In addition to his mail-related duties, a post rider was expected to act as a travel guide for anyone who wished to accompany him. One such person was Sarah Kemble Knight, a twice-widowed shopkeeper's daughter from Boston who at the age of thirty-eight traveled the lower Post Road to New York in 1704. Frightened of water travel, Sarah Knight chose horseback for her trip to New York to settle the estate of her deceased second husband. After she left Boston in the afternoon of October 2, it took Knight three days to reach the Pawcatuck River and cross into Connecticut. Her observations of her travels through the colony, recorded in a daily journal, provide a firsthand look at the difficult travel conditions that still existed along the lower post road in eastern Connecticut six years after the order of the General Court:

> Thursday, October 5th: I Ridd on very slowly thro' Stoningtown, where the Rode was very Stony and uneven. . . . Here I heard there was an old man and his Daughter to come that way, bound to N. London; and being now destitute of a Guide, gladly waited for them. . . . About seven that Evening, we come to New London Ferry: here, by reason of a very high

wind, we mett with great difficulty in getting over—the boat toss't exceedingly, and our Horses capper'd at a very surprising Rate, and set us all in a fright. . . . Being safely arrived . . . in N. London, I treated neighbor Polly and daughter for their divirting company, and bid them farewell.

Friday, October 6th: about eight this morning, with Mr. Joshua Wheeler my new Guide . . . wee advanced on towards Seabrook. The Rodes all along this way are very bad, Incumbered with rocks and mountainos passages . . . after about eight miles Rideing, in going over a Bridge, under which the River Run very swift, my horse stumbled, and very narrowly 'scaped falling over into the water, which extreemly frightened mee. . . . From hence wee went pretty briskly forward, and arriv'd at Saybrook ferry about two of the Clock afternoon . . . and about seven at night come to Killingsworth . . . and Lodgd there that night.

Saturday, October 7th: wee set out early in the Morning . . . and we soon after came into the Rhode, and keeping still on, without anything further Remarkabell, about two a clock afternoon we arrived at New Haven, where I was received with all Possible Respects and civility. Here I discharged Mr. Wheeler with a reward to his satisfaction, and took some time to rest after so long and toilsome a Journey.[29]

Sarah Knight spent six days traveling to New Haven on the first portion of her journey. She remained there with family for several months before resuming her trip to New York in early December. Sarah Knight finally arrived in New York after three more days on the road, but not before encountering "many and great difficulties, as Bridges which were exceeding high and very tottering and of vast Length, steep and Rocky Hills and precipices." In the area of western Greenwich known as Horseneck, she traversed "a mountainous passage that almost broke my heart in ascending."[30] Yet, difficult though it was, Sarah Knight's overland journey could hardly have been attempted without the existence of the post service and the king's best highway.

Eighteenth-Century Expansion

In the eighteenth century, the Connecticut economy expanded from one that was mainly agricultural to one in which market capitalism played a larger role, and an increase in trade produced a demand for more roads, ferries, and bridges.

THE COLONY'S ECONOMY EXPANDS

During the first half of the eighteenth century, as the population of Connecticut continued to climb and settlers moved into the eastern and western uplands, the economy of the colony changed. As the population of older towns reached a level greater than that necessary for self-subsistence, larger amounts of farm produce, dairy products, cattle, horses, and livestock were available for trade to other colonies, in particular to the islands of the West Indies, where a ready demand existed for the kinds of subsistence products that Connecticut had to spare. In addition, as the last of Connecticut's farmland was put to the plow, a land shortage developed that led the sons of established farm families to migrate north and west to Vermont, New York, and Ohio; or to find work outside the farm in small-scale industries, such as metal-working, clock repair, cloth-making, and distillation of rum.

With this growth in trade and small-scale industry came disparities in wealth between farmer and merchant, merchant and trader. The economic transformation these changes represented was felt first in older, more established communities and later in other towns across the colony as settlement expanded. By the 1760s, the combination of increasing population and limited farmland had transformed the economy of Connecticut from one based largely on subsistence agriculture to one that included significant (and increasing) amounts of intercolony trade and small-scale manufacturing. Although this economic expansion directly involved no more than 10 percent of Connecticut's work-age population, it concerned the trading of agricultural products and livestock throughout the colony and therefore impacted a large portion of the colony's total population.

As part of the expansion, Connecticut towns began to differentiate themselves according to their economic function. First were urban centers such as Hartford, New Haven, Middletown, New London, and Norwich, port towns where merchants conducted trade directly with comparable ports outside the colony. Next were secondary centers, such as Windham, Danbury, Lebanon, and Litchfield, that acted as inland marketplaces where trade goods were collected from and dispersed to surrounding communities. In addition, ports like Glastonbury, Haddam, Fairfield, and Saybrook that traded outside the colony, but only for themselves, could also be considered secondary centers. Last of all were the mainly agricultural towns, such as Sharon, Simsbury, Hebron, and Woodstock, that traded surplus products for imported goods in secondary or urban centers. These inland farm towns constituted the majority of Connecticut communities.

In each town, whatever its economic function, the local tavern was the prime location for conducting the business affairs of the community. Whereas a country town might have five such taverns, a secondary town supported twice that number and an urban center a dozen or more. By midcentury, as the initial settlement of the colony came to a close, no Connecticut man lived more than a three-mile walk from one of these economic watering holes, or from the flow of opportunity and ideas that they represented.[31]

NEW ROADS, FERRIES, AND BRIDGES

Connecticut's economic expansion quite naturally had an impact on the colony's transportation needs. The increasing activity associated with trade resulted in a growing volume of wagon and livestock traffic that required the construction of new roads, ferries, and bridges as well as the improvement of existing ones. In the same way that overland travel in the early days of the colony had largely been determined by the distance to the local gristmill, meetinghouse, and militia training field, overland travel in the eighteenth century was now largely influenced by the distance between inland town and market center and between market center and port town.[32]

In the decades up to 1750, most new roads in the colony appeared east of the Connecticut River, as towns in the Windham Hills sought access to the ports of Norwich and Stonington to trade their surplus produce; to Boston for surplus cattle; and to Providence for surplus butter. After 1750, the appearance of new roads shifted to the western uplands, where the excess grain of Litchfield County and the pig iron produced by Salisbury-area furnaces were hauled to the Hudson River for transport by water to New York. In addition, a new road from Newtown to Danbury was opened specifically for driving cattle to New York City. In 1761, an effort was made to divert this Hudson-bound traffic to the port of Derby by the construction of a cart road from Canaan to Derby and the removal of navigation hazards from the lower Housatonic River. The scheme failed. Travel to New York City remained easier via the Hudson. But the very attempt suggests the competitive spirit that was abroad in Connecticut in the years before the revolution.[33]

Other road construction included the improvement of an existing road from Durham to Middletown to facilitate the shipment of horses and cattle to the West Indies and a road from Hartford to Albany via Simsbury, New Hartford, Norfolk, and Canaan, prompted by the need to transport troops and munitions westward during the French and Indian War.[34]

As before, such intertown roads were constructed using statute labor under the supervision of highway surveyors. These newer country roads were still located along a path of least resistance, but in New London County, at least, an effort was made to improve their design by reducing the surface damage caused by flowing water. This was accomplished by constructing earthen bumps on the sloped portions of a road so as to direct rainwater off the roadway. These swells were often placed on a diagonal "to give less resistance to the wheels, & turn off the water more effectually & with the least injury" to the road. "Cavities on the sides, near the swells catch the wash, & retain the sediment," which allowed the earth that accumulated in these cavities to be thrown back on the road "from time to time, upon the swells, or where it is most wanted," thereby aiding in road repair.[35]

Overall, the quality of country roads in Connecticut was still less than adequate, and could vary considerably from route to route, or from town to town along a given route. John Fitch, the Windsor native who later gained neither fame nor fortune as an inventor of the steamboat, told of a road gang incident of his youth that gives us a picture of colonial life in the 1750s, as well as an appreciation for the role of rum in road-building:

When I was a lad of about seven or eight years of age [Governor Wolcott] used to go to Hartford by my fathers house dressed in a scarlet coat. My oldest brother with many others was mending the highway at Grindle Hill close by my fathers and it was the custom at the time and since in them parts for such people to keep a bottle of rum and offer every traveler which passed a dram. From which they expected a generious price for the dram and frequantly received as much as would buy a whole quart. On this day Governour Woolcutt passed that place who was saluted agreable to custom and gave them one copper only for the dram he drank. What makes me remember it so perfectly well was my oldest brother who was possessed with quite as much meanness as either my father or Governour Woolcutt brought the copper to my fathers and punched a hole thro' it and got a piece of scarlet cloth and went and sat a post in the ground so near the road that every traveler must see it. I

stood by and see him punch the hole in the copper and went with him to see them plant the post and nail the copper and scarlet rag and heared many invectives thrown out against him [Governor Wolcott] for his meanness.[36]

With the increase in travel brought on by a developing market economy, additional ferry crossings also appeared throughout the colony. By 1750, the number of ferries in Connecticut had grown from eleven (fifty years earlier) to twenty-six, and would peak at thirty by the end of the eighteenth century. In 1764, the colony established its first ferry across Long Island Sound, from Norwalk to the town of Huntington on Long Island. In addition, some busier crossings began to operate two boats, one from either shore, and offered scheduled service as opposed to service on demand. As with highways, the towns in which the ferries operated retained responsibility for seeing that updated ferry regulations and fares set by the General Assembly were put into practice.[37]

At the turn of the century, the operations of several heavily traveled ferry crossings were transferred from individual to town ownership, including ferries across the Housatonic River between Stratford and Milford (1791) and across the Connecticut River between Saybrook and Lyme (1794), Hartford and East Hartford (1805), and Middletown and Portland (1812). One reason for this transfer was the need to finance improvements at ferry landings and to provide larger boats to accommodate the wheeled carriages that had begun to appear on the roads. To equalize such service between two towns, operation and revenue were assigned to the town on one side for one direction and to the town on the other side for the other direction. Towns that operated their own ferries often used the toll revenue to subsidize the cost of their public schools or to pay for bridge repairs. Still, the majority of Connecticut ferries were operated by individuals under a grant of exclusive privilege.[38]

Besides additional ferry service, more than thirty bridges of note were built in Connecticut between 1720 and 1789. The construction material of choice remained timber, and the design was of the king post or queen post variety. With confidence gained from experience, bridge builders attempted longer spans by using multiple sections resting on a series of stone or timber piers built midstream. A multiple-span bridge with a total length of 250 feet was erected over the Quinebaug River at Norwich in 1728—at a height of twenty feet above the water, so as not to interfere with boat traffic. Additional multispan bridges were constructed in Derby, Lisbon, and Farmington.[39]

As the need for longer and stronger bridges became apparent, dependence on statute labor for their construction became impractical. Instead, towns looked to local or itinerant artisans to build their bridges for them, and such bridge builders needed to be paid. However, the useful life of a timber bridge built during the colonial period was only seven to ten years, by which time damage from weathering, ice flows, and spring floods (and from sea worms to bridges on wooden pilings) had taken their toll. This meant that after a bridge was built, finding funds for reconstruction remained an ongoing worry for town officials, particularly in communities with several crossings, or a span of considerable length.

On occasion, local businessmen who hoped to benefit from the construction of a particular bridge pooled their funds to build it, as was the case in Windsor in 1748, when three men were allowed to replace an existing ferry by building a cart bridge across the Rivulet, so long as the new structure remained "a free bridge forever." More common were instances in which towns were admonished by the General Assembly for not paying sufficient attention to the condition of their bridges, particularly those located along intertown roads.[40]

As a result, alternative methods of financing were tried. One of the earliest was the use of bartered labor, in which an individual agreed to build or repair a particular bridge in return for a parcel of town land, or an exemption from his town taxes. This method was used in Woodstock in 1721, when Samuel Morris built and maintained three bridges in town in exchange for "being exempted from paying any rates whatsoever, whether country, town or ministry" for ten years; and in Pomfret, the following year, when John Sabin was granted three hundred acres of land in exchange "for his service in making of a bridge over Quinabaug River, on condition he keep the same in repair fourteen years next coming." A variation on the bridge-for-land exchange occurred in 1759 in New Haven. There, the sewer commissioners of the town agreed to build a dike and dam across the East River, thereby making two thousand acres of marshy meadow land useable, if the proprietors of the meadow agreed, in turn, to build and maintain "a good and sufficient cart-bridge" near the dam to connect the two thousand acres to the town proper.[41]

A second means of paying for bridge construction that was used more widely as the century wore on was to allow the person who constructed a bridge to collect a toll for its use. The idea was first utilized in Connecticut with the construction of a stone arch bridge in Middletown in 1697. The colony's second toll bridge was built in Plainfield in 1728. Toll bridge crossings were authorized and regulated by the General Assembly.

The toll bridge was considered an equitable solution to the problem of bridge financing, since it shifted the burden from the town as a whole to those who actually used the bridge, regardless of where they lived. As a result, toll collection became a common form of bridge financing, with the length of time a toll privilege was in effect varying from bridge to bridge. On occasion, toll privileges were granted in perpetuity, which meant that the town had to buy out the owner of the bridge at some future date should it ever want to free the crossing. Such was the case with the colony's first toll crossing in Middletown; the town eventually purchased the bridge from the builder's widow for two hundred acres of town-owned land sixty years after the toll was first established.[42]

The toll collection method was used to finance the construction of bridges in Lyme (1731), Simsbury (1734), Norwich (1737), New Milford (1741), and

Advertisement for a bridge lottery. (Courtesy of the Connecticut Historical Society, Hartford, Connecticut)

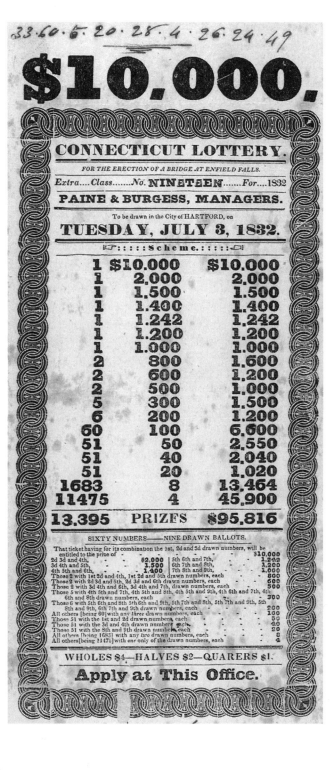

Sharon-Cornwall (1757), among others. In Simsbury, where a group of men financed the construction of a toll bridge, the General Assembly afterward allowed them to form a proprietorship, complete with the election of officers and the holding of business meetings. This was an early and rare case of the corporation concept being used in colonial transportation. A similar bridge proprietorship was also authorized for a toll bridge in New Milford.[43]

Another popular way of raising bridge building funds in the second half of the eighteenth century was with a lottery. This method was first legalized in Connecticut in 1747 and was used thereafter to fund many public works projects, including bridge construction. Lotteries were used to build a bridge in Windsor in 1762 and one across Norwich Cove in 1772. By the end of the century, lotteries had been used in the construction or repair of more than a dozen bridges throughout Connecticut.[44]

In situations where a bridge crossed the boundary between two towns, and the towns could not agree on the need for or method of construction—often because they did not want to pay for the work—the matter was referred to the county court for resolution. If the court agreed that the crossing or repair was necessary, the selectmen of the towns involved were ordered to complete the work. Beginning in 1761, such towns were allowed to levy a tax on their grand list to raise the necessary bridge funds. Once built, the bridge was typically maintained by the two towns in proportion to their grand lists. Later, towns were allowed to levy a bridge tax for an expensive reconstruction even if the structure did not cross a town boundary.[45]

Throughout the eighteenth century, Connecticut towns made use of these various financing methods—barter, toll, lottery, and the occasional tax levy—to construct and maintain the bridges in their communities, often using one method to build a bridge and another to fund its repair or reconstruction. Meanwhile, towns that had little need for expensive bridge crossings considered themselves blessed by circumstance.

POST ROAD DEVELOPMENTS

The upper, middle, and lower post roads through Connecticut remained the triune spine of the colony's intertown road network throughout the eighteenth century. But as traffic increased, variations appeared in each route to service new towns, or to make travel easier overall. On the upper Post Road, a detour from the New Haven to Hartford route veered east from North Haven through Durham, Middletown, and Cromwell and rejoined the old route in Wethersfield. Along the middle post road to Boston, a more direct route was established through Mansfield, Pomfret, and Thompson, south of the existing road.

Because of the difficult travel conditions encountered along the eastern portion of the lower Post Road, Connecticut and Rhode Island acted jointly to reroute the King's Highway between New London and Providence away from the shoreline and through Norwich instead, thereby avoiding both the inconvenience of a Thames River ferry crossing and the stony road conditions that existed east of New London. When completed in 1714, this inland branch of the lower Post Road from Norwich through Voluntown and Preston became the locally preferred route to and from Providence for the remainder of the century.[46]

In the summer of 1753, Benjamin Franklin traveled the lower Post Road through Connecticut while touring New England as the new deputy postmaster of the English colonies. In an effort to standardize postal rates according to distance traveled, Franklin and several assistants drove the lower post route in a carriage and placed stone markers at each mile point. In 1761, the colony's General Assembly ordered towns located on any post route in Connecticut to erect stone markers along the side of the road that were at least two feet high and indicated the distance to the county seat. As with the increasing number of bridges and ferries, the placement of milestones along the colony's post roads was another indication of the increase in traffic generated by the colony's growing population and expanding economy.[47]

In November 1773, Hugh Finlay, the surveyor of all the king's highways in North America, traveled through Connecticut as part of an inspection tour of postal operations in New England. Traveling from Newport to New London along the stretch of roadway that had so troubled Madam Knight seven decades before, Finlay noted:

> Continued my route towards New London where I expected to arrive in the evening, but I found the road past all conception bad so that from daybreak until sunset I made but 33 miles and put up at a little tavern 4 mile east of New London. The road is one continued bed of rocks and very hilly. It is impossible for a Post to ride above 4 mile an hour in such road, and to do even that he must have a good horse, one used to such a rocky path.

Not only had conditions not changed in three-quarters of a century, in Finlay's opinion the post road in this location was "on the whole the most difficult and as dangerous as any in America."

Continuing to New Haven, Finlay was further inconvenienced when the post rider he hoped to meet in New London was delayed. Finlay suspected that the rider's tardiness was caused by the personal business he was conducting along the way, and as he rode on ahead without him, his suspicion was confirmed by people who inquired of Finlay "if I had not met the Post driving some oxen; it seems he had agreed to bring some along with him."

> This man . . . at 72 is strong and robust, he has been in the service 46 years. . . . It is well known that he has made an estate by his riding. . . . He does much business on the road on commission, he is a publick carrier, and loads his horse with merchandise for people living in his route; he receives cash, and carry's money backwards and forwards, takes care of return'd horses, and in short refuses no business however it may affect his speed as Post.[48]

Finlay's assessment of John Hurd of Stamford, New England's most famous post rider, suggests the growing volume of business being transacted in the colony, while his description of the lower post road through New London county is weighty testimony to the poor travel conditions still to be encountered in portions of Connecticut late in the eighteenth century.

FREIGHT WAGONS AND STAGECOACHES

The earliest public transportation in the Connecticut colony (other than ferries) appeared in 1717, when Captain John Munson of New Haven, an officer in the local militia, was given permission by the General Assembly "to set up a waggon, to pass and transport passengers and goods between Hartford and New Haven." As with most ferries, Munson was given a seven-year grant of exclusive privilege to operate the service, provided that he made at least one round trip per month (except in winter) and completed each round trip within one week. Should someone infringe on Munson's privilege by charging a fee to carry freight between these two towns, he could be fined. Likewise, should Munson not meet the terms of his grant, he too was subject to a fine.[49]

Unfortunately, little more is known of Munson's operation, which likely traveled the Post Road from New Haven to Hartford. The rising level of economic activity suggests that similar wagon services existed in other parts of the colony. One such wagon service is thought to have run from Norwich to Providence along the inland route of the lower post road. Another may have operated about this time in northeastern Connecticut from Pomfret to

Providence. Such were conditions in eastern Connecticut that the thirty-six miles from Pomfret to Providence, half a day's journey on horseback, required two days by wagon.[50]

Stagecoach services first appeared in Connecticut in the 1760s, and focused mainly on travel between New York and Boston via the upper post road. The service began as a two-week round trip, but was sufficiently popular for the proprietor to increase the service to two trips per week to and from each city. The cost was 3 pence per mile, or about 3 pounds for the journey from New York to Boston. Stagecoach service was also begun along the north shore of Long Island from New York to Sag Harbor, where packet boats were available for the crossing to New London. Once in Connecticut, passengers could continue their stagecoach journey to Providence, and on to Boston. This combination land-sea-land route avoided both the difficult river crossings along the shoreline in Connecticut and a rough and stormy sea voyage around Point Judith. Stagecoach service also originated around this time along two different routes between Providence and Hartford.[51]

The wagon-like stagecoach of the eighteenth century was little more than a large wooden box on springs. A canvas or leather top with windowless side flaps provided the only protection from rain and cold. Seats were of the bench variety, and often had no backs. Without a side entrance, passengers had to climb over the driver and one another to enter or exit the vehicle. And the ride over the rough and ready roads of colonial Connecticut was bone-jarring to be sure. Yet such was the demand for travel on the eve of the revolution that even such crude services were attempted and utilized.[52]

From Colony to Nation

Following the expulsion of the French from North America, the tax policy of King George III turned the desire for continued economic expansion in the American colonies into a call for political independence.

ROADS TO INDEPENDENCE

Following the defeat of the French in 1763 and their expulsion from colonial North America, England found itself with an overseas colony that stretched from the Atlantic seaboard west to the Mississippi River, a territory that was as costly to maintain as it was vast. After generations of salutary neglect by the mother country, during which time the English colonies, Connecticut in particular, had been allowed considerable freedom in the conduct of their affairs, the British government under George III began a policy of strict oversight of trade, while enacting revenue-raising measures such as the Stamp Act, the Townsend Act, and the Tea Act to help pay for their American empire. With each new act, the colonists stiffened their resistance, as they sought to retain the autonomy and economic prosperity they were accustomed to. By April 1775, when news of the armed skirmishes between British troops and colonial militia at Lexington and Concord reached New Haven, what had begun as a rebellion against unfair taxes and trade restrictions had become a revolution for political and economic independence.

The war impacted Connecticut transportation in several ways. With communities along Long Island Sound, such as Fairfield, New Haven, and New London, open to invasion by sea, wartime activities such as the collection and distribution of troops and supplies shifted to inland towns. As a result, enterprising businessmen looking to profit from these activities gravitated to Norwich, Hartford, Windsor, Litchfield, and Danbury, adding to the economic stature of these towns.[53]

The war also placed an added burden on Connecticut's existing road network. Because of the colony's position in the region, troops, cattle, and wagons loaded with provisions moved across Connecticut in all directions. One notable military expedition across Connecticut was the march of General Jean-Baptiste de Rochambeau and several regiments of French troops on their way to Yorktown. In the summer of 1781, Rochambeau led a group of some five hundred officers, four thousand infantry, and six hundred cavalry troops from Providence to Danbury via Voluntown, Windham, Hartford, Southington, and Middlebury. Marching twelve to fifteen miles a day, the troops traveled with a train of two hundred wagons, carrying tents, food, and other supplies, each wagon pulled by a team of six oxen. One can only imagine the impact of the army as they trampled across hundreds of miles of dirt roads in Connecticut.[54]

With most able-bodied men preoccupied with fighting the English, it was difficult to keep supply routes in even the most rudimentary repair using statutory labor. Even before the war, the General Assembly in 1774 had for the first time allowed towns to levy a highway tax to raise the funds needed to repair and maintain their roads and bridges. Permission first had to be requested from the General Assembly and was granted for a limited time only, usually three years. Before the start of hostilities, only one or two towns had made use of the new highway tax, but by the end of the war nearly half

This roadside monument in Southington marks one of the many locations where Rochambeau's army camped in June 1781 on its march across Connecticut.
(Photo by the author)

the towns in the colony had used the tax to fund road repairs. Most of these towns were located in the Connecticut River valley or along inland routes to Providence, Boston, and the Hudson River.[55]

After the war, the funding of highway repairs through direct taxation remained a popular idea. In an environment of economic independence, with commerce and moneymaking on the rise, the use of forced labor to fix roads seemed regressive, while a graduated tax based on the value of the property a man owned appeared a fair alternative. As a result, the number of towns petitioning the General Assembly for permission to levy a highway tax continued to rise even after the war ended, reaching a total of seventy-one towns by 1795, with several towns making use of the levy more than once. In that year, the legislature incorporated the principle of a town highway tax into the general laws of Connecticut, allowing each town the right to levy the tax any time it chose by majority vote. In that way, the highway tax gradually came to replace the medieval principle of statute labor as the accepted means of financing roadwork.[56]

CONNECTICUT CIRCA 1800

Generations of English settlers had altered the natural landscape of Connecticut dramatically. By 1800, forest coverage had been reduced by two-thirds, from 95 percent of the colony's land area to 30 percent. As the habitats provided by this ancient forest had disappeared, so had the native wildlife, such as black bear, white-tailed deer, wolves, and beaver, all of which were in steep decline at the end of the colonial period. Other species, including the moose, mountain lion, passenger pigeon, and wild turkey, had nearly become extinct in Connecticut. Meanwhile, Connecticut's Ninnimissinuwock people, whose way of life had been interwoven over thousands of years with the flora and fauna of this natural landscape, had likewise all but disappeared.[57]

The natural landscape the first Puritans had considered "a hidious & desolate wildernes, full of wild beasts & wild men" had been replaced by a manmade landscape of family farms, church parishes, schools, and all manner of commerce and commercial buildings.[58] For the purpose of governance, the landscape was now divided into more than one hundred separate communities, organized into eight counties, a patchwork of civil jurisdictions stitched together by some one thousand miles of unimproved but passable country roads, and several dozen bridge and ferry crossings. As noted in the *American Gazetteer* of 1804, Connecticut had become

> checkered with innumerable roads or highways crossing each other in every direction. A traveller in any of these roads, even in the most unsettled parts of the state, will seldom pass more than half a mile or a mile without finding a house, and a farm under such improvements, as to afford the necessaries for the support of a family. The whole state resembles a well cultivated garden.[59]

Of all these roads, the three-pronged upper, middle, and lower post roads from New York to Boston, together with the high road to Albany northwest from Hartford, provided the main transportation corridors linking the new state of Connecticut to the independent nation of which it was one small part.

Also by 1800, the European-style economy of Connecticut had grown to sustain a population of more than 250,000 persons (almost entirely of En-

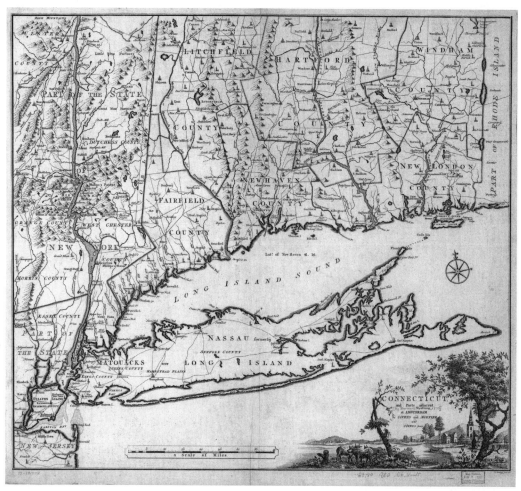

Connecticut c. 1780. This map by Dutch mapmakers Covens and Mortier shows Connecticut at the end of the colonial period, including the three post routes to Boston and their local variations. (Courtesy of the Library of Congress)

glish descent) who were distributed more or less evenly over the largely agricultural landscape. Yet within this cultivated English garden, the seeds of diversification and urbanization had already been planted. In 1784, the municipalities of New Haven, New London, Hartford, Middletown, and Norwich were incorporated as the state's first cities, a clear indication that the evolving civic interests of the merchant class in those ports had become of greater relative importance than the traditional needs of local farmers.

The charters for these five cities transferred to them certain political decisions that had been the concern of the state government. In each city a mayor, aldermen, and a common council were empowered to govern in such matters as markets and commerce, jury service, highways and wharfs, fire protection, and public health, among others. Likewise, the mayor and aldermen sat once each month as a city court to hear certain judicial matters affecting their local jurisdictions.[60]

As for transportation, Connecticut, like the nation of which it was now a part, emerged from the revolution precariously balanced between two worlds: a colonial past of minimal construction and shoestring financing of roads that had yet to produce an adequate highway network, especially along the hundreds of miles of intertown routes so essential to regional trade and travel, and an uncertain future of economic expansion that required the movement of more and heavier goods over greater distances, which required more and better roads, bridges, and ferries. Connecticut overcame this transportation dilemma through a legal revolution that was every bit as significant as the political one that made Connecticut a state.

Chapter Two **Turnpikes and Stagecoaches**

In the aftermath of the revolution, there was deep concern that if the new nation could not function as an economic whole it would soon dissolve. Providing adequate overland transportation was the key to making commerce possible on a national scale. Burdened by the repayment of state war debts, and divided by sectional rivalries that made consensus difficult, the federal government was unable to adopt an effective policy for the funding of internal improvements. Instead, the states turned to the chartering of joint-stock corporations to solve their transportation problems. Connecticut was an early leader in turnpike construction and, due to its unique settlement pattern, experienced a longer period of construction and for its size built more turnpike roads than any other state. Meanwhile, the privately owned stagecoach services that operated over this turnpike network allowed Connecticut to take part in the business of the new nation.

The Turnpike Solution

With the national government preoccupied with repaying the nation's war debt, responsibility for highway improvements fell to the individual states, who adapted the British concept of a turnpike toll road to their own needs.

LOOKING TO ENGLAND

The poor travel conditions that existed in Connecticut and in the new nation following the Revolutionary War represented more than mere inconvenience. In the early days of the republic, as the federal government attempted to establish a national economy free from the control of European nations, the lack of the adequate transportation so essential to internal commerce was in a very real sense a threat to the fledgling union of the thirteen former colonies.

While federalists and republicans alike recognized the urgency of internal improvements, the national government could do little until the war debt of the individual states had been repaid, a crucial first step in establishing the credibility of the new nation as an international trading partner. To this end, the new national government assumed responsibility for some $25 million in state war debt (including $1.6 million from Connecticut) that it proceeded to repay, year by year, using revenue collected from custom duties. With federal revenues thus committed, solving the nation's transportation crisis fell to the states, most of which were also cash poor following the revolution. Unable to raise the large amounts of money needed for road improvements through taxation, the states looked to their English heritage for a solution and adopted the toll road concept as the means of improving roads in America.

England had created its first toll road in 1663, under the reign of Charles II, along the Great North Road between London and Scotland, a heavily traveled road difficult to maintain through statute labor. Under this law, all toll revenue was collected by county commissioners and applied directly to repairing the road in question. By the start of the eighteenth century, several other publicly operated turnpikes had been created in Britain, mainly in the vicinity of London.[1]

During the eighteenth century, as toll roads in England proliferated, the concept established under Charles II changed dramatically. In the place of publicly operated county turnpikes, the government created privately operated turnpike trusts. The power to collect tolls and order repairs, previously held by accountable county justices, was given to groups of private individuals who were permitted to appoint surveyors, demand statute labor of local towns, and mortgage tolls to raise capital. Eventually, the power of these private trustees was increased to include the right to raise capital through subscription, to purchase land, and to divert an existing road to a new location, all with no credible oversight.

By the end of the eighteenth century, as the former English colonies in America were about to embark on their own turnpike construction, private turnpike trusts in England had produced a plethora of roads that were ineffectively administered by groups of men who were often corrupt. So when Connecticut and other states began to charter their own toll roads, they were careful to adapt the turnpike concept to more moderate, conservative ends.[2]

CONNECTICUT'S FIRST TURNPIKES

Connecticut's first turnpike was the Mohegan Road, created in May 1792 to run on the west side of the Thames River along the existing road from New London to Norwich. The Mohegan Road was the first turnpike created in New England and the second in America. That fall, the General Assembly also created the Greenwich Road, the state's second turnpike (and America's third) along a portion of the Post Road in the town of Greenwich. Both early turnpikes were located on the state's most prominent travel corridor, the lower post road between New York and Boston, and each covered a segment of the route that was badly in need of attention.

In fashioning its first turnpikes, Connecticut rejected the contemporary British model of privately operated turnpike trusts in favor of the public trust model developed under Charles II, and county commissioners were appointed by the legislature to operate both the Mohegan and Greenwich turnpikes. As might be expected when asking travelers to pay for use of a road that had been free, the legislature required that each road first be put into good repair by the towns involved before its tollgate could be erected. In this way, the tolls collected were used to repair damages caused by the very travelers who had paid the tolls. To fund the initial repairs, a lottery was authorized for each of the two roads, with the proceeds used to make each roadway turnpike ready.[3]

The impact on the Mohegan Road, which for decades had been difficult to keep in good repair because it ran through reservation lands of the Mohegan tribe, was immediate and dramatic. Timothy Dwight, the well-traveled president of Yale College, noted that before the road had been converted into a turnpike between Norwich and New London "few persons attempted to go from one of the places to the other, and then return, on the same day. The new road is smooth and good; and the journey is now easily performed in little more than two hours. These towns, therefore, may be regarded as having been brought nearer to each other more than half a day's journey."[4] The impact on the Greenwich Road, already a well-traveled highway, was at first not as dramatic, though turnpike improvements no doubt made travel easier. It was not until 1806, when the Greenwich Turnpike was absorbed by the Connecticut Turnpike Company, that funds were available to eliminate the biggest obstacle on the route: the steep and stony switchback in western Greenwich known as Horseneck Hill that had intimidated Sarah Knight and other travelers throughout the colonial period.[5]

Yet the very existence of a turnpike ensured that whatever the level of improvement, it would be maintained into the future through the collection of toll revenue. Having achieved a measure of success with its first two turnpikes, Connecticut established a third toll road in October 1794 to run from Norwich to the town of Preston. This turnpike was an extension of the Mohegan Road and a further improvement to the lower post road route that ran inland from New London to Providence via Norwich and Plainfield. As with the state's first two turnpikes, the Norwich Road was to be operated by county commissioners, who were authorized to set up their tollgate only after the existing road had been improved.[6] However, the towns involved took no action to improve the roadway. Instead, the following year the legislature chartered the New London and Windham County Society, a privately owned turnpike company, to operate over the inland post route from Norwich through Preston and Plainfield to the Rhode Island line in the town of Sterling. This private turnpike corporation was permitted to erect two tollgates on the route, but not until it had spent 1,200 pounds improving the road to the satisfaction of the county court. In return for its investment, the company was allowed to collect tolls until such time as its shareholders had received a 12 percent annual return on their investment, which included the ongoing expense necessary to keep the road in good repair. The operation of the turnpike road was supervised by a legislative committee appointed for that purpose.[7]

Why did Connecticut turn from the model of Charles II, with turnpikes operated by county officials as a public trust, to the quasi-public, profit-oriented model of the New London and Windham County Society? The first reason was a practical one. Following the creation of the Norwich Road as a publicly operated turnpike, Rhode Island authorized a turnpike to be constructed along the route from Providence to the Connecticut line as a private corporation, which caused Connecticut legislators the following year to both extend their turnpike to the state line and to charter their route as a private corporation as well.[8]

However, there was another, deeper reason behind the change: the need to raise the capital necessary to bring each turnpike road to acceptable standards before a toll could be collected. By relying on lotteries or statute labor to accomplish these repairs, public trusts were susceptible to the same difficulties that had produced such poor roads in the first place. Chartering the turnpike as a private corporation allowed the state to tap pockets of private wealth that were available for investment from the very persons in the community—merchants, ship captains, and small factory owners—who would benefit most from the proposed road improvement.

In addition to the New London and Windham County Society, Connecticut that year chartered corporations to build the Oxford Turnpike, from Southbury to Derby; the Hartford, New London, Windham & Tolland County Turnpike, intended to go from Hartford to Norwich (but constructed only from Bolton to Franklin); and the Norwalk & Danbury Turnpike, to run between those two towns. By the end of the decade, the state had authorized more than a dozen turnpike corporations. With the chartering of these turnpike companies, the Connecticut legislature and private investors from one end of the state to the other who purchased shares of these corporations together demonstrated their willingness to subscribe to the turnpike solution as a way out of the transportation crisis that so threatened Connecticut's economic future.[9]

Turnpikes in Connecticut

Because of its particular pattern of settlement, Connecticut built one of the densest turnpike networks of any state.

AN OVERVIEW

From 1795 to 1839, Connecticut issued 119 charters for privately operated joint-stock turnpike corporations. Of these, all but nineteen resulted in operating turnpikes, giving Connecticut one of the highest ratios of turnpikes completed to turnpikes chartered in the nation, significantly higher than the 50 percent completion ratio for the rest of New England. While the turnpikes incorporated in Connecticut during these years were chartered according to no particular plan or scheme, the timing of the charters reflected the level of local interest behind each project. In retrospect, the chartering of these turnpikes over more than four decades can be seen to have occurred in three phases.[10]

In the first phase, from 1795 to 1803, forty-seven turnpike companies were incorporated, all but four of which resulted in operating turnpikes. Construction in this phase radiated from three major population centers: Hartford, New Haven, and Norwich, with secondary areas of activity in Litchfield and Willimantic. In this rush of early turnpike-building, which lasted barely a decade, roads in nearly all the state's major travel corridors were privatized, and more than half of the turnpike mileage to be built in the state was completed, including a daunting cross-state route from Danbury to Thompson that involved half a dozen different turnpike companies.

The second phase of turnpike construction extended from 1805 to 1817. This period, which included the war years with England, saw a drop in the number of turnpikes chartered to twenty-six. But even in these slow years, all but two charters resulted in operating turnpikes. Many of the turnpikes constructed in this phase radiated from Middletown, which had been all but ignored in the earlier phase. Other construction consisted of shorter turnpikes scattered throughout the state.[11]

From 1818 to 1839, a time when turnpike construction in many states had come to a halt, Connecticut experienced a third and final burst of turnpike building, as forty-nine additional charters were issued and thirty-three new turnpikes built. Construction included three east-west routes in eastern Connecticut, along with a concentration of shorter, north-south feeder roads in Fairfield County. By 1839, when all was done, Connecticut had produced an astonishing sixteen hundred miles of toll roads, or more than 40 percent of all the turnpike mileage in New England.[12]

Competition played an important role in covering so small a state with such a network of turnpike roads. As early as 1807, a visitor to Connecticut wrote that he found "in almost every direction a turnpike road; for these roads being here made objects of private gain . . . they are established with avidity, on the smallest prospect of advantage."[13] Without a dominant center of population and trade, turnpike improvements in Connecticut occurred between many different centers of more or less equal size and attraction across the state. The centers that had the best competitive advantage after the war acted early, hoping to maintain their economic status by funneling trade from their hinterlands to points where goods could be collected and distributed. Likewise, inland market towns such as Litchfield and Willimantic sought connection to attractors beyond the state's borders, as early toll roads were constructed westward toward Albany and Hudson River ports, toward Providence in the east, and to the economic centers of New York and Boston. In subsequent phases of construction, smaller towns sought similar competitive advantage, until after four decades the state became saturated with turnpike roads.[14]

Also contributing to the state's extensive turnpike network was the low cost of turnpike road construction in Connecticut as compared to elsewhere, which allowed investors in ever smaller towns the opportunity to enter the turnpike lottery. Construction costs were kept low by utilizing existing road

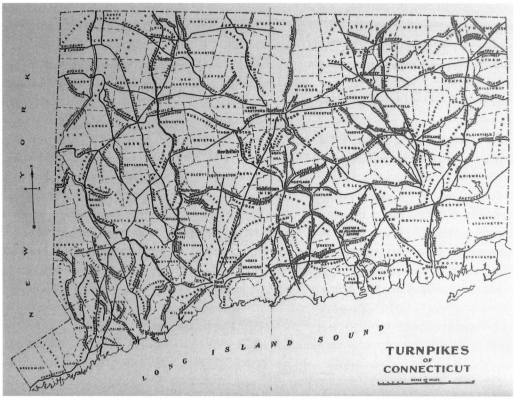

Connecticut turnpikes, from Frederick J. Wood, Turnpikes of New England *(1919).*

locations wherever possible, thereby reducing the cost of land acquisition, and in many instances by requiring local communities to bear the cost of land acquisition and bridge construction. Together, the higher than average mileage needed to connect numerous population centers and the lower than average construction costs made intense turnpike building possible in Connecticut.[15]

In cross-section, the Connecticut turnpike was a simple design: a convex earthen roadbed, crowned at the centerline, and sloped toward drainage ditches that ran along both sides of the roadway. While much turnpike building consisted of little more than an upgrade of an existing roadway, some turnpikes were constructed, in whole or in part, on a new alignment, which often required cutting a path through wooded areas, leveling hills, and filling in boggy marsh lands, all of which was accomplished with little more than an ox-drawn cart or wagon and locally crafted picks, shovels, and hoes. In the event an outcropping of bedrock intruded, blast holes were hand-drilled into the obstacle, and gunpowder was used to shatter the rock. Other construction equipment included a flattened metal disk called a one-horse shoe on which large rocks could be hauled away; an ox-drawn scraper to smooth the dirt surface of the roadway; and a plow to dig out drainage gutters along the edges of the roadway.

Construction was often accomplished by farmers looking to supplement their income whom the turnpike company hired for their labor and the use of whatever tools and animals they brought with them. As time went on, independent contractors appeared to organize road construction and to provide the labor force necessary to build and maintain turnpikes. On the Talcott Mountain and Greenwoods turnpikes construction was divided into sections, with each section assigned to a different contractor in the hope that a friendly rivalry between the crews would result in a higher quality of work.[16]

BRIDGES AND FERRIES

The proliferation of turnpike roads was an impetus for much new bridge construction. Longer, multispan bridges were now attempted across some of the state's wider rivers to remove the inconvenience of a ferry crossing and thereby reduce travel time for wagon shipments and stagecoaches. Since these bridge projects exceeded the funding capability of most towns and individuals, the joint-stock corporation was extended to toll bridge building as well, and in 1796 the state chartered its first joint-stock bridge company to erect a bridge between New Haven and East Haven. Similar companies were chartered at Niantic in 1797 and Enfield in 1798. In total, Connecticut chartered some thirty joint-stock bridge companies during the turnpike era.[17]

The construction material of choice for turnpike bridges remained timber. To increase the durability and longevity of timber crossings, some builders began to enclose the king or queen post trusses they erected in wood, a practice on shorter bridges that simply involved boxing in the wooden truss on either side of the roadway with weather boarding. By replacing a rotted board or two now and again, the life of a timber bridge was extended significantly, and several boxed bridges are known to have been built in Barkhamsted over the east and west branches of the Farmington River. Soon, the practice of enclosing a bridge truss to prolong its life was extended to roofing the entire length of a span, thereby creating the quintessential symbol of

Burr truss used in the Connecticut River bridge built at Hartford in 1808, from George E. Wright, Crossing the Connecticut (1908).

nineteenth-century New England, the covered bridge. It is estimated that more than forty covered highway bridges were built in Connecticut, the majority in the valleys of the Housatonic, Naugatuck, and Farmington rivers.[18]

Some builders tackled the problem of bridge longevity by experimenting with truss designs. Connecticut produced several bridge designers of note, including Theodore Burr (1771–1822) of Torringford, and Ithiel Town (1784–1844) of Thompson. Burr, a self-taught house-builder and millwright, designed a truss whose main feature was a wooden arch of considerable heft that ran lengthwise through a span of rectangular timber braces, adding the strength of arch construction to a more typical timber truss. Burr used his design to erect the first bridges of significant size over the Hudson, Mohawk, Delaware, and Susquehanna rivers, and he built the longest single-span wooden bridge in the world—across the Susquehanna at McCall's Ferry, Pennsylvania—in 1815. While the Burr truss became a popular design of the period, it had the disadvantage of requiring large timber beams for the central arch and skilled workmen to assemble the large beams into the desired shape.[19]

Ithiel Town, an architect and builder of churches in New Haven, eliminated the difficulty of Burr's arch design by inventing a simplified lattice truss. His truss consisted of three-inch timber boards crisscrossed at an angle

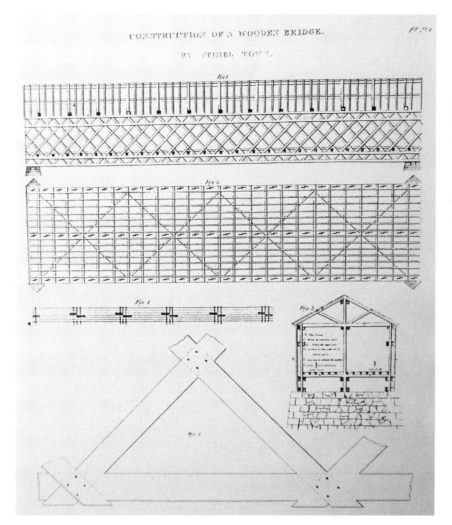

Lattice truss design patented by Ithiel Town in 1826, from Town's "A Description of Ithiel Town's Improvement in the Construction of Wooden and Iron Bridges," 1821.

of eighty degrees and set within a sturdy wood frame. The lattice boards were pinned together using two-inch-round wooden pegs, with the weight of the bridge deck acting to keep peg connections taut. The Town truss was first used in Connecticut in 1823 on the Hartford & New Haven turnpike at the Mill River in Hamden. Town promoted his design aggressively throughout the East, and he collected a royalty of $1 per foot for its use. Its ease of construction made the Town truss popular, and made Ithiel Town a wealthy man.[20]

Another Connecticut bridge-builder of note was Ezra Brainerd of East Haddam, who built one of the most unique structures of the period to carry the Middletown, Durham & New Haven turnpike across the Pamaecha River in Middletown. Unlike a Burr truss, in which a wooden arch was inserted within a rectangular frame, Brainerd used a rectangular truss formed into the shape of an arch over the entire length of the span. Built in 1814 at a cost of $3,000, the Middletown bridge was described as being

> of one arch, the chord of which is 160 feet, supported by butments formed almost wholly by the natural, rocky, and nearly perpendicular banks of the river. The floor is 27 feet wide, elevated 50 feet above the stream. The bridge is formed wholly of pine; and, by its situation and style of workmanship, constitutes a principal ornament of the southwestern part of Middletown city.[21]

Brainerd went on to build the first crossing of the lower falls on the Genesee River in Rochester, New York, using a similar arch structure that stood two hundred feet above high water. It was the highest wooden arch bridge ever attempted. Unfortunately, the Rochester bridge collapsed after only fifteen months, a costly reminder of the experimental nature of bridge construction in the turnpike period.[22]

Two bridges of note were built in Hartford during this time. The first was the Hartford Toll Bridge, which crossed the Connecticut River between Hartford and East Hartford and opened in 1810. Designed by Connecticut native Jonathan Walcott, this bridge was supported from beneath by an arch truss, with an open roadway edged with an iron rail fence. After the bridge was washed away by a spring freshet in 1818, it was replaced by a covered span built by Ithiel Town using a Burr arch design. In what was an unusual configuration, the bridge was separated into two lanes of travel by a third arch truss that ran along the midline of the span. To allow for navigation north of Hartford, an additional pier was built on the west end of the bridge to accommodate a thirty-foot uncovered draw section.

The second notable bridge in Hartford was the Great Bridge, built on Main Street over the Hog (Park) River in 1831. This one-hundred-foot-long stone bridge was the largest stone arch span constructed in the United States to that time. Stone arch bridges were used sparingly during the turnpike period because they were costly and time-consuming to construct. But they were durable, so much so that the Great Bridge stands as a functioning bridge to this day.[23]

With a rise in bridge construction, the number of ferries in Connecticut had fallen from a high of thirty at the turn of the century to twenty by 1821, after which the number remained the same for some fifty years.[24] Beginning in 1821, the General Assembly appointed two commissioners for each ferry in the state to inspect its boats and landing facilities and oversee its general operation. But unlike turnpike and bridge commissioners, who had the authority to remove the toll on a facility until repairs were completed to their satisfaction, ferry commissioners were only bound to notify the selectmen of the appropriate town, who in turn were responsible for making the repairs in a timely fashion. In 1847, the General Assembly delegated the authority to establish new ferries, relocate existing ones, and set toll schedules to the county courts.[25]

The majority of ferries were still operated by individuals or towns as grants of privilege, but with some interesting exceptions. The Pettipaug ferry across the Connecticut River at Essex was given to the Essex Turnpike Company to run as part of its charter. Likewise, in 1808, the town-operated ferry across the Connecticut River at Middletown was taken over by the Colchester & Chatham Turnpike Company, which operated the ferry until 1852, when a separate corporation, the Middletown Ferry Company, was chartered to provide the service. This appears to be a rare instance during the turnpike era of a Connecticut corporation being chartered solely to operate a ferry crossing.[26]

THE JOINT-STOCK CORPORATION AND COMPETITION

As important as the turnpike was in making commerce and travel easier in Connecticut, equally important was the joint-stock corporation, the legal entity that was used after the revolution to finance business ventures such as manufacturing, banking, insurance, and transportation. The English and other European nations had previously used the joint-stock corporation in a limited way in their settlement of the New World, but the expanded use of such corporations in all types of enterprise during the nineteenth century was revolutionary.

Under a charter obtained from the state, a joint-stock corporation was authorized to sell a specific number of shares at a prescribed price per share to raise the capital necessary to provide the service for which they had been chartered. Managed by a board of directors and supported by shareholders with a vote in corporate affairs equal to the number of shares they owned, the joint-stock corporation made possible the pooling of capital and the underwriting of business ventures whose cost was beyond that of any one person or partnership.

Connecticut took quickly to the concept, and by 1800 had chartered forty-five joint-stock corporations (more than any other state to that time). More than half of these charters were devoted to the building of turnpike roads and toll bridges. Indeed, Connecticut was comfortable enough with this new legal entity to enact the Joint-Stock Corporation Act in 1837, the first such law in the nation, which allowed manufacturing companies to incorporate according to regulations outlined in the General Statutes, without the need for a formal state charter. All other types of corporations continued to require the granting of a charter by the state.[27]

What made the joint-stock corporation a revolutionary concept was its unique identity under the law, which evolved over time as a result of litigious conflicts mediated by state and federal courts. The u.s. Supreme Court decision in an early landmark case, *Dartmouth College v. Woodward* of 1819, defined the legal identity of a joint-stock corporation. The Court ruled that the granting of corporate powers by a state was a contract under the Constitution, which meant that no state could pass a law impairing the obligation of a charter once it had been executed. Unless a charter specifically included a provision that allowed for its modification by the state, a corporation could regulate its internal affairs without interference, including whether or not it continued to exist. Coupled with the fact that corporate stock could be transferred and inherited, this ruling meant that a state-chartered corporation under the law was both timeless and self-governing, not unlike the state that had created it.[28]

Equally important to the legal identity of a joint-stock corporation was the concept of limited liability. At first, the liability of a corporation was considered to be the sum total of the assets of all its shareholders, so early lawsuits often listed each shareholder as a defendant. However, the concept was later modified by state and federal courts to allow a corporation to sue and be sued under its own name, as a citizen of the state in which it had been incorporated. In this way, the liability of a joint-stock corporation was limited to the total of its corporate assets, and no more. This fundamental aspect of modern corporate law was affirmed in Connecticut by the state Supreme Court of Errors in 1823, in *The President, Directors and Company of the Middletown Bank v. Magill and Others.* After this decision, Connecticut businessmen were able to invest in a joint-stock venture knowing that they risked no more of their personal wealth than the value of the shares they purchased.[29]

Another aspect of the legal revolution that took place in the first decades of the nineteenth century was the emerging concept of competition. Initially, charters granted by the state for toll roads and bridges were presumed to be exclusive to the corporation receiving the grant, much as the right to operate a ferry or stagecoach service granted to an individual in colonial Connecticut had been an exclusive privilege. This view remained intact in Connecticut as late as 1802, in a decision of the Connecticut Supreme Court of Errors concerning a charter granted to one Reuben Sikes to operate a stagecoach over the upper post road between Hartford and Boston. When Thomas Perrin began to operate a stage service between Hartford and Albany over a portion of the Hartford-to-Springfield road used by Sikes, Sikes sued. Though the two services were not in competition, running as they did in opposite directions, the court decided that Perrin's service was in violation of the privilege given to Sikes to operate exclusively over the road between Hartford and the Massachusetts line.[30]

As the demand for turnpikes and bridges increased, the presumption of exclusive privilege was seen as restricting economic growth. In Connecticut, the changeover came in 1828 with the decision of the Connecticut Supreme Court of Errors in *Enfield Toll Bridge Company v. Connecticut River Company*. This ruling allowed the defending river company to proceed with its charter to lock the falls on the Connecticut River at Enfield, despite the fact that the privilege had been granted to the bridge company twenty years earlier (but had so far not been implemented). In support of its position, the court noted: "The public have a deep interest in the commodious navigation of *Connecticut* river, and it is peculiarly inequitable, that the rights of a community should be sacrificed, to insure the franchise of the plaintiffs from all possible damages."[31]

Whereas a grant of exclusive privilege had once been considered necessary to attract the finances and commitment needed to provide a transportation service in the public interest such as a ferry or a stagecoach, the public interest was now considered better served by competing, nonexclusive services. Where one charter impinged on another, the remedy was for the aggrieved company to sue for damages in a lower court, where each case was judged on its own merits. A similar conclusion by the u.s. Supreme Court in *Charles River Bridge v. Warren Bridge* in 1837 placed the full weight of federal law behind the new principle of competition.[32]

The establishment of the joint-stock corporation as a legal entity of limited liability, together with the emerging principle of competition and damages as the best way to provide for economic growth and serve the public interest, redefined the legal landscape of the United States in the first quarter of the nineteenth century, and constituted a legal revolution every bit as significant as the political one that had established the former English colony as a nation in its own right, under the rule of its own laws. As a result, the state-chartered joint-stock transportation company became the accepted means for providing the internal improvements such as turnpikes and toll bridges that were so essential to sustaining the independence of the new nation.

THE REGULATION OF TURNPIKE COMPANIES

The chartering of privately owned joint-stock corporations to provide the state's transportation infrastructure, essentially a public service, while charging a toll for what had been free, was a situation ripe for abuse. In Connecticut, the state took a sensible and conservative approach to the regulation of turnpike corporations. Where the acquisition of land was required, the laying out of a turnpike road was done by a committee appointed by the General Assembly that also assessed the dollar value of the damages paid to the owners of the land taken. Should an owner consider the offer unfair, he was allowed an appeal to the county court. Once the assessments were determined and accepted by the legislature, a time limit was set in which damages had to be paid to all affected landowners before construction could begin. In this way, Connecticut kept public control of the most sensitive aspect of turnpike construction, the determination and acquisition of the road's right-of-way.[33]

With land issues settled, the turnpike company was free to build, widen, or repair the road in question, and here too the state maintained control by not allowing tolls to be collected until the road had been completed to the satisfaction of a public oversight group, be it a committee of the legislature or a county court. Once the road was in operation, exemptions from tolls were given to residents traveling to a town meeting, to a religious service, or to and from their field or local gristmill, so long as they traveled no more than four miles on the turnpike.[34]

Relying on the legislature or county court to ensure that each turnpike company adequately maintained its road and bridges once the road was open, however, proved impractical. As early as 1802, Governor Jonathan Trumbull, Jr., noted that the condition of existing turnpike roads "already is an abject of considerable complaint. . . . For, unless the roads are kept in

constant and sufficient repairs, the toll collected at the gates, is a species of imposition on the traveller which should not be authorized by law."[35]

To remedy the situation, the General Assembly in 1803 appointed three commissioners (later two) to each turnpike to monitor its operations. These commissioners had the power to inspect their road at least once each year; to order the company to make repairs as necessary; and should the company not respond, to throw open the tollgates until such time as repairs were completed to the satisfaction of the commissioners. Turnpike commissioners also audited the books of their company each year and reported the results to the legislature. For their time, the commissioners were each paid $3 per day by the turnpike corporation to which they were assigned. This policy of relying on appointed commissioners to regulate turnpike corporations became the accepted method of oversight for all state-chartered transportation corporations throughout the nineteenth century.[36]

While using such conservative measures to regulate what were the state's first public utilities, legislators also remained conscious of the need to attract investors on an ongoing basis. One way this was accomplished was by allowing a 12 percent rate of return on a company's total investment, including the cost of ongoing maintenance. While the profit limit was lowered in later years on most turnpike charters to 8 percent, it remained higher than the 6 percent return available to investors in banks and most other corporations.[37]

In addition, the state accommodated the political nature of road-building by allowing the company to negotiate with the town in which its road was located some of the conditions under which it was to operate. While land damages were usually the responsibility of the turnpike company, some charters assigned that cost to the towns involved. It was likewise with bridges, whose construction was often a substantial part of a turnpike's total cost. In most instances, a turnpike company was made responsible for new bridges built along its route, while existing structures remained the responsibility of the town. In some cases, a turnpike company took responsibility for all bridges, existing as well as new; in some others, all bridges were the town's responsibility.[38]

A pledge by a local community to pay for bridge construction was even used on occasion to entice a turnpike committee to locate its road through a particular part of a town. Such was the case with the village of New Cambridge, which offered to build two bridges for the Farmington & Bristol Turnpike Company in order to make a route through its village more compelling than a competing route that required fewer bridges.[39] To a limited extent, even the amount of the tolls to be charged might be tailored to the perceived needs of a particular turnpike company, though the amount of variance from one charter to another was slight. But in no instance did Connecticut subsidize the construction of its turnpikes and toll bridges with a contribution of state funds.

This combination of conservative regulation and liberal enticement resulted in an overall policy toward turnpike and toll bridge corporations that was effective in protecting the public interest, while at the same time providing for the state's economic growth.

MOBILITY BECOMES COMMONPLACE

Before the 1750s, overland travelers moved mainly on foot or horseback, with the occasional farm wagon, cart, or winter sled for hauling goods. In the last half of the century, English-made carriages appeared in Connecticut, purchased by the colony's wealthier residents. Carriage travel in Connecticut remained unusual until after the revolution, but horse-drawn vehicles were present in sufficient numbers to require a toll category for carriages to be added at all ferry crossings in 1760, and to the list of taxable personal property in all towns in 1771.[40]

The construction of turnpike roads created a demand for better-wheeled vehicles of all kinds, from the one-horse chaise or wagon to larger carriages and coaches, while economic expansion provided more Connecticut residents with the means to own such vehicles. Carriages imported from England were copied and improved on in American workshops for use on American turnpikes. During this period New Haven became established as a national center for the turnpike-driven carriage industry.

One prominent carriage-maker was James Brewster, a wagon-maker from Northampton, Massachusetts, who relocated to New Haven in 1809. Convinced that he could improve on the two-wheeled carriages being made in that city by underpaid artisans, Brewster opened a carriage shop at Elm and High streets where he began producing a quality line of two- and four-wheel carriages using higher-paid craftsmen. To educate his employees in their craft, Brewster formed the Young Men's Mechanical Institute, where professors from Yale College gave after-work lectures on scientific topics to his artisans. The company prospered, and Brewster moved to larger quarters on the banks of the Mill River, where he manufactured high-end phaetons, victorias, and coaches for the affluent of New York City, Philadelphia, and Charleston. With the help of two sons, Brewster later opened plants in Bridgeport and New York and exported carriages to distant markets in Mexico, Cuba, South America, Africa, and Australia.[41]

One of the larger makers of mass-produced carriages in New Haven was G. & D. Cook & Company, founded in 1845 and located in a two-story building at Grove and State streets. By introducing an assembly line production of sorts in which each craftsman was responsible for a single part of the finished product, the Cook brothers improved their productivity and the quality of their vehicles. By 1860, business required the company to relocate to a large eighty-five-thousand-square-foot factory, where productivity increased from one carriage per day to ten. By this time, the company catalog contained 145

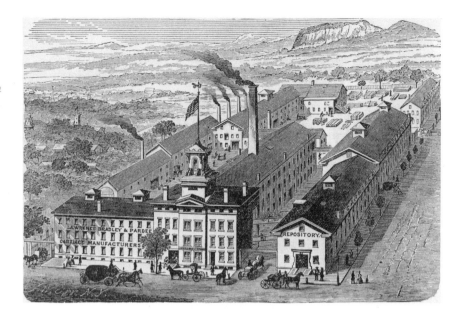

different carriage models, including a basic wagon that sold for less than $100, a farmer's buggy for $175, and more ornate barouches, rockaways, bretts, and coaches for $200 to $1,200. As with Brewster, the Cooks shipped most of their products via New York for sale in the south and west.[42]

In addition to these and other carriage-makers, numerous firms operated within the city in a support capacity, specializing in the production of certain carriage parts, which were sold in bulk to larger manufacturers. Specialty firms included the wood-carver James H. Campbell, lamp-maker A. J. Cutler, hardware-maker C. Cowles & Co, the New Haven Spring Company, and the New Haven Wheel Company, one of the largest wheel-producing firms in the nation. A description of the company's factory noted that "their machinery is new, much of it invented by themselves or manufactured expressly for their own use, and is capable of turning out wheels, spokes, hubs and fellowes with astonishing rapidity and remarkable accuracy. They keep constantly on hand a stock of about a million spokes finished in the rough."[43]

The carriage-making industry was also a notable presence in Bridgeport and Norwalk, where some twenty carriage shops and related businesses operated, and in Norwich, where the Mowry Axle & Machine Company manufactured quality axles and springs as well as carriage-building tools and machinery. As turnpike travel became commonplace, every Connecticut town had a carriage craftsman close at hand, if only for repairs. By 1860, carriage-making was the fourth largest industry in Connecticut, and more than forty carriage shops were in business in New Haven alone.[44]

In the early decades of the nineteenth century, stagecoach service spread rapidly throughout the seaboard states, with the proliferation of turnpike roads making stagecoach service faster and more reliable. In addition, the expansion of the U.S. postal network between 1792 and 1828 facilitated the spread of reliable stagecoach service and the turnpikes on which mail stages traveled. Indeed, the spread of postal routes created the nation's first communication network, via which the weekly stage brought the latest in news and commerce to almost every community of any size.[45]

In Connecticut, stage service was first resumed after the war on the upper post road between New Haven and Springfield, Massachusetts, operated by the Hartford innkeeper Jacob Brown. Before construction of the Hartford & New Haven Turnpike, the one-way trip required two days, with an overnight stay at Brown's inn in Hartford. But it was the forty-four-year-old Enfield native and tavern owner Levi Pease who brought scheduled stagecoach service to the full Post Road between New York and Boston, and ultimately to all of New England.[46]

Beginning in 1783, Pease entered into a partnership with the blacksmith Reuben Sikes to operate a four-day stage service on the upper post road between Hartford and Boston. The stage departed Hartford every Monday morning and arrived in Boston on Thursday evening. Return service left Boston the following Monday and reached Hartford on Thursday, where a connection was made with Brown's stage to New Haven. At first, business was spotty, and on portions of the route the coach carried no passengers at all. But believing that reliability of service was the key to success, Pease and Sikes adhered to their schedule, and slowly ridership improved. By October 1784, the first through stagecoach route was established between New York and Boston, with the help of Jacob Brown, whose service now ran from Hartford to Stratford, and an operator in New York who provided service as far north as Stratford Ferry. Travel time from New York to Boston was six days, at a cost of 4 pence per mile, or 6 pounds for a full-length, round trip.[47]

Pease's status as the stage master of the Boston Post Road was secured when the Continental Congress transferred the U.S. mail from post rider to stagecoach in 1785. The Congress awarded Pease the mail contract for all of New England, which gave him a steady, supplemental income for his busi-

This mural in the Bridgeport Post Office, painted by the Works Progress Administration in the 1930s, depicts early mail service on the upper Boston Post Road.
(By permission of the U.S. Postal Service. All rights reserved)

ness, while at the same time requiring that the frequency of his service and travel time between New York and Boston be improved.

By the turn of the century, mail and stage service between New York and Boston operated daily (except Sundays) with the mail stage traveling the route as far as New Haven each day, and then to Boston via the upper or lower post road on alternate days. Maintaining daily service from New York to Boston involved more than a dozen stagecoach proprietors who were under contract to Pease for a portion of their revenue. By the time Connecticut's first turnpikes had appeared, reliable daily stage service between New York and Boston was a fact of life.[48]

Using Boston as his hub, Pease expanded his stagecoach operations into Maine, Vermont, and New Hampshire and westward to Albany. He also established an express business, with his stages carrying bundles, bank notes, and other documents for a reasonable commission. At first, a conductor who traveled with the stage handled the express business. Later, agents were stationed in towns along each route.[49]

A description of a stagecoach trip from Boston to New York made in 1794 by Josiah Quincy, president of Harvard College, gives a sense of the adventure and discomfort of this new form of public travel:

I set out from Boston on the line of stage lately established by an enterprising Yankee, Pease by name, which at that day was considered a method of transportation of wonderful expedition. The journey to New York took up a week. The carriages were old and shackling and much of the harness was made of ropes. One pair of horses carried the stage eighteen miles. We generally reached our resting place for the night, if no accident intervened, at ten o'clock and after a frugal supper went to bed with a notice that we should be called at three the next morning, which generally proved to be half past two. Then, whether it snowed or rained, the traveller must rise and make ready by the help of a horn-lantern and a farthing candle, and proceed on his way over bad roads, sometimes with a driver showing no doubtful symptoms of drunkenness, which good-hearted passengers never fail to improve at every stopping place by urging upon him another glass of toddy. Thus we travelled eighteen miles a stage, sometimes obliged to get out and help the coachman lift the coach out of a quagmire or rut, and arrived at New York after a week's hard travelling, wondering at the ease as well as the expedition of our journey.[50]

Traveling the same route by stagecoach a few years later, French visitor Brissot de Warville encountered the same hazardous stretch of Horseneck Hill in west Greenwich that had troubled Madam Knight on horseback a century before:

The agreeable part of our journey ended at Fairfield. For thirty-three miles from this town to Rye [New York], we had to fight our way over rocks and precipices. I did not know which to admire more, the driver's daring or his skill. I cannot conceive had he succeeded twenty times in preventing the carriage from being shattered, or how his horses could check the coach when going down the veritable stairways of rocks. The word "stairways" is no exaggeration. One of these, known as Horseneck, is nothing but a steep slope of boulders; if the horses slipped, the coach would tumble 200 or 300 feet down into the valley below.[51]

Breakdowns also were common. One of the most frequent involved a coach's through brace, one of several leather springs that ran under the stage and allowed the body of the coach to swing gently even as the wheels were jolted by an uneven road surface. Given enough jostling, a brace would snap, and an impromptu, on-the-road repair had to be made. As one traveler

Sign of the Red Horse Tavern, from Stephen Jenkins, The Old Boston Post Road *(1913). This old tavern on the upper post road in Sudbury, Massachusetts, operated for more than two centuries under several owners whose initials appear on the sign.*

recalled: "the defect was supplied by breaking down an honest man's fence, and thrusting a rail under the carriage, while the passengers stood almost up to the ankles in mud, holding it up."[52]

As turnpike construction in Connecticut progressed, stagecoach routes multiplied, as both passenger and mail service were extended to towns throughout the state. An 1827 publication listing stage routes, fares, and timetables for all New England—its very existence a sign of the times—noted twenty-six stage routes within and through Connecticut. These included daily service (except Sundays) between centers such as Danbury and Norwalk, New Haven and Hartford, and Hartford and Albany; and thrice weekly service to towns such as Litchfield and Middletown. Numerous intermediate stops along each route created an overland transportation network that extended throughout the more populated portions of New England and the Hudson River valley.[53]

The locus of stagecoach travel in each Connecticut town was the local tavern, usually run by a man of some standing in the community. Tavern stops were typically twelve to eighteen miles apart, and the stage proprietor often owned locations where passengers spent the night. Drivers announced the arrival of their coach by blowing on an English-style trumpet horn, and might use the number of staccato blasts to convey to the tavern-keeper how many passengers to expect for dinner. At table, the driver ate with his passengers, a custom that class-conscious travelers from abroad were quick to note as a sign of the new nation's democratic principles.[54]

In its heyday from 1820 to 1840, stage-coaching was a large-scale enterprise, and a source of livelihood for a significant number of individuals: proprietors, drivers and ticket agents, coach manufacturers and blacksmiths, tavern owners and stable hands, and the farmers who raised the horses and grew the oats, corn, and hay that kept them running. Stage-coaching was America's first transportation subculture, the means by which a considerable portion of the nation along the eastern seaboard became readily mobile and better informed. In a time before the telegraph, when travel and communication were one and the same, such mobility influenced the spread of news, the conduct of business, and the tempo of everyday life for traveler and nontraveler alike.[55]

The Decline of Toll Roads

The turnpike toll road idea was ultimately abandoned as unprofitable, but not before serving an important role in the state's transportation development.

FEDERALISM TRIUMPHANT?

Unlike other states, Connecticut after the revolution did not formulate a new state constitution. Instead, governance of the state continued as usual under the colony's charter of 1662, with the General Assembly firmly controlled by a small group of Congregational Church elite commonly referred to as the "Standing Order." It was not until 1818 that Connecticut enacted its first state constitution, providing for three independent branches of government and the separation of church and state.

As part of the long process of debate and protest that led to the overthrow of the Standing Order, an anonymous writer with obvious republican leanings exercised his frustration in 1802 by writing a six-act farce entitled *Federalism Triumphant, or The Turnpike Road To a Fortune*. The play poked fun at those in the Standing Order who worked to block universal suffrage and the organization of an opposition party. As one character put the matter:

Damn the people! . . . if all the states in the union were to swerve to that cursed jacobinical doctrine of Democracy, and Connecticut stand alone— the combined *good sense* of the *well born,* our steady habits, and well arranged systems, so powerfully supported by the clergy—will overpower the loose, scattered, unconnected, disjointed and disorganized schemes, of all the Jacobins which this state can muster.[56]

As the play's subtitle suggests, the writer used the turnpike corporation as the symbol of all that was wrong with the self-serving Federalist ideology that gripped the state. As an example of turnpike promoters who "preach the common good but mean their own," the author cites James Hillhouse, u.s. senator from New Haven and majority investor in the Hartford & New Haven Turnpike. His alter ego in the play, a character named Jammy Hillroad, proclaimed to a friend:

those turnpike Companies must establish the Aristocracy of Connecticut, by those alone, we maintain our steady habits, the priests will flinch when they see no prospect of an established religion and tythes, but in the Turnpike Company, there is a permanent *prospect* of wealth.[57]

Federalism Triumphant was an amusing contribution to the overthrow of the Standing Order, and its characterization of Federalist turnpike promoters as the state's new aristocracy was not wholly unjustified. Men of power and wealth, such as James Hillhouse, did invest in turnpike roads to further their own interests. However, the message implicit in the play's subtitle, that turnpike investments were themselves a road to fortune, was often far from the truth.

While Connecticut turnpikes had better earnings on average than those in other New England states, the success and life span of individual toll roads varied greatly, as one might expect given the number of turnpikes in the state. Only twenty of the state's one hundred operating turnpikes produced profits from 3 to 10 percent for ten years or longer. One truly exceptional road, the Talcott Mountain Turnpike, earned an average of nearly 11 percent for four decades running. It was even reported that the road's revenue was so great in certain years that company directors chose to spend more than necessary on repairs rather than risk exceeding their 12 percent return rate and having the road become a public thoroughfare. But such success was rare, and well tempered by the four in five turnpike companies that operated with little or no return on their investment.[58]

Locating a tollgate at a point where the surrounding terrain made it difficult to avoid increased the likelihood of a turnpike company becoming financially successful. Many less profitable roads suffered from losing a portion of their traffic to a shunpike, a short detour around a tollhouse that allowed persons in the know to avoid a toll. Together with the normal exemptions allowed local travelers, a well-used shunpike could do serious harm to a company, as it did to the Farmington & Bristol Turnpike, where directors petitioned the state legislature for permission to change the location of their tollgate because they were "in such a situation that the traveler by leaving the road for only a half a mile, can avoid the gate [and] this is practiced by a great proportion of those who travel on it."[59]

The main reason that the revenue of most turnpikes was inadequate to both maintain the road and produce a profit for company investors was the revival of public road-building that occurred during the turnpike era, and for which the turnpike movement was in part responsible. By taking responsibility for intertown roads, turnpike companies freed towns from a burden, allowing them to divert funds that would have been used to service through travelers to the care of local roads instead. As one Goshen resident noted in 1812: "The common roads in this town have for the past ten years been in a state of rapid improvement. This has been owing partly, to the running of two turnpike roads through the town . . . which not only throws more labor on the common roads but gives us . . . a precedent [for their improvement]."[60] At the same time, turnpike construction helped establish a road-building industry whose contractors were experienced and available to work on local roads as well as turnpikes.

The revival of public road-building that accompanied the turnpike era resulted in a network of local roads that offered a free, if less direct, alternative to turnpike travel, a situation that made the traveling public resent having to pay any turnpike tolls at all. After the town of Hamden lost a spirited battle to keep the Cheshire Turnpike from going through its community, the town's officials built a public road specifically intended to circumvent the tollgate of the Cheshire Turnpike. Lest anyone miss the point, the street was named Shunpike Road.

As might be expected, turnpike companies eventually challenged the construction of bypass roads as injurious to their corporations. When a lawsuit brought by the Salem & Hamburg Turnpike against the town of Lyme for building a road parallel to its existing turnpike reached the Connecticut Supreme Court of Errors in 1847, the court ruled against the turnpike company, thereby extending the newly established principle of competition to the realm of public road building.[61]

REPEALING TURNPIKE CHARTERS

Faced with disappointing income and the cost of ongoing maintenance, some turnpike companies began to abandon their roads as early as 1819. By the time the last Connecticut turnpike had been chartered in 1839, some twenty companies had already abandoned all or part of their turnpikes. Since most charters stipulated that turnpike roads would become public again only after the company had achieved a profit of 12 percent per annum on incurred expenses—and it was soon obvious that most turnpikes were not profitable enough for that to happen—lawmakers recognized that they had inadvertently created a legal dilemma for themselves. How was an unprofitable turnpike, whose charter was an inviolate contract under the law, to be returned to public use?

In 1835, the General Assembly took a first step toward undoing this legal tangle by inserting the following provision within a law that confirmed the legality of all existing tollgates in the state: once the shareholders of a turnpike company voted to accept the new law, their company's charter became subject to repeal, alteration, or amendment by the legislature. How many companies availed themselves of this opportunity is not known, but presumably many did not, for various additional laws followed providing the means by which turnpike roads might be released from corporate control. Taken together, the laws suggest the problems being experienced by travelers and turnpike contractors alike during this period.[62]

First, the legislature authorized sheriffs to demand payment of outstanding debts from the turnpike company treasurer (1837); then, if the company's bills were not paid, a receiver could be appointed by the county court to collect enough tolls to cover the debt and repair the roadway (1841); or on the complaint of twenty electors of a town in which a turnpike was located, its tollgates could be opened, and if repairs were not made within thirty days to the satisfaction of the turnpike commissioners, the town was authorized to make the repairs, charge the company, and keep the tollgates open until the debt was paid (1844); or a company could agree to transfer its turnpike to the town as a public highway, but only if the agreement, which might include compensation to the company for its assets, was formally accepted by the shareholders of the company *and* the inhabitants of the town (1853); or a

Mohegan Turnpike Report, 1847. (Mohegan Turnpike Records, Connecticut State Library)

turnpike company could open its tollgates voluntarily and then apply to the county commissioners to abandon all or part of its route (1854); or should a company cease to take tolls and do repairs for one year, such neglect would constitute abandonment of its corporate powers, and the road would become a public highway (1856); and lastly, a failure to comply with a commissioner's request for repairs within sixty days constituted abandonment, and the road became public (1863). In this ad hoc fashion, Connecticut's privately operated turnpike network eventually was returned to public ownership.[63]

In the decommissioning of Connecticut turnpikes, the state's first and last toll roads deserve special mention for their remarkable achievements, one as a unique publicly operated turnpike, the other as a small but successful privately owned turnpike corporation.

The Mohegan Road from Norwich to New London (1792) was not only Connecticut's first turnpike but the only turnpike in the state, and perhaps in the nation as well, to exist as a public turnpike operated by county commissioners throughout its life. This occurred because a portion of the route traversed reservation lands of the Mohegan tribe, which made private ownership of the road impractical. Account statements indicate that every penny earned by this public turnpike was spent on road repairs and related expenses. In addition, an excess of toll revenue during the road's early years allowed the county to extend the route further into Norwich, relieving the town of additional road expense. After a useful life of sixty years, the turnpike was made a public road again in 1852, by which time reservation lands had been subdivided into individual properties.[64]

The Derby Turnpike (1798) between the towns of Derby and New Haven was the last state-chartered turnpike corporation to surrender its road. With just one tollgate, well situated above Maltby Lake, the road had a long and profitable existence, paying dividends to its shareholders for nearly a century. The company was finally bought out by the towns of New Haven, Derby, and several other surrounding communities for $8000, a price that was slightly more than the road's original construction cost. The tollgate of Connecticut's last privately owned turnpike was removed on February 9, 1897.[65]

IMPACT OF TURNPIKE ROADS

Without question the transportation improvements of the early nineteenth century—turnpike roads, toll bridges, stagecoach service, and fewer ferry crossings—significantly improved the comfort and speed of overland travel in Connecticut, and made possible a degree of commerce and personal mobility that could not have been reached without such improvements. The impact can be sensed by reading between the lines of an account by Benjamin Silliman, a science professor at Yale College, who traveled overland from Hartford to Quebec in the autumn of 1819. Heading west from Hartford along the high road to Albany, Silliman wrote: "The fine turnpike on which we commenced our journey, was, but a few years since, a most rugged and uncomfortable road; now we passed it with ease and rapidity, scarcely perceiving its beautiful undulations, which gradually rising, as we receded from the Connecticut river, brought us, within an hour to the foot of Talcott mountain." In Simsbury, Silliman left the turnpike to take a country road through the Farmington Valley, and the contrast suggests the degree of development taking place in turnpike corridors:

> We had now left the Albany turnpike, and the great thoroughfare of
> population and of business, and purposefully deviated into one of those
> wildernesses, which, intersected by roads, and sprinkled with solitary
> houses, afford the traveller an interesting variety, and easily transport
> him back in imagination, to the time when the whole of this vast empire
> was a trackless forest. . . . In the afternoon, during a ride of sixteen
> miles, which brought us to Sandisfield, in Massachusetts, we never left
> the banks of the Farmington river, which owing to its windings, and our
> own, we crossed during the day, no fewer than seven times, and on as
> many bridges.[66]

Overall, the impact of the toll road and toll bridge on Connecticut was a positive one. These privately constructed roads and bridges provided adequately and at minimal cost for the surge of travel created in the first decades of the nineteenth century by a society increasingly commercial in its outlook. With only limited assistance from the state, merchants, bankers, and all manner of businessmen took the risk necessary to provide the infrastructure required for the new state of Connecticut to integrate itself and its economy into that of the region and the nation. Though many investors did not profit, some did, as the buying of shares in a corporate enterprise became an accepted way of making money. And because most investors were local businessmen, those who did not profit directly from turnpike investments benefited from the increase in trade and business that turnpikes nurtured.

Turnpikes also made reliable stagecoach service available to most Connecticut residents. As stage-coaching and the communication it fostered spread over the landscape, the social fabric of the nation was able to coalesce at a time when distance itself threatened political independence. Turnpikes, and the carriages and wagons that traveled them, made mobility commonplace, and travel time an American commodity. As Levi Pease began his career in 1784, a trip by stage from New York to Boston took a bonerattling six days. A decade later, express service in a comfortable coach took only half that time. By the time of Pease's death in 1824, travel time between New York and Boston had been cut in half again, to thirty-six hours. Meanwhile, turnpike travel and the growing affluence of many Americans made carriage manufacturing one of the state's largest industries, and New Haven the carriage-making center of New England.[67]

In addition to solving Connecticut's first transportation crisis, the construction of toll roads and bridges established the publicly regulated joint-stock corporation as a model for subsequent transportation improvements. What began as a necessity dictated by the financial difficulties of state and federal governments became accepted public policy. As turnpike building was under way, the joint-stock model was applied to other modes of transportation, as Connecticut prepared for its third revolution in as many generations, this one symbolized not by a political system, or by legal principles, but by a new technology powered by a new source of energy: steam.

Along with the political and legal revolutions that overtook Connecticut in the first decades of the nineteenth century came a technological revolution based on the mechanization of manufacturing and the power of the steam engine. Steam power revolutionized both industry and transportation, beginning with the advent of the steamboat, to which two Connecticut natives, John Fitch and Samuel Morey, made important contributions. Early steamboat service in Connecticut was delayed by challenges to the New York steamboat monopoly of Robert Fulton and Robert Livingston, but by the 1830s steamboat travel was firmly established on Long Island Sound, and along the Connecticut River as far north as Hartford. Meanwhile, the success of the Erie Canal sparked a canal fever throughout the new nation. In Connecticut, two canals were constructed, sponsored by the state's rival capitals, New Haven and Hartford. The result was a battle of wills that extended from the uppermost reaches of the Connecticut River in Vermont to the capitol building in Washington, D.C., and in the end defeated the best intentions of both canal corporations to provide New England with its first regional transportation system.

The Factory Village: Resettling the Land

The founding of two hundred factory villages in Connecticut created a new wave of settlement on the landscape, while the use of steam power in manufacturing began the urbanization of Connecticut's cities.

As the forces of market capitalism took hold in Connecticut, aided by the chartering of joint-stock corporations and the emerging legal concept of competition, the production of goods moved from small shops to large factories. But what is often referred to as a revolution in industrial production was in fact more a revolution in technology that impacted both the production of manufactured goods and the means of distributing them. This technological revolution was the result of the widespread use of machinery in the manufacturing of many different products, together with the adaptation of steam power to the transportation of these manufactured goods. In the half century from 1790 to 1840, this technological revolution began in Connecticut with the manufacture of textiles and military arms and the advent of the steamboat and steam locomotive, all of which combined to transform the state's economy and its landscape yet again.

Mechanized production in the manufacture of textiles was introduced into America by Samuel Slater, an apprentice in the English textile industry who built southern New England's first cotton mill in Pawtucket, Rhode Island, in 1790. Using machinery developed by English inventors, entrepreneurs such as Slater, Francis Cabot Lowell, and others soon built textile mills throughout the region. In Connecticut, most of these mills were located in the eastern highlands of the Quinebaug and Shetucket river valleys, where fast-running streams were used to power textile machines such as the spinning jenny and the power loom. These machines brought the spinning and weaving processes involved in the manufacture of cotton cloth and woolen apparel, previously a part-time cottage industry performed by women at home, under one roof in large factories where raw materials were now converted into finished products by a full-time workforce of mostly female employees. In the decade from 1810 to 1819, more than 120 cotton and woolen mills were opened in Connecticut alone.[1]

A steady supply of raw material for the growing number of textile mills in the north was ensured by the invention of the cotton gin by Connecticut native Eli Whitney in 1793. This simple box-like machine, operated by hand cranking, made it easier to separate the tightly knit fibers of short-staple cotton from its seed. This made it possible for southern planters to replace their cultivation of long-staple cotton, which was restricted to wetter coastal areas, with a hardier crop of short-staple cotton that could be planted throughout the South. This symbiosis between southern landowners and northern mill owners enhanced by the cotton gin ensured profits for both parties, as it deepened the culture of slavery and slave labor on which their mutual success and interdependence rested.

A major step in the mass production of manufactured arms was taken by the U.S. military, driven by a desire for standardized weapons. In conjunc-

The cotton gin, invented by Eli Whitney, was an essential piece of technology in the production of southern cotton for northern textile mills. In the process, the cotton gin spread the culture of slavery throughout the South. (Courtesy of the Library of Congress)

tion with federal armories in Springfield, Massachusetts, and Harper's Ferry, Virginia, the War Department promoted what became known as the American System of Manufactures, in which rifles and small arms were built by means of the sequential production of interchangeable parts using machine tools of various types. As the method caught on, it was used by private companies in the manufacture of textiles and rugs, and in other industries as well. By identifying mass production as the key to financial success, the American System of Manufactures became the foundation of market capitalism in America.

The War Department worked with outside contractors, one of whom was Connecticut's Eli Whitney, who was given a contract to manufacture thousands of muskets for the U.S. army. To build the guns, Whitney opened a factory on the outskirts of New Haven and hired a workforce of forty men. He arranged the work in assembly line fashion and created a series of machine tools and templates that allowed each workman to visualize the part he worked on, and to cut and drill that part so that the resulting pieces were interchangeable.

Like Connecticut's early textile mills, Eli Whitney's gun manufactory was

VIEW OF ROCKVILLE, FROM FOX-HILL.

water powered. The factory was located near a timber dam on the Mill River
in Hamden, adjacent to the Hartford & New Haven Turnpike. On the one-
hundred-acre site Whitney constructed a factory village that included a
forge, several workshop buildings, five stone houses where married workers
could live with their families, and a boardinghouse for unmarried workmen.
Whitney himself lived with three nephews and several apprentices in a farm-
house across the road from what was the first manufacturing village in
America.[2]

As industry of all types was mechanized, the concept of the factory village
was repeated in versions large and small across the Connecticut landscape,
easily recognized by the suffix "ville" attached to a location's name. Some
factory villages, such as Fluteville in Litchfield (1830), Augerville in North
Haven (1836), and Spoonville in East Granby (1840), were named for the
products made there. Others, like Rockville in Vernon (1794), Oakville in
Waterbury (1852), and Glenville in Greenwich (1854) took their name from a
feature of the local landscape.

But the large majority of factory villages were named for their founders:
Humphreysville, a sheep farm and woolen mill in Seymour (1806) founded
by David Humphreys, former aide-de-camp to George Washington; Yales-
ville, a tin ware factory in Wallingford (1809) founded by Charles and Hiram
Yale; Collinsville, an axe and shovel factory on the Farmington River in Can-
ton (1826) founded by the Collins brothers; Fitchville, an ironworks factory in
Bozrah (1828) founded by Asa Fitch; and Terryville, a clock factory in Plym-

outh (1835) founded by the well-known clock-maker Eli Terry. And of course, Whitneyville, which remains a neighborhood of Hamden to this day.[3]

As the technological revolution unfolded, more than two hundred manufacturing villages were established in Connecticut, and few townships were without at least one of these town-within-a-town manufacturing communities. In the same way that the practice of town founding in the colonial period had reflected the economic (and spiritual) needs of Connecticut's Puritan settlers, the proliferation of manufacturing villages in the nineteenth century reflected the economic needs of the new secular American spirit based on market capitalism.

Like much early American technology, the steam engine was first developed in England and later modified by American mechanics—in particular the low-pressure steam engine as perfected by the Englishmen Matthew Boulton and James Watt in the 1760s. Because waterpower was so plentiful in most of Connecticut, the use of the stationary steam engine in manufacturing occurred later here than might have otherwise been the case. By 1810, reports from some fifty Connecticut towns made note of only one stationary steam engine then in operation. The engine was located at a woolen factory of eighty employees in Middletown, where it ran the company's carding, spinning, and weaving machinery. The steam engine consumed three-quarters of a cord of oak wood during a twelve-hour workday, and the company's owners were sure to note that "the consumption of fuel was a serious drawback upon the profits."[4]

Offsetting the cost of wood-fueled steam power was its portability. As the Middletown example suggests, the stationary steam engine allowed entrepreneurs in lowland towns to also participate in the technological revolution. By 1838, there were forty-seven stationary steam engines in operation in the state, many in lowland towns, eleven in New Haven alone. When George Newhall opened his carriage factory in the Newhallville section of New Haven in 1851, he became the first carriage-maker in Connecticut to utilize steam power. Steam technology then spread to other carriage factories in the city. But it was not until the availability of cheap coal as a fuel source following the Civil War that steam vapor surpassed flowing water as the main source of manufacturing power in Connecticut.[5]

The economic growth in Connecticut that resulted from machine production and the spread of factory villages was mirrored in a substantial increase in the state's population. Previously forced to emigrate westward by a short-

Steam ferry on the Connecticut River, from George E. Wright, Crossing the Connecticut (1908).

age of farmland, Connecticut's increasing population could now find employment in the growing number of mills and factories in the state. By 1860, the population of Connecticut nearly doubled to 460,000 persons, from 250,000 in 1800. A full two-thirds of this increase occurred in the central valley and along the coastal slope west of New Haven; these areas grew at a rate twice that of the state as a whole.[6]

As manufactured goods made their way from upland mills to distribution centers in lowland valleys and to port towns, much of this growth was concentrated in the state's cities. At the start of the nineteenth century, Connecticut's five existing cities, Hartford, New Haven, Middletown, New London, and Norwich, held only 10 percent of the state's total population. As manufacturing grew, two additional cities were incorporated in Bridgeport (1836) and Waterbury (1853), and by the onset of the Civil War these seven cities contained more than one-quarter of the state's total population. Half the population increase that occurred during this period was absorbed by these seven cities alone.[7]

By any measure, the onset of market capitalism in the nineteenth century had a significant impact on the number of people in the state and where they lived. Of the 150 towns that existed in Connecticut in 1860, about one-third were involved in industrial production of one kind or another, to one degree or another. Meanwhile, more effective farming methods, including crop rotation, were introduced in the remaining one hundred towns to increase the productivity of Connecticut farmland and thereby the state's ability to feed a growing population.[8]

By 1830, the pattern of triangular trade with the West Indies that characterized the state's economy during the colonial period had been replaced by a triangular interdependence among the three main sections of the new nation: the industrial Northeast, the cotton South and the grain-producing Midwest. But the emerging national economy was not without its growing pains. As production outpaced consumption and more goods were produced in one region than could be consumed in another, economic growth underwent repeated cycles of speculative expansion followed by economic slowdown. Before the Civil War, the nation experienced three of these boom-bust cycles: in 1819–21, 1837–43, and 1857–60. Periodic crashes continued to occur in the decades following the war.

Maintaining a high level of industrial production required the ability to ship products long distances reliably and cheaply. While turnpike construction made the shipping of goods overland easier, earthen roads were not well suited for the long haul, particularly if the freight was heavy or bulky. Through the application of the steam engine to the problem of long-distance transportation, the power of steam helped provide the very reliability and shipping capacity necessary for the full realization of the technological revolution. The story of steam transportation on water and over land occupies the remaining chapters of this book. This story begins in Philadelphia in 1787, when the Continental Congress was busy inventing a new nation, while the Connecticut native John Fitch was busy inventing a new mode of transportation: the steamboat.

The Advent of the Steamboat

The steamboat monopoly created by Robert Fulton and Robert Livingston led to a landmark decision of the u.s. Supreme Court that opened interstate commerce to unfettered competition.

FROM FITCH TO FULTON

Robert Fulton and Robert Livingston began the first financially successful steamboat service in America on the Hudson River between New York and Albany in 1807. But like most inventions, the steamboat had many parents, two of whom, John Fitch and Samuel Morey, merit mention as Connecticut natives whose work predated that of Fulton and Livingston, and contributed to the success of the Fulton-Livingston partnership.

John Fitch (1744–98) was born in South Windsor, Connecticut, the youngest son in a poor farming family. His ambition and thirst for knowledge exceeded the opportunities available to someone of his social standing. In 1769, at age twenty-five, Fitch left behind a wife and two children in Connecticut to seek his fame and fortune in the wider world.[9] By the onset of the American Revolution he had become a successful silversmith in Trenton, New Jersey, but he lost both his business and his savings in the Battle of Trenton. After several attempts to regain his financial footing, first as a profiteer at Valley Forge and later as a surveyor and land jobber in the Ohio River valley, Fitch finally settled in Philadelphia. In 1785, he had the idea of building a steam-powered boat, an invention he was convinced would open the waters of the Ohio and Mississippi rivers to trade and settlement, and in the process bring him the fame and fortune he so desired. He later wrote: "I have frequently thought that Heaven has been preparing me for this great undertaking from my Childhood."[10]

With the assistance of Henry Voigt, a local clock-maker, Fitch completed his first working steamboat in 1787. Forty-five feet long and twelve feet abeam, the boat was powered by a small, homemade steam engine, with steam generated by an onboard water tank and a wood-burning brick furnace. A pawl-and-ratchet mechanism attached to the engine converted the rectilinear motion of the piston to the rotary motion necessary to move the boat forward. The boat's propulsion system consisted of twelve paddles, six on either side of the boat, connected to the engine through an overhead wood frame. As the piston moved up and down, the paddles moved through the water, six in, six out, in alternating fashion, pushing the boat forward.

On August 20, 1787, Fitch demonstrated his steamboat for delegates of the Constitutional Convention, who were meeting just a few streets from the Philadelphia waterfront in Independence Hall. He was hoping to gain support for his invention and convince the delegates to include a patent clause to protect inventors such as himself in the Constitution they were drafting. The trial run, with some convention delegates on board, was the first time a steamboat was operated in American waters. A week later, back in Connecticut, the president of Yale College, Ezra Stiles, noted in his diary: "Judge Ellsworth, a member of the Federal Convention, just returned from Philadelphia, visited me, and tells me . . . he there saw a Steam-Engine for rowing

boats against the stream, invented by Mr. Fitch, of Windsor, in Connecticut. He was on board the boat, and saw the experiment succeed."[11]

While the demonstration showed it was possible to run a boat against the flow of a large river using the power of steam, this first steamboat's speed was only four miles per hour, too slow for practical application. For a steamboat to be viable, it had to operate at twice that speed or more to compete with overland travel by stagecoach. For three years Fitch and Voigt persevered, overcoming financial and technical difficulties to achieve their goal: a working steamboat that operated at eight to ten miles per hour. Commenting on a trial run of this second steamboat, propelled by oar-shaped paddles mounted in the rear, Fitch noted: "altho the Wind blew very fresh at N.E., we reigned Lord high admirals of the Delaware, and no Boat on the River could hold sway with us, but all fell a-stern."[12]

With this success, the company Fitch organized to fund his steamboat experiments made the new boat passenger-ready, and by June 1790 Fitch and Voigt were operating a thrice-weekly steamboat service from Philadelphia upriver to Burlington, Bristol, Bordentown, and Trenton, New Jersey. The Fitch steamer left Philadelphia each Monday, Wednesday, and Friday and returned the following day. The service ran for three months, during which John Fitch and his steamboat logged about two thousand miles traveling up and down the Delaware River. It was the first scheduled steamboat service in the world.

So that he might profit from his invention, Fitch early on obtained exclu-

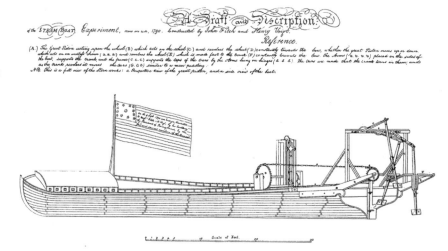

sive rights from the legislatures of Pennsylvania, New York, New Jersey, and Virginia. To satisfy the size requirement of the Virginia monopoly, which included the right to operate on the Mississippi and Ohio rivers, Fitch set about building a third and larger boat. But when a storm destroyed the boat before it was completed, Fitch and his company placed their fate instead in the hands of the newly established U.S. Patent Board, headed by Thomas Jefferson.

In one of the first requests to the new Patent Board, Fitch applied for protection as the original and sole inventor of the steamboat. However, two other men, James Rumsey of Virginia and John Stevens of New Jersey, had conducted steamboat trials of their own. Though neither man began as early as Fitch or had as yet built a viable steamboat, they too sought protection from the board. Unwilling to choose a priority inventor, the board instead issued identical steamboat patents to all three men.

Since none of the three inventors had the money to mount an expensive legal battle to prove the priority of his claim, and since the existence of other identical patents made it difficult for the men to raise the capital necessary to continue their work, the net result of the nation's first patent conflict was to discourage further steamboat development until the fourteen-year term of the first patents had elapsed. Dejected by the government's refusal to recognize the priority of his work, Fitch ultimately retreated to Kentucky, where he took to drink and died a pauper.

The second native of Connecticut to invent a working steamboat was Samuel Morey (1762–1843). Born in Hebron, Morey moved as a child with his family to Orford, Vermont, where from a young age he displayed an aptitude for mechanical invention. Unaware of the work of Fitch and other steamboat experimenters, Morey built a steam engine of his own design in 1790, and within two years was operating a small steamboat on the Connecticut River near Orford at a speed of four miles per hour.[13]

At the suggestion of Benjamin Silliman, professor of science at Yale College, Morey went to New York City, where he worked for three consecutive summers perfecting his steam engine and experimented with different methods of propelling his boat through the water. Called home in 1795 by an illness in the family, Morey brought his steamboat to Hartford for safekeeping, where he ran it in the presence of curious onlookers. It was the first time a steamboat was operated in Connecticut waters.

The following year, Morey returned to New York and exhibited his boat to a few interested persons, including steamboat enthusiast Robert Livingston and his brother-in-law, patent holder John Stevens. Livingston was a member of a well-known New York family and was chancellor of New York State. After a short excursion on Morey's boat from lower Manhattan to Greenwich Street on the west side of New York City, Livingston offered Morey $7,000 for the right to use his patented engine design on the Hudson River. Livingston promised an even greater sum if Morey succeeded in building a boat capable of reaching eight miles per hour. Morey rejected the offer, but was encouraged enough to continue working on his steamboat design.

In 1797, Morey built a second steamboat in Bordentown, New Jersey, propelled through the water by two paddle wheels mounted amidships, one on either side of the vessel. After a trial run on the Delaware, Morey noted: "I found that my two wheels answered the purpose very well, and better than any other mode that I had tried." Morey exhibited the boat at Philadelphia, and from that time "considered every obstacle removed, and no difficulty remaining or impediment existing to the construction of steamboats on a large scale." Morey's paddle-wheel steamer caught the attention of several Philadelphia businessmen interested in operating a steamboat company, but in the end his supporters were unable to raise the necessary funds. Disappointed, Morey returned to Vermont, where he continued to work on other inventions.[14]

The following year, Robert Livingston petitioned the New York state legislature to transfer the monopoly it had granted earlier to John Fitch to him, on the grounds that Fitch had left the region and was no longer actively pursuing his invention. Given the chancellor's influence, the transfer was made with little fuss. Over the next two years, Livingston and his brother-in-law John Stevens conducted several steamboat trials in New York City, hoping to satisfy the state monopoly. Neither attempt resulted in a working steamboat, and the partnership was dissolved when Robert Livingston was appointed u.s. minister to France to negotiate the Louisiana Purchase.[15]

It was in Paris that Livingston first met Robert Fulton and the two men struck a deal to pursue Livingston's New York steamboat monopoly. Fulton's ambition and skill as a mechanic together with Livingston's financial resources and political influence proved a winning combination. After purchasing a steam engine manufactured by Boulton and Watt in London, Livingston and Fulton returned to the United States to execute their plan. In the summer of 1807, the North River Steamboat Company founded by Livingston and Fulton ran the first commercially successful steamboat in America on the Hudson River between New York and Albany. Within a few years, Fulton and Livingston built additional steamboats and opened additional routes in New York, and on the Mississippi and Ohio rivers, where they had secured exclusive operating privileges.[16]

CHALLENGING THE MONOPOLY

It took more than a decade of legal challenges by steamboat operators, climaxing in a landmark decision by the u.s. Supreme Court, to defeat the monopoly of Livingston and Fulton and open the nation's waterways to unfettered steamboat competition. Several of these challenges inadvertently provided Connecticut with its first steamboat services.

In the summer of 1811, John Stevens began to operate a steam-powered ferry from Hoboken, New Jersey, to lower Manhattan, in competition with a steam ferry licensed by Livingston and Fulton. Though clearly in violation of the New York monopoly, Robert Livingston allowed his brother-in-law to run the service unmolested for more than two years. After Livingston's death in 1813, Fulton took legal action against Stevens and threatened to seize his steamboat, the *Juliana,* unless he stopped running the service. To protect his steamboat, Stevens surreptitiously sent the *Juliana* to Connecticut with his son James, who made a daring nighttime run past British warships patrolling Long Island Sound during the War of 1812. Stevens described the event in a letter to another son:

James started from here with the *Juliana* on Thursday last, 9 o'clock, and arrived at Killingworth, within 10 miles of the mouth of the Connecticut, at 10 o'clock Friday morning. In proceeding from thence, he was chased by six barges filled with men—they got within four miles of him. He, however, arrived at Saybrook safe, at 3 o'clock in the afternoon, and proceeded from thence up the river to Middletown.[17]

Two weeks after the New Jersey steamer arrived in Connecticut, a notice appeared in the *Connecticut Courant* advertising daily steamboat service between Hartford and Middletown aboard the *Juliana.* The trip carried a one-way fare of 75 cents and took three hours on the downstream run and four and one-half hours on the upstream return. The captain of the *Juliana* also made intermittent stops as requested. Little else is known of Connecticut's first scheduled steamboat service, except that advertisements for the *Juliana* continued through November 1813, and presumably so did the *Juliana.*[18]

Following the end of America's second war with England in 1815, the monopoly put one of its own boats, the *Fulton,* into service in Connecticut waters between New York and New Haven. The *Fulton,* whose namesake was now also deceased, was a marked improvement over the *Juliana.* Measuring 134 feet in length and 36 feet abeam, the *Fulton* traveled the seventy-five miles from New York to New Haven in eleven hours, and accommodated fifty to one hundred passengers on its overnight voyage. Below deck, a forward cabin acted as a gathering room and dining hall, while settees in the rear of the boat were converted into sleeping berths, with two small cabins set aside for female passengers. On deck, the black-hulled *Fulton* stored the cord upon cord of wood needed to raise steam for the nonstop voyage. But like most early steamers, the *Fulton* was also sloop-rigged, with a full set of sails, as insurance against difficulties with the boat's one steam engine.

Two years later, a second monopoly boat, the *Connecticut,* replaced the *Fulton* on the New Haven run and provided thrice weekly service to New York, while the *Fulton* ran a connecting service from New Haven to New London on alternate days. With the two steamers, owned and operated by an out-of-state corporation with which Connecticut businessmen could not compete, the monopoly established its full presence in Connecticut waters.[19]

A challenge by John Langdon Sullivan, son of an ex-governor of Massachusetts and chief engineer of Boston's Middlesex Canal, also left its impact on Connecticut. To tap a lucrative market not served by the monopoly, Sullivan patented a steam tugboat system designed to pull sloops and barges laden with freight up and down the nation's major rivers. For several years, Sullivan petitioned the legislature of New York for the right to operate his tugboat business on the Hudson, using the power of steam to tow freight from Albany to New York City. Steamboats owned by the monopoly were prohibited by law from carrying freight, so Sullivan saw his service as non-competitive. But even after the death of Livingston and Fulton, the monopoly's founders, its political clout was such that Sullivan's reasonable request was repeatedly denied.[20]

In 1818, Sullivan retreated to Hartford, where he sought investors interested in establishing his steam-powered tugboat system on the Connecticut River. As an enticement, Sullivan noted that his steam tugboats were powered by a rotary engine designed by Samuel Morey, from whom Sullivan had purchased the patent rights. At a meeting of local businessmen, Sullivan discussed his plan for a line of moderate-sized tugboats to pull barges up and down the Connecticut River from Hartford to Saybrook, and a fleet of smaller tugs to run on the upper river above Hartford.

Eager to join New Haven in the steam age, several Hartford businessmen agreed to the plan, and later that year they were granted a state charter as the Connecticut Steamboat Company, the state's first steamboat corporation. The company built a tugboat, the *Enterprise,* that was put into service between Hartford and Saybrook in the summer of 1819.[21] Meanwhile, Sullivan obtained a charter of his own to build a bypassing canal around the rapids at Enfield to make steamboat travel possible north of Hartford. Once the canal had been completed, Sullivan planned to establish a freight monopoly on the upper river as far north as Northampton, Massachusetts.[22]

However, Sullivan's charter for a canal around the Enfield rapids put him in competition with the Enfield Toll Bridge Company, whose earlier charter contained a similar provision. Although the bridge company had not acted on the provision and was later relieved of its responsibility to build the canal by the legislature, Sullivan's legal standing in the matter was not clear. This uncertainty, together with the financial panic of 1819, made it difficult for Sullivan to raise the capital needed to build the canal. Thwarted yet again, Sullivan returned to Boston, leaving behind as his legacy in Connecticut the formation of the state's first steamboat company, and the idea for a multi-state tugboat monopoly on the upper Connecticut River.[23]

In 1820, a legal challenge to the monopoly finally reached the u.s. Supreme Court, and it seemed that the steamboat issue would be resolved. The suit originated in New Jersey, where Aaron Ogden, a licensee of the monopoly, sued his competitor Thomas Gibbons for operating an unlicensed steam ferry across the Hudson between New Jersey and New York. Rather than capitulate to the monopoly, Gibbons had chosen to run his ferry under a standard coasting license issued by the federal government, thereby presenting the Supreme Court with a clear legal issue: did the power of the federal government to regulate interstate shipping trump that of an individual state to issue a restrictive patent governing steamboat operations?

As the Court continued to postpone a hearing of the case, the Connecticut legislature acted in 1822 to pressure the monopoly (and the Court) by passing a retaliatory law that banned steamboats licensed by the New York monopoly from operating in Connecticut waters. As a result, the *Connecticut* and the *Fulton* were withdrawn from service and assigned to Rhode Island, where they were used to establish the first steamboat service between New York City and Providence: a one-way trip of twenty-five hours![24]

With the monopoly banned from Connecticut, a group of New Haven packet owners bought their own steamboat and started a combination steamboat and stagecoach service between New Haven and New York. The men ran their steamboat, the *United States,* as far as Greenwich, where they transferred passengers to a waiting stagecoach for the remainder of the journey. Like the service of the monopoly it replaced, the steamer-stagecoach service ran thrice weekly, and cost $4 for a one-way trip. On alternate days, the *United States* traveled from New Haven to New London and Norwich to gather additional passengers. Not willing to be outdone, the monopoly instituted a mirror image of this service by running a sail-driven packet boat from New Haven to Oyster Point, Long Island, where a monopoly-owned steamer waited to bring passengers into New York City through New York waters.[25]

In March 1824, the Supreme Court under Chief Justice John Marshall handed down its long-awaited decision in *Gibbons v. Ogden.* By defining commerce in broad terms as any form of commercial intercourse, the Marshall Court ruled that the movement of passengers and freight from one state to another clearly fell within the commerce clause of the Constitution and was subject to regulation by the federal government, not individual states. A proper coasting license, like the one under which Gibbons operated, was all that was needed to conduct interstate commerce. The fact that the service involved new technology and a new mode of transportation was irrelevant. "The laws of Congress for the regulation of commerce do not look to the principle by which vessels are moved." With that, Marshall made state patents, such as the one granted by New York to John Fitch and later transferred to Robert Livingston, null and void.[26] Meanwhile, the u.s. Patent Board was available to protect inventors and their new technologies.

STEAMBOATING AFTER GIBBONS V. OGDEN

Once news of the high court's decision reached New Haven, the *United States* made its first full-length trip into New York. As the steamer chugged into New York harbor, flags flew, passengers cheered, and an onboard canon fired a victory salute. That spring, the owners of the *United States* obtained a state charter as the New Haven Steamboat Company, purchased a second steamer, the *Hudson,* and in conjunction with the *United States* began daily service to New York. The *Fulton* and *Connecticut* were returned to service on the New Haven run, but customers boycotted the boats, and the steamers of the former monopoly were soon returned to service between New York and Providence. In Hartford, meanwhile, the Connecticut River Steamboat Company, chartered in 1823, built its first steamer and initiated that city's first steam-powered service to New York. The Hartford boat was named the *Oliver Ellsworth,* after the Connecticut justice who had ridden on the first steamboat operated by John Fitch in Philadelphia forty years earlier.[27]

In the decade after *Gibbons,* seven additional corporations were also chartered to provide service from Connecticut ports to New York. To the west of New Haven, they were the Norwalk & New York Steamboat Association (1824), the Stamford Steamboat Company (1825), the Bridgeport Steamboat Company (1824), and the Ousatonic Steamboat Company (1835); and on the Connecticut River, the Hartford Steamboat Company (1824). In eastern Connecticut, the steamboat operators included the Norwich Steamboat Company (1826) and the New London & Norwich Steamboat Company (1832). In addition, two companies were chartered to operate steam-powered tow services on the Connecticut River: the Hartford & Greenfield Tow Boat Company (1823) and the Steam Navigation Company of Middletown (1825).[28]

An account of a trip from New York to Hartford by two Englishmen who were visiting America to report on its prisons indicated how quickly the steamboat became an accepted mode of travel on Long Island Sound, well integrated with existing stagecoach service:

> I left New York for Hartford in Connecticut with Mr. Crawford (the Commissioner for Inspecting the Prisons) and his coadjutor Mr.

Newman. We went by steam-boat to New Haven (eighty-four miles) and the rest of the way (about forty) by stage. The whole fare (by sea and land) was three dollars each. It was eight o'clock P.M. when we arrived at the end of our journey, having started at seven in the morning. . . . At the hotel where we put up, the first on entering Hartford, we found everything extremely good. The rooms were clean and well furnished, and the people of the house particularly civil.[29]

As noted in the account, the fare from New York to Hartford was less than it had been under the monopoly, no doubt a result of the competing services now available to travelers.

As the steamboat became a permanent fixture on the waters of Long Island Sound, the need for companies to continually upgrade their fleets to accommodate a growing volume of passenger and freight traffic became the driving force behind technological innovations in engine and hull design. During the 1830s, a second generation of steamboats appeared that were larger, faster, and more comfortable than early experimental models. The newer boats had more than one deck, and an enclosed deck space to keep cargo from the weather. Some were equipped with two boilers and two engines for faster speeds and carried private cabins below for passengers willing to pay extra for additional comfort. But most telling, Long Island Sound steamboats were no longer rigged with masts and sails, a sure sign that the steam engine had achieved status as a reliable source of motive power.

The largest steamer on the sound in this period was the *New York,* a 230-foot day steamer put in service by the New Haven Steamboat Company in 1836. A vivid glimpse of the *New York* is provided by Charles Dickens, who traveled aboard it from New Haven to New York in the 1840s:

The great difference in appearance between these packets and ours, is, that there is so much of them out of the water: the main-deck being enclosed on all sides, and filled with casks and goods, like any second or third floor in a stack of warehouses; and the promenade or hurricane-deck being a-top of that again. A part of the machinery is always above this deck; where the connecting-rod, in a strong and lofty frame, is seen working away like an iron top-sawyer. There is seldom any mast or tackle: nothing aloft but two tall black chimneys. The man at the helm is shut up in a little house in the fore part of the boat (the wheel being connected with the rudder by iron chains, working the whole length of

New Arrangement...Commencing on Monday, August 4th, 1845.

FOR

RIDGEFIELD,
WILTON & NORWALK.

Fare through $1.00

The Old Line of Stages will leave Ridgebury every

MONDAY, THURSDAY & SATURDAY

AT HALF-PAST TWO O'CLK. A.M.,

And RIDGEFIELD at FOUR o'clock, passing through WILTON and arriving in
NORWALK in time for Passengers to take the Steamboat for New-York.

**Returning, leave Norwalk on the same days, on the arrival of the boat
from New-York.**

AUGUST, 1845.   **D. HUNT, Proprietor.**

the deck); and the passengers, unless the weather be very fine indeed,
usually congregate below. . . .

There is always a clerk's office on the lower deck, where you pay your
fare; a ladies' cabin; baggage and stowage rooms; engineer's room; and
in short a great variety of perplexities which render the discovery of the
gentlemen's cabin, a matter of some difficulty. It often occupies the
whole length of the boat (as it did in this case), and has three or four

tiers of berths on each side. . . . After exhausting (with good help from a friend) the larder, and the stock of bottled beer, I lay down to sleep; being very much tired with the fatigues of yesterday.[30]

Connecticut passed its first steamboat laws in the 1830s. The statues addressed mainly safety issues, such as landing passengers using a small boat when a shore landing was not possible; the passing of other steamboats on the right; the carrying of lifeboats; and the display of lights at night.[31] However, regulating the dangers inherent in steam technology was not easily accomplished.

From 1827 to 1833, three steamboat disasters occurred on Long Island Sound, all the result of boiler explosions. The most damaging involved the *New England,* whose double copper boilers exploded in the early hours as the steamer approached the town of Essex on an overnight run from New York to Hartford. Debris from the explosion shattered portions of the boat, and gallons of boiling water spilled into cabins below deck where passengers slept. Fifteen persons were killed, and ten others were severely scalded.

Public awareness of the danger from exploding boilers presented steamboat operators with a public relations challenge. Owners of the *Victory* and the *Oliver Ellsworth,* Connecticut steamers equipped with low-pressure engines, were quick to note that fact in their advertisements. Since it was also known that explosions resulted from the carelessness of a boiler man who ran with the safety valve open to increase speed, ads for the *Ellsworth* proclaimed that the steamer had "an extra safety-valve, exclusively under the control of the commander," surely an uncommon design feature of the time. Boat designers, meanwhile, took pains to locate engines and boilers on the overhanging portion of a boat's hull to minimize injury and damage in the event an explosion occurred.[32]

Given the federal control of interstate commerce asserted by *Gibbons,* repeat boiler explosions brought calls for the federal regulation of steamboat technology. In 1838, Congress enacted a law requiring inspectors (chosen by federal judges) to inspect the hulls of steamboats in their district once every year and their engine machinery every six months. The law established the national government as the primary regulator of steamboats, but the lack of specific standards for the construction and operation of steam engines and boilers limited the law's effectiveness.[33]

It was not until 1852 that Congress passed comprehensive legislation concerning steamboat safety. The new law appointed two inspectors for each

New-York & Boston
STEAM BOAT LINE, via
HARTFORD.

The New Steam Boat
OLIVER ELLSWORTH,
Daniel Havens, Master,

Leaves *NEW-YORK* on Tuesdays and Fridays
4 P. M.
Leaves HARTFORD on Mondays and Thursdays
at 11 A. M.

The Oliver Ellsworth is a boat of the first class, is fitted up in elegant style, and has su
erior accommodations for passengers.

Experience has proved her engine to be strong and powerful, constructed upon the Bolto
nd Watt, or *low pressure* principle ; having an extra safety-valve, exclusively under the cor
rol of the commander of the boat; and for convenience and safety is probably not surpasse
y any boat in this country.

The commander of the Oliver Ellsworth has had great experience in the navigation o
ong Island sound, and has by his gentlemanly deportment and polite attention, given un
ersal satisfaction to passengers.

Stages will be in readiness, on the arrival of the Steam Boat at Hartford, to forward pas
engers to Boston, Vermont, and New-Hampshire.

HARTFORD. March, 1826.   *CHAPIN & NORTHAM*, Agents.

customs district, one to inspect the hull of the boat, its passenger safety equipment, and overall seaworthiness and another to inspect the material, workmanship, and strength of the boat's boilers and related machinery. The law included specifications for the stamped iron used in steam boiler construction, the maximum pressure of steam engines, and the use of gauges by which the engineer monitored the pressure of his engines. The act also created a national board to oversee the inspectors, outlined new procedures for the licensing of steamboat engineers and pilots, and provided stiff penalties for those caught in noncompliance with the regulations. In Connecticut, federal steamboat inspections began on March 1, 1853, and were administered by the New London customs district.[34]

It was the commercial activity of New York City, fed by the textiles, shoes, brass buttons, tin ware, and metal tools produced in the factory villages of southern New England, that drove the demand for larger steamers with more cargo space. The steamboat also spurred passenger travel in the New York–Boston corridor by offering greater comfort than a bumpy, dusty stagecoach trip. Although stagecoaches provided important feeder service to steamboat ports, and two-masted packet boats still sailed Long Island Sound in large numbers carrying passengers and cargo, their heyday was past. The future of Connecticut transportation, whether over water or land, lay in the power of steam, and the competitive spirit of the privately owned, publicly regulated corporations that built and operated the services that steam power made possible.

Canal Fever

The success of New York's Erie Canal sparked a flurry of canal construction throughout the nation during the 1820s, including the building of the Farmington and Enfield canals in Connecticut.

INFLUENCE OF THE ERIE CANAL

In 1806, with payment of the nation's revolutionary war debt almost completed, Congress took a first step toward the federal funding of turnpikes and canals by authorizing the construction of the "National Road," extending from Cumberland, Virginia, across the Appalachian divide to the Ohio River. The work was undertaken with the consent of Pennsylvania and Ohio, the two states in which the road was located, and paid for with revenue from the sale of public lands in Ohio. But President Thomas Jefferson, a strict constructionist with regard to the powers the Constitution conveyed to the national government, considered such internal improvements beyond the scope of federal power as it existed. Though he signed the National Road bill into law, he recommended that Congress pass an amendment to the Constitution to allow the national government to fund such projects on an ongoing basis.[35]

Instead, Congress directed the secretary of the treasury, Albert Gallatin, to evaluate the issue of internal improvements and recommend a plan for the construction of projects deemed to be of national importance. After gathering information on improvements contemplated by each state, Gallatin presented his findings in his 1808 *Report of the Secretary of the Treasury on the Subject of Roads and Canals.* The report proposed two dozen turnpike and canal improvements along the eastern coast and across the Appalachian divide that Gallatin believed would bind the established seaboard states together from Maine to Georgia, as well as connecting them to the trans-Appalachian west. Gallatin estimated that the projects could be accomplished within ten years at a cost of $20 million.[36]

Sectional rivalries and a second war with England prevented action on Gallatin's plan until 1816, when Senator John Calhoun of South Carolina introduced legislation to fund the projects using revenues from the chartering of the Second National Bank. Exhorted to action by Calhoun's rhetoric, Congress enacted his proposal by a slim margin in both houses. As with the National Road, Calhoun's bill relied on the consent of the states involved to empower the actions of the national government. President James Madison, however, vetoed the bill, saying: "If a general power to construct roads and canals, and to improve the navigation of water courses, with the train of powers incident thereto, be not possessed by Congress, the assent of the States in the mode provided in the bill cannot confer the power." With too few votes to override the veto, the first congressional attempt to establish a national transportation plan was defeated.[37]

New York State was an avid supporter of the Gallatin plan and of the cross-state canal proposed to connect the western territories with the Hudson River at Albany via Lake Erie. After Madison's veto, the New York legislature proceeded with the Erie Canal on its own and funded the project largely on the credit of the state. Engineered by Connecticut native Benjamin Wright, the Erie Canal was a financial gamble of unprecedented proportions. Three hundred fifty miles long, with eighty-three locks and eighteen aqueducts to carry it over rivers and streams, the Erie Canal cost an astounding $7 million. The

Middlesex Canal in Massachusetts, the largest American canal then built, had cost less than 10 percent of that sum.

Construction of the Erie Canal began on July 4, 1817, and the first stretch, from Rome, New York, to the Hudson River at Albany, opened in 1823. The Erie was an immediate success, collecting $1 million in toll revenue during its first year of operation. The canal was completed to Lake Erie two years later, and by the end of the decade tolls from freight and passenger traffic had repaid the entire cost of construction. By grabbing trade that otherwise might have gone down the Mississippi or through the Great Lakes to Canadian ports, the Erie Canal turned New York City into the nation's premier port, and added to the reputation of the state that had made it all happen without federal assistance.[38]

In the heat of the fever induced by the construction of the Erie Canal, other states in the nation dreamed of similar riches, and canal projects were begun in Pennsylvania, Ohio, Indiana, Virginia, and—to a lesser degree—in New England. By 1840, using engineers who had honed their skills on the Erie Canal, these states had built a total of over thirty-three hundred miles of canals at a cost of $125 million. Unfortunately, few if any achieved the degree of success the Erie had.[39]

At the height of canal fever, the Connecticut legislature granted charters for the construction of six canals in the state: the Farmington Canal (1822), the Ousatonic Canal (1822), the Sharon Canal (1823), the Enfield Canal (1824), the Quinebaug Canal (1826), and the Saugatuck & New Milford Canal (1829). Despite the enthusiasm of their hometown promoters, four of these canal projects never raised funds sufficient to begin construction.[40] They were:

The Ousatonic Canal. Intended to connect manufacturing villages on the upper Housatonic and the iron furnaces of the Salisbury area with the port of Derby, this canal line was surveyed by Benjamin Wright, after which a charter was granted. The cost of the sixty-six-mile canal was estimated at $600,000, including sixty locks. It was expected that the canal would be extended to Stockbridge, Massachusetts, at an additional cost of $34,000, putting the Ousatonic's northern terminus within forty miles of Albany and the Erie Canal. Subscriptions were opened on July 1, 1822, but the response was insufficient, and the canal's commissioners never called a meeting to organize the company. The canal's charter expired unfulfilled after ten years.

In 1839, an effort was made to revive the project with the incorporation of the smaller Ousatonic Canal & River Company, whose charter ran from Derby northward for only twelve miles, but even this modest proposal failed to materialize.

The Sharon Canal. This short, two-mile-long canal was the tail end of a larger proposal for the New York & Sharon Canal incorporated in New York in April 1823. The project was to run from the Croton River in Pawling, New York, to Great Barrington, Massachusetts, where it would connect to the great Boston–Albany canal being planned in that state. But the proposal never progressed beyond a preliminary survey, and the charter for the portion of the project in Sharon soon expired.

The Quinebaug Canal. Intended to run north from the Thames River at Norwich to Worcester, Massachusetts, this canal was to be used for the shipment of raw materials and finished products in and out of the many textile mills situated along the Quinebaug River. The idea languished for three years before supporters were organized in both states and a preliminary survey of the route was made. In 1826, a charter was granted in Connecticut to the Quinebaug Canal Corporation but was repealed at the request of its own supporters, who thought the provisions so "obnoxious . . . as to render it useless and worse than useless." In its place, the Quinebaug Canal Bank was chartered to help raise funds for construction. But political delays in Massachusetts doomed the project.

The Saugatuck & New Milford Canal. This Fairfield County canal was chartered to extend from Saugatuck Harbor in Westport through Weston, Reading, Danbury, and Brookfield to the center of New Milford. A survey of the route was made and costs were estimated at $417,000 for a canal with all stone locks, $329,000 for a canal with stone and timber locks, and $271,000 for a canal that used inclined planes for the lifting and lowering of boats. Commissioners were appointed to oversee construction, but subscription books for the project were never opened, and the charter expired after ten years.

Unlike New York and other states that financed their canals in whole or in part on the credit of the state, Connecticut gave no financial assistance to its canal promoters. Capital for canals in Connecticut was intended to come solely from the shareholders of the corporations chartered to build them.

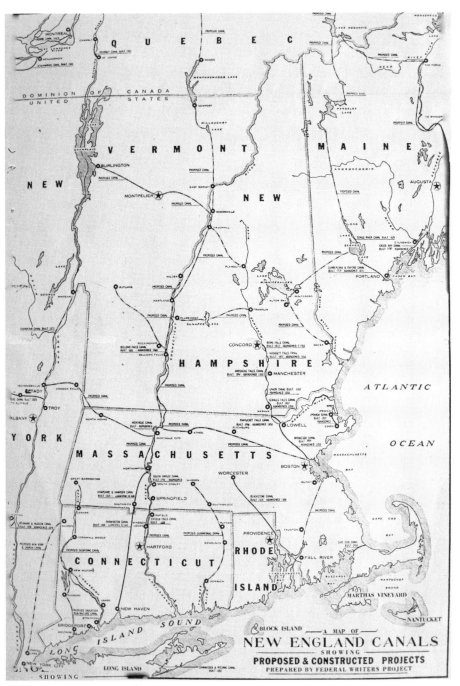

New England canals, from Connecticut: A Guide to Its Roads, Lore and People *by the Workers of the Federal Writers' Project (1938).*

The state offered only indirect assistance by making canal stock tax-free until such time as a company's profits reached 6 percent per annum. In addition, Connecticut allowed for the incorporation of canal banks, a specified portion of whose capitalization was pledged to the purchase of stock in a particular canal company.

Given these preconditions, building canals in Connecticut was a risky business. And because of the state's size, one terminus of any canal of significant length would likely be located in another state, making the project even more difficult to organize and finance. In addition, by the time the state chartered its first canals, inland regions of Connecticut were well served by turnpike roads, with more being built. Turnpikes not only competed with canals for investment dollars, but were built with less fuss and at less expense.

What is surprising, then, is that two Connecticut canals were built: the Farmington Canal, an ambitious proposal by the merchants of New Haven to divert trade away from their rival, Hartford; and the Enfield Canal, a river improvement sponsored by Hartford businessmen looking to follow in the footsteps of John Sullivan and open the Connecticut River above Hartford to the steamboat. Given the long-standing, spirited rivalry between these twin capitals of Connecticut, which would be brought to a fever pitch by the possibility of federal funding for their canals, the building of the Farmington and Enfield canals became one of the most competitive episodes in nineteenth-century corporate transportation.

NEW HAVEN AND THE FARMINGTON CANAL

In the course of geologic history, the city of New Haven was twice cheated. With the lifting and erosion of New England's central valley, the Connecticut River etched its course in the landscape by cutting through a trap rock ridge at Northampton, Massachusetts, to flow on the east side of the ridge and past the future sites of Hartford and Middletown. Had the river remained west of the ridge at Northampton, it would likely have flowed south to New Haven, making that city the main port of central New England. Likewise, during the process of glaciation, New Haven was denied access to an inland waterway when glacial debris diverted the Farmington River from its heading southward toward New Haven and into the Connecticut River at Windsor instead.

When canal fever reached New Haven in the 1820s, merchants saw the possibility of giving their city the inland waterway that nature had denied it. Building a canal from tidewater at New Haven to the Connecticut River at

Northampton created in effect a manmade tributary of the Connecticut River west of the trap rock ridge that could establish New Haven as the logical destination of trade originating along the upper reaches of the Connecticut River.

In January 1822, representatives of New Haven and sixteen other towns in the Farmington valley met to discuss plans for such a canal. A survey of the route by Benjamin Wright followed, and by May the group had received their charter as the "President, Directors and Company of the Farmington Canal." The next year, the Hampshire & Hampden Canal Company was chartered in Massachusetts to construct the portion of the canal in that state.[41]

An ambitious plan from the start, the canal was a true engineering challenge. With a cross-section twenty feet wide by four feet deep, excavating the eighty-mile canal meant the removal of three million cubic yards of earth and fourteen thousand cubic yards of rock. Those sections where the canal rose above grade required the placement of an additional one million cubic yards of earthen fill. The work would be performed using tools no more sophisticated than homemade shovels, wheelbarrows, and horse-drawn wagons and would be done by hundreds of itinerant Irish laborers from the Erie Canal and by farmers along the route looking to earn extra income.[42]

The elevation profile of the route required that the canal rise and fall more than five hundred feet from tidewater in New Haven to its junction with the Connecticut River at Northampton. Given that the wooden construction materials of the day could provide no more than ten feet of lift per lock, keeping the canal's water surface level throughout its length required sixty locks—twenty-eight in Connecticut and thirty-two in Massachusetts—each lock seventy-five feet long and twelve feet wide. The locks were made from an outer wall of heavy stone and an inner lining of timber planks. Water in the locks was held in place by two sets of hefty wooden doors, each with two wickets through which water could be let into or out of the lock.

Highway and stream crossings required building more than two hundred bridges and stone arch culverts to carry the canal over smaller streams. Eight aqueducts also had to be constructed to carry the canal and its towpath over wider waterways. The largest in Connecticut was a stone arch structure over the Farmington River that consisted of seven 40-foot spans.

Because the Farmington Canal crossed between two watersheds, the water supply entered the canal at its highest point, near the Massachusetts border. For the Connecticut portion of the canal, water was provided by the Farmington River, which was brought to the canal at the state line via a

The Farmington Canal crossing the Farmington River. (Courtesy of the New Haven Museum)

three-mile feeder canal from a dam constructed below Unionville. In Massachusetts, Congamond Ponds, the Little River, and the Westfield River all supplied water for the Hampshire & Hampden Canal. Where streams intersected, their water was used to counteract loss from evaporation and seepage. Likewise, spillways were placed along the route to carry off excess rainwater.[43]

Recognizing the scope and complexity of the project, the Connecticut legislature appointed a board of six commissioners to oversee construction and supervise operation of the canal once it was completed. The commissioners' duties included working with engineers to finalize the canal's location; determining lands to be taken and awarding fair compensation for all damages; locating tollhouses and private crossings; directing the construction of bridges and highway relocations; opening the subscription books of the company and recording the names of all investors; calling the first meeting of the corporation once sufficient funds had been pledged; inspecting construction work and filing final location surveys and cost figures for the project; licensing boats operating on the canal; setting tolls for boats and tariffs for all goods shipped; and inspecting the condition of the canal and related structures at least once each year and ordering repairs as necessary. Like turnpike and bridge commissioners, canal commissioners had the authority to make the canal free if recommended repairs were not made to their satisfaction.[44]

Raising funds for the project, however, was difficult. The Farmington Canal alone was estimated to cost $420,000, the Hampshire & Hampden Canal an additional $290,000. Neither figure included land costs. When the subscription books for the Farmington Canal were opened in July 1823, the company was encouraged by an initial spurt of stock pledges, but subscriptions slowed before enough funds could be raised to begin construction. Lest the project falter at the start, the directors of the canal obtained a charter for the Mechanics Bank of New Haven, which was allowed to purchase up to $200,000 in Farmington Canal stock. With the bank's help, the directors of the Farmington Canal had enough capital pledged by April 1825 for construction to begin.[45]

Then something odd happened. Suddenly, the company recruited James Hillhouse to join its board of directors, elected him president, and gave him added authority as superintendent of the project. Hillhouse, a native of New Haven, a former U.S. senator, and an astute politician, had resigned a position as head of the Connecticut School Fund to take over the canal project. No sooner had Hillhouse arrived than talk began of extending the canal to upper New England from Northampton, Massachusetts, to Barnet, Vermont, and then overland to Lake Memphremagog on the Vermont-Canada border. Hillhouse also implied that corporations in Canada were ready to continue the canal to the St. Lawrence River and thereby establish a water route from New Haven to the West via the Great Lakes independent of the Erie Canal. The fact that the New Haven route was twice as long did not dampen its supporters' enthusiasm.[46] What happened to cause this change of leadership and scope on a project already considered overly ambitious? In a word: competition. To no one's surprise, it originated in Hartford.

Steamboats on the Upper River

Hartford businessmen responded to the challenge of the Farmington Canal by attempting to establish a steamboat monopoly on the upper reaches of the Connecticut River.

HARTFORD'S RESPONSE: A RIVER MONOPOLY

From its source in upper New England to tidewater at Hartford, the Connecticut River falls more than two thousand feet. On the way, as the river carves its niche into the valley's sandstone floor, it encounters outcroppings of harder, erosion-resistant rock, and the result is a stretch of white-water rapids that are an obstacle to navigation. One such rapids north of Hartford in Enfield was considered the limit of ship navigation on the Connecticut River from the time the Dutch explorer Adriaen Block first encountered it in 1608.

During the colonial era, the difficulty posed by the Enfield rapids was overcome by building a warehouse at the foot of the falls on the east side of the river; furs and pelts headed south from Springfield, Massachusetts, were brought down the rapids by raft and stored in this warehouse until they could be loaded onto ships headed downriver. Goods headed upstream were unloaded at the warehouse, stored if necessary, and then carted overland to Springfield. As commerce increased, this strategy was used to accommodate trade of all types moving up and down the river. By the 1760s it was not unusual for a dozen sailing ships to be docked at the foot of the falls, at the location known as Warehouse Point.[47]

Enfield Falls was not the only obstacle to upriver trade. Above Springfield the river was obstructed at Turner's Falls and South Hadley Falls in Massachusetts and at Bellows Falls, Sumner's Falls, and Olcott's (Wilder) Falls in Vermont, until one reached the town of Barnet, above which a fifteen-mile stretch of rapids was considered the true limit of any kind of upriver navigation. Between 1795 and 1810 canals were built bypassing each of these rapids in Massachusetts and Vermont, improving navigation along a two-hundred-mile stretch of river above Springfield.

During this time, three attempts were also made to improve navigation at the Enfield rapids: by lottery in 1791; again in 1798, when the construction of a bypass canal was included in the charter of the Enfield Toll Bridge Company; and in 1818, when John Sullivan was granted his charter as part of a plan to introduce steam tugboats to the upper river. None of these efforts came to fruition. It was just this situation—a relatively obstacle-free upper river interrupted by a major navigation hazard just north of Hartford—that the merchants of New Haven sought to exploit with their construction of the Farmington Canal.[48]

To counter New Haven's threat, Hartford businessmen came together in 1824 and obtained a charter for the Connecticut River Company, hoping to execute the plan John Sullivan had earlier proposed and then abandoned. Their goal was to construct a canal around the rapids at Enfield, combine all river canals above Hartford under one company, and operate a line of steamboats to tow freight on the upper river between Hartford and Barnet, Vermont. By rebuilding the locks to a uniform size, standardizing tolls, and utilizing the power of steam to tow freight at eight miles per hour (twice the speed of a horse-drawn canal boat) the company hoped to create a monopoly on the upper river whose service would be superior to the canal service being planned by New Haven. As with the Farmington Canal, a board of three commissioners was appointed by the legislature to oversee the activities of the company.[49]

Was the market upriver sufficient to warrant such an expenditure of time and money? To answer that question, the group conducted a survey of conditions upriver, only to concede that "notwithstanding all that has been done by the proprietors of the present locks and canals, the amount of transportation on the river has diminished since their construction." The main reason for the drop-off in trade was the construction of turnpike roads across central Vermont and New Hampshire that carried trade to port towns such as Portland, Maine, Newburyport, Massachusetts, and Boston—the primary destination for trade in upper New England. Such roads had lessened the cost of overland transportation from that of pre-turnpike days, when the river was the cheapest route to market.

Still, despite the facts, the report remained optimistic and concluded: "The fact that the navigation above Hartford has declined, notwithstanding a large expenditure in partial improvements, seems . . . to prove with the certainty of experience, that divided operations, and small efforts to improve the river, will not supply the great want, a cheap and expeditious carriage to and from market." Their answer was a "thorough and general improvement of the navigation" of the kind proposed by the Connecticut River Company.[50]

To muster support for their plan, the directors of the Connecticut River Company held a two-day convention in Windsor, Vermont, in February 1825. The affair was well attended by two hundred merchants, businessmen, and public officials representing dozens of river towns in the four-state region. To understand what happened at the convention, one must look to Washington, D.C., where legislation had recently been enacted concerning the federal funding of internal improvements. In the midst of ongoing bickering over transportation issues, Congress in April 1824 had passed the General Survey Act, which created a board of engineers to survey and prepare cost estimates for road and canal projects of national importance. Many, including the directors of the Connecticut River Company, believed the General Survey Act was the first step in the development of a national transportation plan, and that projects chosen for surveys under the act would later receive federal construction funds.[51]

As a result, the Windsor convention heartily endorsed a proposal to expand the scope of the river project north of Barnet to the Canadian border, so

19th CONGRESS,   [Doc. No. 154.]   HO. OF REPS.
1st Session.   DEPT. WAR.

SURVEY—CONNECTICUT RIVER, &c.

LETTER

FROM

THE SECRETARY OF WAR,

TRANSMITTING

A Report of a Survey of Connecticut River,

FROM

Barnet, in Vermont, to Lake Connecticut.

AND, ALSO,

A Canal Route

FROM

MEMPHRYMAGOG TO CONNECTICUT RIVER.

APRIL 12, 1826.

Read, and laid upon the table.

WASHINGTON:

PRINTED BY GALES & SEATON.

1826.

as to impress Washington with the national significance of their multistate project. It was the convention's endorsement of the expanded upriver plan in February 1825 that prompted the directors of the Farmington Canal to recruit James Hillhouse as their president that April and to expand the scope of their project to match that of the Connecticut River Company. That summer, as requested by the two companies, federal engineers surveyed two routes through Vermont to the Canadian border: one along the Connecticut River above Barnet, another via an overland canal from Barnet to Lake Memphremagog.[52] Meanwhile, the Connecticut legislature endorsed the Connecticut River Company's expanded plan, increasing capitalization to $1,500,000 and allowing the incorporation of the Connecticut River Banking Company to help raise capital for the project.[53]

THE CAUSE IS LOST

To prove that steamboats could indeed navigate the upper river (some thought the channel too shallow) the Connecticut River Company proceeded to build its own steamboat, a flat-bottomed, seventy-five-foot stern-wheeler named the *Barnet* that needed a mere twenty-four inches of water in which to operate. Named for its intended destination, the *Barnet* began its maiden journey in November 1826. After clearing the rapids in Enfield with the help of several dozen pole-men, the steamer proceeded without incident to Springfield, Massachusetts, and then to Brattleboro, greeted at each stop by cheering citizens eager to see their first steamboat. Delayed for a time by ice, the *Barnet* reached Bellows Falls, Vermont, in mid-December, but there her voyage ended. The steamer had been built too wide to fit through the canal locks in that town.[54]

Despite the embarrassment, the *Barnet* proved the viability of steamboat travel on the upper river, and the following summer the company directors began construction of the Enfield Canal. It consisted of a six-mile-long channel on the west side of the river that bypassed the upper and lower rapids of the Enfield falls. The canal included one lock at its headwaters and three more at its lower end, for a total drop of thirty-three feet. In between were several miles of calm water and a one-hundred-foot aqueduct over Stony Brook. At the head of the canal, a seven-hundred-foot wing dam extended to the middle of the Connecticut River to facilitate access to the canal. As with the Farmington Canal, the work of digging the channel and removing the earth, one wheelbarrow at a time, was largely accomplished by Irish canal workers.

The Enfield Canal opened on November 10, 1829, and to mark the day two new stern-wheel steamers built for the occasion and filled with dignitaries and supporters from Hartford and Springfield made their way through the canal as hundreds more cheered onshore. After the celebration, sixteen toll-paying vessels laden with merchandise passed through the locks on the canal's first day of operation.[55] After four attempts in as many decades, the last physical obstacle to upriver travel on the Connecticut River had been removed.

To control trade on the upper river, however, the Connecticut River Company needed to gain political support in each upriver state for its steamboat monopoly, and that was no simple matter. After the Windsor convention, the company secured a charter from the Vermont legislature that defined its intent in greater detail. With a capitalization of $1,500,000 and limits of operation that extended from Hartford to Barnet, the company was empowered to purchase existing river canals (with the approval of one-half of the stockholders); build a new system of locks on the river to accommodate boats with dimensions sixty-six feet long by sixteen feet wide; collect tolls according to a rate schedule in the Vermont charter; and own their own steamboats. To oversee the company, the charter created a board of twelve commissioners, three from each of the four river states, and stipulated that any action taken by the company required the approval of a majority of the commissioners of the state in which the action was to take place.[56]

To become law, the Vermont charter required confirmation by the other river states. Two states, Connecticut and New Hampshire, endorsed the new charter with certain provisos. In addition, a congressional committee on roads and canals in Washington issued a report in March 1827 recommending that the federal government purchase one-third ($500,000) of the company's stock once the Vermont charter became official. Reiterating the history of the project, the congressional report noted: "The improvements contemplated by this act of incorporation are among the most important to the New England States that can be presented to the consideration of the National Legislature." All that remained for the project to get under way was "an application now pending before the Legislature of Massachusetts for their assent and confirmation, the grant of which, though resisted by local jealousies and supposed conflicting interests, cannot reasonably be doubted."[57]

Despite the committee's optimism, here the company's plan ultimately faltered. For two years, river company supporters waged a battle of political wills in the Massachusetts legislature against the interests of Bostonian merchants and the promoters of the Hampshire & Hampden Canal. After the

Supreme Court decision in *Gibbons,* a public distaste for monopoly made the Connecticut River Company proposal even more difficult to swallow. In the end, the legislators of Massachusetts allowed the Connecticut River Company to combine the two canals in that state (Turner's Falls and South Hadley) into one company, but did not approve the multistate proposal.[58]

With their plan to combine all river canals under one corporation defeated, the Connecticut River Company tried to salvage at least the second part of their proposal: the creation of a steam tugboat service along the upper river between Hartford and Wells River, Vermont, to compete with the Farmington and Hampshire & Hampden canals. To accomplish this, Connecticut River Company supporters obtained a second charter in Vermont for the Connecticut River Valley Steamboat Company in 1829.

The following year, the Connecticut River Company held a second convention in Windsor, Vermont, and there adopted a plan to build five steamboats, each boat to operate on a different stretch of river, towing freight and carrying passengers between existing canals. The price tag for construction of the five steamers was a modest $20,000. Funds were raised through subscriptions, and in the spring of 1831 the tugboats were put into service. The volume of business was disappointing, and revenues proved insufficient to cover the operating expenses of the company. When a second stock assessment was called, stockholders declined to invest further. After one year of operation, the Connecticut River Valley Steamboat Company was forced to quit its business.[59]

While the Connecticut River Valley Steamboat Company was occupied with its tugboat plan, two attempts were made by others to reach Barnet, Vermont, by steamboat. First, the *Vermont,* a small stern-wheeler with a draft of only twelve inches, steamed upriver as far as Windsor, Vermont, where it became stuck in the locks north of town. Later, the first steamer built specifically to fit through all of the locks on the river, the *John Ledyard,* traveled upstream as far as Wells River, where it ran aground on a sandbar. Despite these heroic efforts, in the end no Connecticut River steamboat ever reached Barnet, Vermont.[60]

Closer to home, the Connecticut River Company met with modest success. Business on the river between Hartford and Massachusetts was brisk. Here steam-powered tugboats hauled barges loaded with livestock, liquor, and cheese up and down the river, while small steamers built by Massachusetts river towns carried passengers downstream to Hartford, and to a connection with New York–bound steamers. Still, this modest success had to be qualified, since many steamers used the Enfield Canal only when traveling upstream, choosing to avoid the downstream toll by riding the rapids instead. As a result, toll revenues were less than expected, despite an increase in local river traffic.[61]

Lower toll revenues adversely affected the Connecticut River Banking Company, which owned $60,000 in Connecticut River Company stock. Because the bank expected to profit from the dividends of the river company, the bank's charter precluded it from issuing notes on the portion of its capital that was tied up in the river company. When it became apparent that no such dividends would be forthcoming, the bank ended its relationship with the Connecticut River Company. Meanwhile, the Connecticut River Company continued to operate the Enfield Canal, supplementing revenues by leasing land it owned between the canal and the river to manufacturers interested in establishing factories near the canal's water supply. Ultimately a dozen factories of various types were constructed along the Enfield Canal.[62]

The Fever Breaks

The construction and operation of the Farmington Canal were plagued with financial difficulties that ultimately led to its demise.

TROUBLE ON THE FARMINGTON CANAL

While the Connecticut River Company battled for their steamboat monopoly, James Hillhouse and his associates were likewise busy seeking approval from the legislatures of Massachusetts, Vermont, and New Hampshire to extend their Hampshire & Hampden Canal northward to Lake Memphremagog. Since the canal company was not allowed by charter to operate its own packet boats, such an extension did not constitute a monopoly, and the necessary approvals were granted with little difficulty. Technically, Hillhouse and his supporters had won the political battle for the upper river—if only they could complete their canal to Northampton.

The first portion of the canal from New Haven to Farmington opened to traffic in 1828. To commemorate the occasion, the packet boat *James Hillhouse* was launched at Plainville. As two hundred dignitaries sipped refreshments on deck, the *Hillhouse* was pulled through the bucolic landscape by four large gray horses ridden by four African-American boys. Additional boats, built and owned by merchants along the route of the canal, were also put into service. By 1830, the entire canal in Connecticut was operational, along with the lower portion of the Hampshire & Hampden Canal in Massachusetts. As apples, butter, cider, and wood flowed south to New Haven, imports such as coffee, flour, hides, molasses, salt, and sugar went upstream as far as Southwick.[63]

However, by then both canal corporations were in dire financial straits. Land purchases and unanticipated expenses on the Farmington Canal (including a washed-out bridge over the Salmon River) increased the cost of that project to $770,000, and the company had fallen behind in its payments to contractors and landowners. One contractor who was owed $16,000 described the trouble he had collecting his fee: "Those having claims against the Company have repeatedly presented their claims . . . for nearly a year without any success. . . . The company having neither money or credit have considered it their duty . . . to keep the chief engineer out of the way so that people could not obtain their estimates and to elude, evade, prevaricate, procrastinate, and totally neglect to pay any old claims." Meanwhile, some landowners who had not yet received the payments due them took their anger out directly on the canal, causing breaks to suddenly appear in the embankments, whose repair only added to the company's financial difficulties. The sale of $100,000 in stock to the city of New Haven allowed the Farmington Canal Company to clear its immediate debts, but $130,000 was still needed to complete the canal in Massachusetts.[64]

To resolve the problem, Hillhouse traveled to Washington (at the age of seventy-five!) to petition his former colleagues for financial assistance. In ten pages of testimony, Hillhouse made an impressive case for a request of $150,000 to complete incidental construction on the canal in Connecticut and $130,000 to bring the Hampshire & Hampden Canal to Northampton. Noting that the federal government had recently purchased shares in three southern canals, Hillhouse testified:

> Whenever individuals have engaged in important internal improvements, and have embarked a large amount of property, the General Government have always afforded their aid, if necessary, to enable them to complete their undertaking. . . . Will the Government of the United States suffer those individuals to be crushed, and an important improvement lost, for want of aid which can be afforded with so little inconvenience and no risk, and is similar to what has heretofore been afforded to other portions of the Union?[65]

Hillhouse also took the opportunity to make a case for the national government's support of the canal's extension to Canada, which he believed could be accomplished under a compact among the four states. With Congress behind the proposal, Hillhouse declared, "can there remain a doubt as to raising funds to carry the canal to the Canada line?" But despite a last-minute reduction in his request to $155,000 for both canals, House and Senate bills authorizing Congress to purchase 250 shares of stock in the Farmington Canal and 1,300 shares in the Hampshire & Hampden Canal were tabled in May 1830, and were never again acted on.[66]

Hillhouse returned to Connecticut empty-handed. But with the incorporation of the City Bank of New Haven in 1831 and its purchase of $100,000 in canal stock, an additional $60,000 in loans from individuals along the route in 1833, and the incorporation of the New Haven County Bank in 1834 with a commitment of $5,000 for the project, work on the Hampshire & Hampden Canal limped toward completion. On July 29, 1835, the Hampshire & Hampden Canal opened to Northampton, a decade after ground was first broken for Connecticut's Farmington Canal.[67] Unfortunately, Hillhouse did not live to see the project completed, having died in 1832.

In Connecticut, the New Haven Packet Boat Company began offering passenger service over the entire length of the canal, with boats leaving daily from Hillhouse Basin in New Haven for the journey to Northampton. With the boat pulled at a slower-than-walking speed, the leisurely one-way trip, including stops at Cheshire, Farmington, and Granby, took twenty-four hours and cost $3.75. While many persons availed themselves of day excursions on the canal, the profit made by packet boat owners from the transportation of freight was much greater.[68]

Even with the project completed, damage from freshets left the Farmington Canal Company and the Hampshire & Hampden Canal Company both heavily in debt, and the two were reorganized into one corporation, the New Haven & Northampton Company, in 1836. With the reorganization, all outstanding debts were paid (many at less than full value), and a cash reserve of $120,000 was created to operate the new company. In the end, the reorganization was accomplished at a loss to the original shareholders of more than $1 million.[69]

In its first years of operation, business on the New Haven & Northampton Canal increased steadily. In 1839, for example, the revenue collector at New Haven cleared one hundred packet boats each month that fall, carrying some four million pounds of goods headed for inland markets. While communities along the canal prospered, damage to the canal from flooding and freshets

NEW HAVEN AND NORTHAMPTON
DAILY
CANAL BOAT LINE,
AND
STEAMBOAT TO CHEAPSIDE.

The New Haven and Northampton Canal Transportation Line have extended their line of Boats to Cheapside, by adding a Steamboat to run from Northampton. They have also a Steamboat running in connection with the above line from the Basin Wharf in New Haven to New York.

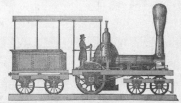

By this arrangement Goods shipped from Albany and Boston by the Western Railroad via Westfield Depot, and from New York and the South via New Haven, will arrive at Cheapside with safety and regularity in the best deck Canal Boats.

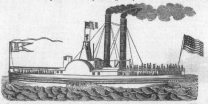

The Steamboat Franklin will leave Northampton for Cheapside landing, on MONDAY, WEDNESDAY, and FRIDAY. Returning, leave Cheapside landing on TUESDAY, THURSDAY, and SATURDAY. The Steamboat SALEM will leave the Basin Wharf in New Haven for New York, every MONDAY and THURSDAY, at 9 o'clock P. M. Returning leave Old Slip, New York, every TUESDAY and FRIDAY, at 5 o'clock P. M. For freight or passage inquire of *J. & N. BRIGGS,* No. 40 South Street, New York, or of *N. A. BACON,* New Haven, or of the Captain on board.

Freight from Boston and Albany will be delivered daily at the Brick Depot, Westfield, and transhipped without delay in the canal boats for Northampton and Cheapside landing, near Greenfield, and in connection with

BEECHER'S DAILY LINE FROM NEW HAVEN,

the present arrangement affords facilities and dispatch hitherto unenjoyed.

The rates of freight generally have been reduced, and Flour from Albany via the Western Railroad, will be delivered at Northampton, *for 34 cents per barrel, and from Albany to Cheapside landing for 40 cents.*

For further particulars inquire at the store house west side of the Deerfield Bridge, at Cheapside, of JOHN R. BOYLE; HENRY BEECHER, New Haven; J. & N. BRIGGS, No. 40 South Street, New York, or of the subscriber at Northampton.

JOSEPH L. KINGSLEY, *General Agent.*

Northampton, April 1, 1845.

For a brief time, the Farmington Canal was part of an emerging regional network that included the steamboat and the railroad. (Courtesy of the New Haven Museum) was exceptionally high, so that during its first four years of full operation, toll revenues recovered barely 20 percent of the company's expenses.[70]

In 1841, Joseph Sheffield, a Connecticut native who had made his fortune as a shipper of cotton in the South, became the president and largest stockholder of the New Haven & Northampton Canal. Convinced that the canal could be profitable, Sheffield arranged with steamboat operators on the upper river to ship their goods via the canal. The following year revenues exceeded expenses for the first time in the canal's history. But the results were short-lived, and Sheffield soon realized what the directors of the Connecticut River Company had known from the start: that in the long term, transportation profits were found in the shipment of goods and not in the collection of tolls. In 1845, Sheffield sought to amend the company's charter so that he could own and operate his own line of packet boats. Little is known of the attempt except that it never materialized, likely because it smelled of monopoly. Soon after, the New Haven & Northampton Canal ceased operation, at an additional loss to shareholders of $288,000.[71]

LESSONS LEARNED

Neither the Farmington Canal nor the Enfield Canal produced the results their investors had anticipated, and for several reasons. Although both projects were earnestly conceived and executed, both were from the start overly ambitious and woefully underfunded, a deadly combination that competition between the two companies—for investment dollars, political support, and limited upriver trade—only made worse. In addition, the General Survey Act encouraged the two rivals to expand their projects even further and as a result to waste years of time and energy on the unlikely possibility of receiving federal assistance.

In their respective spheres, however, both projects were a boon to economic activity. The Farmington Canal benefited dozens of shippers and merchants throughout the Farmington valley from New Haven to Granby, while the Enfield Canal served a substantial amount of river traffic between Hartford and northern Massachusetts. Had the two companies confined themselves to more limited objectives, their projects could have been completed in a timely manner, and to the advantage of their stockholders.

The Connecticut River Company's attempt to become a multistate corporation was a well-executed effort by a group of businessmen to deal with the issue of regional transportation at a time when the national government, divided by sectional rivalries, was unwilling to do so. James Hillhouse's attempt to obtain federal funds for the completion of his canal project can be seen as a valiant, if futile, effort to influence national policy on behalf of Connecticut and New England. While both companies were defeated by their best intentions, their efforts represent an important and often overlooked episode in American transportation history.

The story of the Farmington and Enfield canals gives a clear glimpse into the problems of providing adequate regional transportation at the onset of the industrial era. As a case study, this episode in Connecticut history epitomizes the conundrum at the heart of privately financed transportation, where profits are readily made from the carrying of goods and passengers, and not from the collection of tolls for the use of a particular infrastructure. Certainly there were notable exceptions to the rule: the Erie Canal on a regional scale and Connecticut's own Derby Turnpike on a state level. But overall, the construction of the Farmington and Enfield canals illustrated the fact that in transportation profits are often made by those who use a facility and seldom by those who build and maintain it.

But was a transportation monopoly by a privately owned corporation contrary to the public interest? Evaluating that question required a mode of transport that was both infrastructure and common carrier in one, a mode with its own right-of-way that carried passengers and freight in vehicles that the company itself owned. If such a mode could have a statewide network under the control of a single corporation, the question of competition versus monopoly might be better evaluated. As it happened, even as the conflict between canalers and riverites was unfolding, just such a mode of transportation was invented in England: the railroad.

Chapter Four The Railroad, Part I

The first railroad charters issued in Connecticut were prompted not by a demand for railroads within the state but by rail construction in surrounding states. The situation was understandable, given that Connecticut had an extensive turnpike network, numerous steamboat services on Long Island Sound, and two canal projects under way whose outcome was still uncertain. Once rail construction began, investors were quick to build railroad lines in the state's north-south river valleys to serve steamboat ports on Long Island Sound, and later along routes east and west of Hartford and New Haven. Uppermost in the minds of most railroad corporations was the ultimate goal of all-rail service between New York and Boston, which was achieved with the opening of the New York & New Haven Railroad in 1848. By 1860, with six hundred miles of track in place, all major commercial corridors in Connecticut had good railroad service. Following the Civil War, rail construction continued as the state extended its rail network to one thousand miles. Within this now overbuilt network, stronger roads exerted control over weaker ones through a variety of financial arrangements, as individual lines consolidated into railroad systems. The state's dominant rail system was that of the New York, New Haven & Hartford Railroad, which grew in leaps and bounds to become a powerful railroad giant known as the Consolidated.

Early Railroading in Connecticut

The first two decades of railroading in Connecticut were concerned with establishing a basic rail network and regulating the safety hazards posed by the new technology.

THE COMING OF THE RAILROAD

As the power of steam became apparent, inventive men on both sides of the Atlantic looked for ways to apply that power to transportation over land. In Connecticut, as early as 1797 Apollos Kinsley used a steam engine of his own design to power a makeshift steam-wagon along Main Street in Hartford. But the size and weight of early steam engines, their constant need for water, and the rutted roads of the day presented severe obstacles to a steam-powered highway vehicle.[1]

The same year, a scale model of a steam engine mounted on a strange-looking land vehicle was found among the belongings of John Fitch after his death. Fitch had constructed the model while living out the last years of his life in Bardstown, Kentucky. The vehicle had four flanged wheels connected to the steam engine's power train by belts of hemp that ran through grooved indentations in each flange. The model survives, and many historians of technology believe it depicts the world's first steam locomotive.[2]

Ultimately, it was the idea of running metal wheels over metal rails that made overland steam transportation possible. The low rolling friction of metal on metal enabled a steam-propelled locomotive of small horsepower to pull a heavy train of railcars over the land at a speed of thirty miles per hour or more, thereby creating the economy of rail transport: high-volume transportation with a low unit cost. This transportation had the ability to unleash the full potential of the technological revolution.

The world's first steam railroad opened near London in 1825, just as the Connecticut River Company was about to embark on its effort to bring steamboats to the upper Connecticut River. When news of the event made its way to Hartford, the company sent a committee to England to evaluate the threat that the Stockton & Darlington Railway posed to their project. But the short, twelve-mile railroad, powered by a steam locomotive built by George Stephenson, operated at barely six miles per hour; and when Stephenson's iron horse proved erratic, the stagecoach-like carriages of the Stockton & Darlington were pulled along even more slowly by real horses. The Connecticut River Company committee concluded, therefore, that their company had nothing to fear "so long as merchandise could be transported by water at the

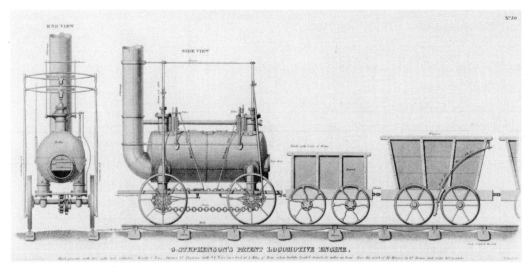

George Stephenson's locomotive operated on England's first railroad, the Stockton & Darlington, which members of the Connecticut River Company visited on their fact-finding trip in 1826. (Courtesy of the Library of Congress)

rate of four miles an hour, no competition by land methods, even by steam traction, need to be apprehended."[3]

The company's investigation of English railroading, and its decision to proceed with construction of the Enfield Canal, though sensible, was premature. By the time the canal was completed in 1829, Stephenson's newest locomotive, the Rocket, had proved itself the fastest in all England, winning the famous Rainhill Trials by traveling at a speed of twenty-nine miles per hour, a feat considered impossible just a few years earlier. With the success of the Rocket, the railroad age began in earnest, and steam locomotives built by Stephenson and other English mechanics were soon imported and put to work on American railroads in Maryland, New York, and Massachusetts.[4]

In 1830–31, the state of Massachusetts took a bold leap into the rail age by chartering New England's first three railroads. Each was positioned to enhance Boston's status as the commercial hub of New England. The first, the Boston & Lowell, was aimed toward upper New England to take the place of the Middlesex Canal in carrying to Boston the traffic generated in the textile center of Lowell. The second was the Boston & Providence, which ran south from Boston to create a shorter land route for the commerce the coastal trades were hauling around Cape Cod. And the third, the Boston & Worcester, was the first link in a rail trunk line to Albany and points west. Each road developed into one of the great railroad systems of New England: the Boston & Maine, the Old Colony, and the Boston & Albany, respectively.[5]

In particular, Massachusetts hoped that the Boston & Worcester, and the Western Railroad, its extension to Albany (chartered in 1833), would divert commerce arriving from the west on the Erie Canal away from New York City to Boston, making Boston the main port of the Northeast for foreign and domestic commerce. However, unlike Philadelphia and Baltimore, which built trunk lines of their own to compete with New York, a rail route to Boston from the west had to first cross New York State, where it could easily be intercepted by the construction of a north-south road to New York City. Recognizing the threat posed by Boston's Western Railroad, New York chartered several railroads of its own: one through the Mohawk River valley to parallel the east-west route of the Erie Canal, and two north-south roads in the Hudson River valley between Albany and New York, thereby providing continuous rail service from the west to New York City.[6]

It was as a result of the competitive activity of its neighbors that Connecticut issued its first two railroad charters in May 1832: one for the Sharon & Salisbury Railroad, to be part of New York's easternmost railroad, which was expected to run through northwestern Connecticut; another for the New York & Stonington Railroad, to run from the Rhode Island state line to the town of Stonington as an extension of the Boston & Providence railroad through Rhode Island. Of the two, only the New York & Stonington was constructed. It opened in 1837 and became Connecticut's first operating railroad.

Connecticut's first two charters illustrate an important point with regard to railroading in the state: rail freight in Connecticut was dependent on the commercial centers of New York, Albany, Boston, and Providence, as traffic filtered down into the state from the Boston-to-Albany trunk line in Massachusetts, or up into Connecticut from a shoreline rail route between New York and Providence, while goods manufactured within the state were sent westward using the same trunk lines. As for passenger traffic, geography ensured that railroads in Connecticut would be mainly local in nature. As Connecticut's Joint Committee on Internal Improvements observed at the time about the state's regional position in the rail age: "The ocean and the Stonington Rail Road on the east, the Western Rail Road on the north, the Hudson River on the west, and Long Island Sound on the south, leave Connecticut entirely insulated."[7] The one major exception, of course, was passenger through travel between New York and Boston.

As railroad construction progressed in both Massachusetts and New York, Boston's hope of becoming *the* port of the Atlantic Northeast faded. Before construction of the Erie Canal, foreign commerce leaving from Boston and New York had been approximately equal. By 1859, imports and exports moving through the port of New York exceeded that of Boston by fivefold, and domestic commerce likewise. Although the tonnage of rail freight reaching Boston grew dramatically during the 1840s and 1850s, barely 15 percent of it originated west of Albany. In the interim, the transformation of New York City that had begun with the opening of the Erie Canal was completed by the railroad, and the city that postal inspector Hugh Finlay had referred to in 1773 as "a little hamlet less important than Philadelphia or Boston" was now the chief Atlantic port of an expanding nation.[8]

More than any mode of transport up to that time, the railroad significantly altered the geography of commerce within the nation. By redirecting trade away from southern flowing rivers and gulf ports, the railroad made east-west transportation across the Appalachian divide easier and affordable. In the Northeast, the railroad made New York City a dominant center of finance as well as trade, while New England became a fringe region tied by its trunk line routes to a nation whose eastern seaboard now ended, for practical purposes, at the Hudson River. Yet within that fringe region, geography allowed one well-positioned Connecticut railroad, the New York & New Haven, to grow into a transportation empire unlike any in the nation.

RAILROAD CONSTRUCTION BEFORE 1860: AN OVERVIEW

The period leading up to the Civil War was the pioneering phase of Connecticut railroading, a time during which the technology of rail transport went from experimental to conventional in the course of a single generation. In its infancy, railroad technology was rudimentary at best. Steam locomotives were built without an enclosed cab for the train's engineer and crew, who stood on an open platform behind the engine's horizontal boiler, raising steam by feeding wood into the boiler's furnace box. Railcars were merely stagecoach bodies mounted on flanged wheels and held together by links of chain, with brakes operated from atop each car by brakemen turning a wheel or pulling on a long, stagecoach-like lever.[9] Locomotive and cars traveled on rails that were little more than flat wrought-iron bars laid in the ground, or on strap rails: thin iron plates ("straps") attached to stringer rails made of wood. And, of course, no equipment yet existed to deal with conditions of ice and snow, as this recollection of an early trip on the New Haven & Hartford Railroad indicates:

> The conductor and baggageman used to sit in front of the locomotive one on each side, and brush off the snow from the rails with brooms as the train slowly crawled along. Each had a pail of sand and sprinkled a handful on the rail when necessary. The driving wheels used to slip round and round. On one occasion, a train got stuck on the Yalesville grade by one inch of snow, and the wood and water gave out before the locomotive could overcome it. At last the crew got out the neighbors, yoked four pair of oxen to the train and drew it—passengers, baggage and all—into Meriden with flying colors.[10]

During the 1840s and 1850s, rail technology improved markedly. Steam locomotives became more powerful, and were equipped with headlights for night operation. The roadbed was now typically made of traditional T-shaped iron rails kept in place by hefty wooden cross ties. Stagecoach-like cars were replaced by long, wooden coaches, with a woodstove in the middle of each car to provide warmth in the winter. In addition, the railroad now had a partner along its right-of-way: the telegraph, which made communication at a distance separate from physical travel for the first time in human history. Connecticut's first telegraph company, the Proprietors of the Electro-Magnetic Telegraph, was incorporated in New Haven in 1846, and by the end of the 1850s, the telegraph was in general use on Connecticut railroads.[11]

Once Connecticut had chartered its first railroads, construction in the state continued apace, as investors focused first on the state's river valleys, building three north-south railroads: the *Norwich & Worcester Railroad* in the Thames-Quinebaug valley, which provided shipping for one hundred textile mills along the line; the *Hartford & New Haven Railroad,* which traveled the established commercial corridor of the central valley from New Haven to Springfield, Massachusetts; and the *Housatonic Railroad,* whose line brought the products of the mills, iron foundries, and marble quarries of the Housatonic valley to Long Island Sound at Bridgeport.[12] Given Connecticut's geography, it was reasonable to begin railroad construction in the state's river valleys, where grades were slight and stream crossings few, which made rail engineering and construction less demanding and less costly. Each of the three rail lines ended in a steamboat port on Long Island Sound, providing early all-steam routes between New York and Boston, in which the railroad and steamboat replaced slower, less comfortable stage-coach service.

By contrast, east-west rail construction through Connecticut was more difficult, due to the numerous river crossings encountered along any shore-line route, and the steep grades required to traverse the inland hills of the state's eastern and western highlands. As a result, the first railroad to cross Connecticut from west to east was not built in the state at all but along the north shore of Long Island. The Long Island Railroad was chartered by New York investors in 1834 to cross the glacial flatlands from Brooklyn to Greenport, Long Island, and was completed a decade later. A short steamboat ride across the sound to Stonington brought passengers to the terminal of the *New York, Providence & Boston Railroad* (opened in 1837 as the New York & Stonington). This short extension from Providence to Stonington brought the railroad into the sheltered portion of Long Island Sound and allowed passengers to travel to Providence and beyond untroubled by a stormy steamboat voyage around Point Judith. For more than a decade, the Long Island Railroad and the steamboat crossing from Greenport made the small whaling village of Stonington a transportation crossroads in eastern Connecticut.[13]

Financing railroad construction, which ranged in Connecticut from $16,000 to $43,000 per mile, was always problematic, especially in the early years when investment capital was limited. Connecticut held to its policy of no direct state aid to transportation corporations, though in one case, the state permitted the incorporation of the Quinebaug Bank of Norwich, a railroad bank that was allowed by its charter to purchase $200,000 worth of stock in the Norwich & Worcester. It was an early response to the issue of railroad financing made in the spirit of canal banks, and was the only instance in which a railroad bank was chartered in Connecticut.[14]

When the nation's second economic crisis hit in 1837, the directors of Connecticut's three north-south railroads suddenly found themselves without available credit to purchase rails and other construction materials. Together the Norwich & Worcester, the Hartford & New Haven, and the Housatonic petitioned the legislature for assistance, each requesting a loan of $350,000 so that construction of Connecticut's first railroads might continue without delay. Their petition was endorsed by the Joint Committee on Internal Improvements, which recommended approval of the mortgage-backed loans up to a total of one-third the construction cost of any railroad with sufficient matching funds; but the legislature rejected the committee's recommendation.[15] State assistance to Connecticut railroads remained indirect, as it had been for turnpikes and canals, and took the form of tax-free stock until such time as the company began to show a specified return on its investment, usually 6 or 8 percent.

In place of state aid, Connecticut allowed individual cities and towns to execute mortgage-backed loans to rail corporations, or to purchase stock in railroads serving their communities. In the years before the Civil War, four Connecticut cities made railroad investments: Bridgeport, Hartford, Norwich, and New London. The investments were made without incident in three of the towns. In the case of Bridgeport, however, the question of town aid to railroads became a scandal of national importance.

To ensure that Bridgeport became the terminus for the Housatonic Railroad, city officials purchased stock in the railroad amounting to $150,000, raising the funds through the sale of municipal bonds.[16] Unfortunately, the city made no provision for the payment of interest on the bonds, intending to use dividends from their rail stock to pay bondholders. When the Housatonic encountered several years of unprofitable operation as a result of the recession, no dividends were forthcoming. In an effort to repudiate their responsibility for the railroad bonds, Bridgeport citizens filed a lawsuit against the railroad, which was denied by the Connecticut Supreme Court of Errors in *Bridgeport v. The Housatonic Railroad Company* (1843). When the city still made no effort to meet its bond obligations, taking steps instead to make itself judgment proof, the bondholders obtained a court order that allowed the city's sheriff to break into local stores, seize merchandise off the shelves, and sell it to the highest bidder to raise the necessary funds. When an affected businessman brought a stop action suit against the sheriff, the matter made its way to the Connecticut Supreme Court of Errors, where in *Beardsley v. Smith* (1844), the court again upheld the rights of the bondholders, ruling that the method of collection, though unorthodox, was legal. Forced by the court to pay its bonded debt, Bridgeport raised the money by imposing a 7.5 percent tax surcharge on all property in the city.[17]

As a result of the two Bridgeport decisions, Connecticut allowed its railroads to issue their own bonds and mortgages up to one-third the amount of construction funds expended, and for the moment financing by the sale of corporate stocks and bonds eliminated the need for further municipal funding. Meanwhile, the two Bridgeport cases set a precedent for state and federal courts in enforcing responsible government action with regard to railroad financing.[18]

As the recession of 1837 waned, railroad builders turned their attention to the difficult task of constructing two east-west rail routes across Connecticut. One was the *Hartford, Providence & Fishkill Railroad,* a midstate road from Providence to Waterbury via Willimantic and Hartford, built with the intention of being extended through Danbury to the Hudson River at Fishkill, New York. The other was a shoreline route from New York City to Providence comprised of three separate roads: the *New York & New Haven Railroad* from New York to New Haven; the New Haven & New London Railroad between those two cities, and the extension of the New York, Providence & Boston from Stonington to Groton (*Shore Line*).

Four more north-south roads were constructed after the recession: in eastern Connecticut, the *New London Northern Railroad* in the valley of the Thames and Shetucket rivers; in the central valley, the *New Haven & Northampton Railroad* along the path of the Farmington Canal; and in western Connecticut, the *Naugatuck Railroad* from Devon to Waterbury and the *Danbury & Norwalk Railroad* between those two towns. One last railroad, the *Southbridge & Blackstone Railroad,* was built southwest from Boston, extending a short distance into Connecticut from the Rhode Island line to Mechanicsville in Putnam. The Southbridge & Blackstone, later known by many different names, was built along the middle post route with the intention of continuing the railroad to Willimantic, where it would connect to the Hartford, Providence & Fishkill.

With the Panic of 1857, early railroad construction in Connecticut came to a close. By then, corporate investors had constructed all or part of twelve railroad lines in every important travel corridor in the state. Total trackage amounted to six hundred miles. Two-thirds of the mileage was north-south roads and one-third east-west, and the total cost of construction exceeded $20 million. These twelve railroads provided service to 90 of Connecticut's 156 towns, and left no town in the state more than fourteen miles from rail access. By the onset of the Civil War, as individual roads were combined into rail networks, the new steam railroad moved from an experimental technology to an established mode of transportation in Connecticut.[19]

REGULATING RISK

Unlike the steamboat, whose technology and power were apparent only at the water's edge, the steam locomotive became a common sight throughout Connecticut as rail construction entered the more populous sections of the state. The iron horse was the most visible and most intrusive aspect of the technological revolution, and it took some getting used to, as this account of the New York & New Haven's first appearance in Stamford indicated:

> The citizens of the village, as well as horses and cattle, were nearly frightened out of their propriety by such a horrible scream as was never heard to issue from other than a metallic throat. Animals of every description went careening around the fields, snuffing at the air in their terror. In a few moments, the cause of the commotion appeared in the shape of a locomotive, puffing off its steam and screaming with its so-called whistle at a terrible rate.[20]

Inherent in railroad technology was a physical risk that found its way into the courtroom, as damage claims of various kinds began to mount up. Whereas responsibility in damage cases had traditionally been assigned to the person or company causing the damage, railroad law evolved a new legal concept that determined responsibility by weighing risk against negligence. The new policy can be traced to two decisions made by the Connecticut Supreme Court of Errors in the 1840s. In the first case, *Boroughs v. The Housatonic Railroad Company* (1842), embers from a passing Housatonic locomotive set fire to a privately owned building that sat near the train line. Since the actions taken by the corporation in building the road had been lawful, and reasonable precautions were taken to control the cinders emerging from the smokestack of the locomotive, the court determined that the railroad was not responsible for the damage caused by the spark-induced fire.

In the second case, *Beers v. The Housatonic Railroad Company* (1849) a train that arrived unexpectedly at a grade crossing killed several oxen that were being herded across the track by a local farmer. Because the time of the train's arrival at the crossing varied from day to day, the court ruled that the farmer could not have reasonably anticipated the danger and therefore the railroad was responsible for the harm it caused. These two Connecticut rulings helped redefine the law in a technological age. New technology was now seen as carrying an inherent level of risk for which no straightforward legal remedy was evident, only a case-by-case adjudication of responsibility that depended on whether or not the individual or corporation causing the damage had acted in a negligent manner.[21]

Connecticut was slow to regulate the physical risk associated with railroad technology. The state's first charters provided three commissioners for each railroad whose duty it was to monitor the location of the route, the payment of land damages, and construction costs. But once the railroad opened, the commissioners' job was over. As for quality of construction, railroads depended on the amount of capital available to them and the general state of rail technology at the time of construction. Since capital and construction materials were scarce throughout the 1830s and 1840s, most of the state's early railroads were first built as cheaply as possible and then rebuilt to a higher standard once revenues began to flow.

One way early railroads conserved dollars was to use strap rails in place of wrought-iron ones. However, the weight of a moving locomotive often caused the iron strap to separate from the wooden stringer rail and curl up into a dangerous "snakehead" that could pierce the floor of a railcar, or derail an entire train. Both the Hartford & New Haven and the Housatonic railroads were initially constructed using wooden strap rails. As late as 1844, the condition of the rails on the Housatonic prompted passengers to warn the public against using the road:

> The undersigned passengers in the cars of the Housatonic Railroad this morning feel ourselves bound to caution the Public against said Rail-Road. Within about three hundred paces of the depot at Newtown the car in which we were seated was throw[n] off the track with great violence, and it was only through the interposition of a merciful Providence that we escaped without the loss of life. The railroad is in a most dangerous condition and we counted in a distance of sixty rods over fifty "snake-heads."[22]

As a result of such complaints, the state enacted its first railroad laws in 1849 and revised these general statutes nearly every legislative session thereafter. Under the laws, commissioners were now appointed to each operating railroad "carefully to examine the whole of said railroad" to see "that the same is kept in suitable repair." Inspections took place twice a year, and requests for repairs were put in writing to the company, along with a time frame for compliance. However, unlike turnpike or canal commissioners, who could revoke toll privileges if their demands were not met, early railroad commissioners did not have that authority. Instead, noncompliance brought a fine of $100 per day until the repairs were made.[23]

In 1853, a train disaster occurred in Norwalk that dramatically altered the course of railroad regulation in Connecticut. At half past ten on the morning of May 6, an express train of the New York & New Haven heading from New York to Boston ran through an open drawbridge over the Saugatuck River and plunged into the river, killing 50 of the 150 passengers on board. A Connecticut physician on board with fellow doctors returning from a meeting of the American Medical Association in New York City recounted the harrowing experience:

> There came then a shaking and a crash and a stop, and in a moment, the work was done. The front of the car and part of the side were broken out, and the floor had broken off just in front of me, one end resting on the bridge and the other on the cars in the water below. So sudden and rapid was the whole affair that we had but time for a moment's thought, and it was over. Helping up those on the inclined floor of the car, who it is believed were not seriously injured, we next went down to those in the water. It was evident that here were two cars full of passengers and that one had fallen on top of the other; the upper one was inclined on its side and evidently nearly filled with water. We immediately commenced taking out the inmates at the windows, and soon got out a large number, some injured, some bruised, and many, ah, far too many, dead. . . . These were, apparently, not killed in the majority of instance by bruises or severe blows, but presented all the symptoms of asphyxia from drowning, and were probably drowned at once . . . thankfulness to God for my preservation . . . was pressed home upon me still more closely when I recognized lying among the dead, him for whom I had given up my seat in New York, and had taken the succeeding car. . . .
>
> Such was the impetus of the train, that the locomotive in passing, struck, it is said, or nearly struck the opposite pier. The engineer jumped off just before the plunge, and it is reported is not much injured. The draw was open for the purpose of letting through a steamboat, which, itself full of passengers, narrowly escaped being crushed.[24]

A board of inquiry determined that the accident was caused by a substitute engineer who failed to observe the red ball signal a half mile before the bridge that indicated the drawbridge was open. In addition to the shocking loss of life, about $300,000 in claims placed a significant financial burden on the railroad.[25]

Within weeks, the Connecticut legislature created the statewide General Railroad Commission to promote and monitor safety on Connecticut railroads. The commission was composed of three men, appointed by the governor, with the authority to inspect each railroad in the state as often as necessary, ask for repairs, question officers of the company under oath, and,

Norwalk Bridge disaster, 1853, from Illustrated News, *May 1853.*

should the company refuse to comply with their recommendations, seek a court injunction to stop the railroad from operating in an unsafe manner. Railroads were also required to notify the commission within twenty-four hours of any accident involving serious injury to either employees or passengers. And by 1856, nearly twenty years after Connecticut's first operating railroad, no Connecticut railroad was allowed to open without a certificate from the General Railroad Commission stating the railroad was "in suitable and safe condition."

While safety was the commission's main concern, it also collected data from each railroad in the state about the equipment it owned, its track mileage, the number of passengers it carried, and the amount of debt it owed, among other items. This information was compiled in an annual report to the legislature and was used to make recommendations for changes in the state's railroad laws. Unlike similar commissions in some states, Connecticut's General Railroad Commission did not have the authority to regulate rates for passenger or freight traffic, thereby allowing for a measure of competition between roads.[26]

In addition to the physical risk to the general public inherent in railroad technology, there was the financial risk to the shareholders of a railroad corporation, a risk that grew in proportion to the ever larger investment of funds needed to construct and maintain the state's railroad lines. The financing of rail construction was a boon to the fledgling New York Stock Exchange, then called the Board of Brokers. From the first listing of railroad stock in 1830, railroad financing dominated New York during the nineteenth century, and by the beginning of the Civil War had transformed that city into the financial capital of the nation. It did not take long before such large sums of money, coming into contact with human nature, made the risky business of railroad financing even riskier.

Robert Schuyler, a New York speculator, perpetrated the state's first significant railroad fraud on the shareholders of the New York & New Haven Railroad. A man of impeccable credentials, Harvard-educated and from an elite New York family, Schuyler was president of the New York & New Haven from its incorporation. However, in the summer of 1854, when one of the railroad's directors inquired into a recent sale of company stock on the New York exchange, it was discovered that Schuyler had issued more stock than the company's charter allowed and had pocketed money he had borrowed against these phony shares. An examination of the company's books found that "by means of false entries, erasures, and other similar practices, an issue of illegal and fraudulent stock has been made within a few months past to the amount . . . of nearly twenty thousand shares, or two million dollars."[27]

Schuyler quickly absconded, first to Canada and then to Europe, where he died the following year in Geneva. But his handiwork remained with the company long after his escape. A series of lawsuits and appeals in the courts held the railroad responsible for the fiasco, with the court convinced that the directors had "handed over to Schuyler the substance of all their authority, and then for nearly seven years laid down to sleep in supine indifference at his feet." As a result of the Schuyler scandal and the Norwalk disaster, the stock of the New York & New Haven sold below par value and paid no dividends for more than a decade.[28]

A Plank Road Interlude

The plank road craze of the 1850s resulted in the chartering of seven new turnpike roads in Connecticut and the construction of one new turnpike, the Waterbury & Cheshire Plank Road.

As railroad construction became more costly, communities with little capital to invest sought a way of reaching market towns or established railroad lines that was more efficient than existing turnpikes. For a brief period from the mid-1840s to the mid-1850s, they embraced the plank road as a low-cost solution to their problem. A plank road was a turnpike road whose smooth surface of wooden planks allowed a teamster and his horses to haul two to three times the load possible on a dirt highway.

The man behind the plank road movement was George Geddes, a civil engineer on the Erie Canal and a New York state legislator. In 1846, Geddes built the nation's first plank road outside Syracuse, New York. With help from Geddes and others, New York State became a hotbed of plank road construction. From 1847 to 1854, 340 companies built some three thousand miles of plank road turnpikes in Geddes's home state. Like the canal fever sparked by construction of the Erie Canal, New York's fascination with plank roads spread throughout the eastern United States.[29]

Between 1851 and 1853, seven plank road corporations were chartered in Connecticut. They were the first charters the state had issued for turnpike construction since 1839. The charters were for the Danbury, Redding, Weston & Westport Plank Road Company (1851); the Stamford, New Canaan & Ridgefield Plank Road Company (1851); the New Haven & Seymour Plank Road Company (1852); the Woodbury & Seymour Plank Road Company (1852); the Waterbury & Cheshire Plank Road Company (1852); the Wallingford, North Haven & New Haven Plank Road Company (1853); and the Salisbury Plank Road Company (1853). Of these seven chartered, only the Waterbury & Cheshire Plank Road was constructed.[30]

This road covered a distance of seven miles, from East Main Street in Waterbury to a point near the West Cheshire station of the New Haven & Northampton Railroad. The plank road provided metal manufacturers in Waterbury access to New Haven via a combined turnpike and rail route whose charges overall were lower than those of the more direct Naugatuck Railroad, then under the control of the New York & New Haven. The Waterbury & Cheshire Plank Road included one tollgate located on the outskirts of Waterbury. Unlike the tolls for other Connecticut turnpikes, those for this plank road were charged according to the distance traveled: 3 cents per mile for a vehicle drawn by two animals, 1½ cents per mile for a vehicle drawn by one animal, ¾ cent per mile for a horse and rider or a led horse, and 1 mill per mile for every mule or head of cattle, sheep, or swine.[31]

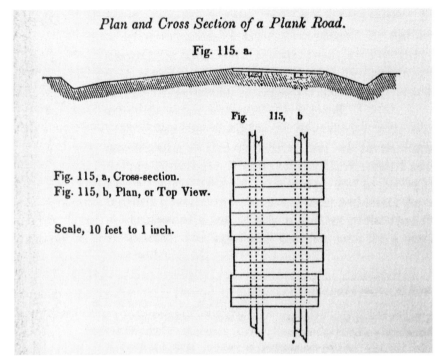

Plan and Cross Section of a Plank Road.

Fig. 115. a.

Fig. 115, b

Fig. 115, a, Cross-section.
Fig. 115, b, Plan, or Top View.

Scale, 10 feet to 1 inch.

Plank road design, from W. M. Gillespie, A Manual of the Principles and Practices of Road Making, 1850.

Few specifics are known about the Waterbury & Cheshire Plank Road, except that bids for the project were solicited in March 1853 and were to be submitted to the company's president, M. G. Elliot, at his office in New Haven, "where the profile, map and specifications can be seen." The ad for bids noted that someone in the office was "in readiness to accompany and point out the route as located by the Directors, if desired," and that the scope of the project required the contractor "to furnish hemlock plank, grade and complete the road on or before the 1st day of September next."[32]

As for the road's design, it was likely a typical plank road, which consisted of an eight-foot travel way of wood planks three to four inches thick placed at right angles across two parallel lines of wooden stringer rails, which were embedded in the earth so that the planked surface was even with the surrounding terrain. The planks were often kept in place only by their own weight. On one side of the roadway a wide earthen shoulder was provided to allow access onto and off the road. The shoulder also served as a turnout from the one-lane road when meeting a wagon coming in the opposite direction. The planks were arranged in sets of three to form a jagged edge that made it easier for wagon wheels to enter and exit the roadway. As with regular turnpikes, ditches were dug on either side of the road for drainage. The cost of a typical plank road was about $1,500 per mile.[33]

After chartering the aforementioned six plank road companies, Connecticut in 1854 enacted a general incorporation law to accommodate additional plank road construction without the need for a legislative charter. It was the first general incorporation act passed in Connecticut for a specific mode of transportation. The law allowed any three or more persons to build a plank road turnpike by complying with provisions of the state statutes governing joint-stock corporations. Having obtained permission from the selectmen of each town through which the plank road was to pass, the corporation was to petition the county court to survey the route and notify all persons whose property was required for the roadway. The right to take the land was then given to the corporation, with the stipulation that it paid all land damages in the manner provided for under state railroad law before construction could begin.[34]

It appears that no plank road companies were incorporated under this general law, and for good reason. The plank road turnpike had a major disadvantage: it wore out. Geddes and his supporters estimated the life of a plank road at eight years, after which the roadway needed to be completely rebuilt. Lest this discourage investors, Geddes claimed the planks deteriorated only in proportion to the traffic that rode on them, implying that a busy road could collect sufficient tolls to replace the planked surface as often as necessary, and with money to spare (as much as 20 percent, according to Geddes) for dividends to its stockholders.

Unfortunately, Geddes was wrong. Experience showed that the wood planks lasted only four or five years, regardless of the amount of wear and tear they received, and unlike a neglected dirt turnpike that was usable despite its potholes and ruts, a weak or broken plank was a danger to horse and wagon, making repairs more urgent. As the short life and high maintenance cost of plank roads became apparent, their popularity quickly diminished. By the time Connecticut enacted a general incorporation law for plank roads, legislators in New York had acknowledged the movement's failure by allowing plank road companies in that state to either abandon their routes or convert them to earthen turnpikes.[35]

The Waterbury & Cheshire Plank Road turnpike remained in existence until 1875, when it was made a free public road. The road's life of more than twenty years indicated some degree of financial success. Only when the Meriden, Waterbury & Connecticut River Railroad was built from Meriden to Waterbury along a parallel route was the company's charter repealed. Whether Connecticut's only plank road remained planked throughout its existence or was converted to an earthen turnpike once the original planking had worn out is not known.[36]

Overbuilding and Consolidation

Continued railroad construction after the Civil War led to an overbuilt network of one thousand track miles and the consolidation of half that mileage under the New York, New Haven & Hartford Railroad.

CONSTRUCTION AFTER 1860: AN OVERVIEW

While still in recovery from the recession of 1857, business on rail lines in Connecticut was disrupted further by the onset of the Civil War. As a result, three of the state's twelve rail lines fell into receivership: the New London Northern; the Hartford, Providence & Fishkill; and the New York, Providence & Boston.[37] But as a war-related economy emerged, traffic on all roads increased to a level beyond that of the prewar years, as Connecticut railroads transported raw materials and manufactured goods for the war effort, as well as troops, horses, and munitions engaged in the Union cause.

By 1865, some Connecticut railroads, including the Housatonic and the Norwich & Worcester, amassed sufficient revenues to pay their outstanding debts, and to provide substantial dividends to their shareholders, all with funds to spare. But wartime profits came at a price: deteriorating safety as a result of deferred maintenance. When an accident on the Shore Line Railroad killed or injured sixty Union soldiers, a reporter visiting the scene noted that "in many places the chairs [the connections between iron rail and wooden cross tie] are broken, the ties are rotten, the iron is poor and the rails are loose."[38]

Such sorrow only added to the greater national tragedy. However, the Civil War did much to improve the financial stability of Connecticut railroads and the culture they represented. Whereas before the war, after a quarter century of building, the General Railroad Commission had found that it was "generally conceded" that Connecticut "has now all the railroads needed for its business," soon after the war the commission reported: "It is now believed that in no State has the limit of construction been even approximately reached."[39]

BLAKE'S PATENT

Stone and Ore Breaker

For reducing to fragments all kinds of hard and brittle substances, such as STONE, for making the most perfect McADAM ROADS, and for making the best CONCRETE. It breaks stone at trifling cost for BALLASTING RAILROADS. It is extensively in use in MINING operations, for crushing

IRON, COPPER, ZINC, SILVER, GOLD, and other ORES.

Also for crushing **Quartz, Flint, Emery, Corundum, Feldspar, Coal, Barytes, Manganese, Phosphate Rock, Plaster, Soapstone, &c.** For circular, with full particulars, address

THE BLAKE CRUSHER CO.,
85 Orange Street, New Haven, Conn.

Invented by Eli Whitney Blake in 1856, the stone and ore breaker used steam power to make the manufacture of railroad ballast and highway gravel possible in large quantities. (Courtesy of the New Haven Museum)

Along with the rehabilitation of existing railroads, seven new Connecticut rail lines were built in the first decade following the Civil War. Three of these were north-south railroads. The *Connecticut Valley Railroad* extended down the western shore of the Connecticut River from Hartford to Old Saybrook, carrying passengers and bulk coal to river towns along the route. The *Shepaug Railroad,* which snaked its way through the state's western hills from Hawleyville to Litchfield, became Connecticut's curviest railroad. The *Connecticut Central Railroad* ran east of the Connecticut River between East Hartford and Springfield, Massachusetts.

Three new lines were also constructed in an east-west direction: the *New Haven & Derby Railroad,* which the city of New Haven built to divert traffic from the Naugatuck Railroad; the *Connecticut Western Railroad,* which ran from Hartford to Sharon through the northwest hills, reaching an elevation of 1333 feet at Norfolk Summit before descending to the Hudson River; and the *Meriden, Waterbury & Connecticut River Railroad,* which brought manufactures from Waterbury and Meriden to the port of Cromwell on the Connecticut River. Additional east-west construction included a major extension of the Hartford, Providence & Fishkill from Waterbury to Danbury and on to the Hudson River, thereby completing the midstate route from Providence begun in the prewar years.

The last of the new roads, the *Air Line Railroad,* occupied a unique position in the state's rail network, running diagonally across eastern Connecticut from New Haven to Willimantic. There it met an extension of the Southbridge & Blackstone from Mechanicsville to Willimantic, also built during

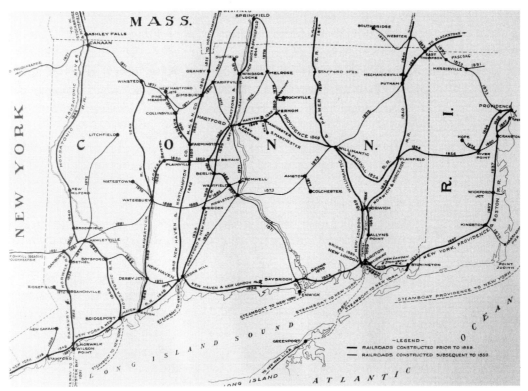

Map of Connecticut railroads, from Sidney Withington, The First Twenty Years of Railroads in Connecticut *(1935). (Courtesy of the Tercentenary Commission of the State of Connecticut)*

the postwar years. Together, the two lines completed the most direct route between New York and Boston.

These seven new railroads, together with the extension of two existing rail lines, added four hundred miles to Connecticut's rail network, bringing total trackage in the state to one thousand miles.[40]

The impetus behind this spurt of postwar building was a return to a state policy of town aid to railroad corporations. With the cost of building railroads on the rise and railroad-issued bonds in Connecticut limited to one-third of the sum expended on construction, railroad corporations were eager for another source of funding, especially for roads that might be of marginal importance relative to the state's existing railroad network. The legislature, meanwhile, believed a return to town aid would encourage competition between established railroads and newer ones that might otherwise not be built.

At least four of the railroads built after the war (one-half of the new mileage) received financial aid from cities and towns along their routes. During a decade of construction, thirty-three towns in the state contributed a total of $5,500,000 to new rail construction. While these thirty-three towns' contributions were less than 10 percent of the state's total railroad capitalization, they amounted to 60 percent of railroad securities issued for new construction.

Two-thirds of the postwar town aid came from three Connecticut cities: Hartford, which provided $1,250,000 for the Connecticut Western and the Valley railroads; Middletown, which contributed $1,370,000 to the Valley and Air Line railroads; and New Haven, whose contribution to the New Haven & Derby and Air Line railroads came to $925,000. It is likely that these four lines would not have been built had it not been for the town aid they received.[41]

But as the decade of postwar construction came to a close, it was apparent that the strategy of building new roads to encourage competition among Connecticut rail lines was not working. During this period, the net earnings of the state's twelve established lines ranged from $1 to $4 million, while those of the postwar roads averaged less than $500,000. Over this period, prewar railroads paid their shareholders dividends of 3 to 10 percent, while the General Railroad Commission noted that "none of the railroad companies incorporated in the past ten years, or since the system of 'town aid' was adopted, have *earned* the interest on their bonded debt." These facts led the commission to conclude: "competition has been tried, and has proved a failure."[42]

To rectify the situation, Connecticut took the unusual step of amending the state constitution in 1877 to prohibit further town aid to railroad corporations. To compensate for the loss of town funding, the legislature increased the limit on railroad-issued bonds to one-half the total cost of construction, and for the first time allowed banks and insurance companies to purchase stock in railroad corporations. Still, the amendment made it clear that towns that had provided aid were still responsible for "any bonds or debts incurred under existing laws." As a result, many towns remained burdened with their postwar railroad debt for decades.[43]

RAILROAD BRIDGES AND FERRIES

Railroad construction stimulated the building of bridges as neither turnpike nor canal construction had done. Whereas earlier a bridge-builder had constructed no more than a handful of major spans in his lifetime, railroad contractors were required to build a dozen or more bridges within a short period of time for each rail line. As a result, bridge-building was transformed from a trial-and-error craft into an engineering profession during the last half of the nineteenth century. The use of iron and, later, steel bridges only added to the need for professional engineers and the mathematical analysis of bridge designs.[44]

In Connecticut, most railroad bridges were built on the design of a Howe truss, a traditional wooden truss whose vertical (tension) members were replaced by wrought-iron rods tightened into the frame of the truss by a turnbuckle. As the wood in the truss aged and shrank over time, the turnbuckle was tightened to take up the slack and return the structure to its full strength. The preferred configuration placed the truss above the deck of the bridge, eliminating damage from floodwaters and floating ice, but on occasion the truss was built under the roadway, especially if there was concern about height restrictions on the line.

Some railroad spans were also built as covered bridges. An estimated forty-seven covered railroad bridges were erected in Connecticut by 1888, three-quarters of them before the Civil War. Of the state's covered railroad bridges, one of the more unusual spans was at Fair Haven, where trains on the Shore Line Railroad crossed the Quinnipiac River on *top* of a long covered span whose truss stood beneath the bridge deck.[45]

Responsibility for seeing that railroad bridges were safely built and properly maintained fell to the General Railroad Commission, which as early as 1867 commented on the difficulty of the task: "the bridges upon the various roads are numerous, amounting to hundreds, and being mostly constructed of wood, require a very rigid inspection . . . as after a few years of use, and exposure to the elements, the life of the timber may be destroyed." The commission then noted that they had "directed all the necessary repairs to be made."[46]

The collapse of a railroad bridge in Connecticut was a rare event, though several occurred. The worst collapse took place in January 1878 on the Connecticut Western in Tariffville. To accommodate a large group of excursionists returning from Hartford, the railroad assembled a ten-car train whose weight required two locomotives to negotiate the hilly terrain of western Connecticut. As the train left Tariffville and crossed the Farmington River on a double span made of two Howe trusses, the second half of the bridge collapsed, sending the two locomotives and three passenger cars into the icy

Connecticut's first iron railroad bridge crossed the Connecticut River at Enfield. (Courtesy of the Connecticut Historical Society, Hartford, Connecticut)

water below. The accident killed thirteen people and injured seventy others. Some witnesses said they saw the locomotive tender derail and hit one of the trusses, thereby collapsing the span; others believed that the bridge, weakened by the elements, was brought down by the extra weight of the two locomotives. An investigation by the General Railroad Commission could not determine the definitive cause of the accident. The accident proved a financial tragedy for the railroad as well. Within two years, claims against the company drove the Connecticut Western into bankruptcy.[47]

In the decades after the Civil War, as locomotives became heavier and longer spans were attempted, a demand arose for all-iron bridges. The first all-iron railroad bridge in Connecticut was built in 1865 by the Hartford & New Haven across the Connecticut River above Hartford to replace a wooden span built twenty years earlier. To minimize disruption on the busy upper road to Boston, the iron truss was built around the old wooden one while the line remained in use. Because the bridge carried only a single track, a turnout was constructed at each end to allow trains from either direction to move aside for oncoming traffic. At $265,000, the cost of the iron bridge was twice that of a wooden span, but the structure was cost-effective nonetheless, since its life expectancy was five times as long.[48]

Connecticut was home to a major iron bridge fabricator, the Berlin Iron Bridge Company, a descendant of the early tin and sheet metal industries of central Connecticut. The company was noted for their patented lenticular truss, a design whose curved upper and lower chords gave the span a unique

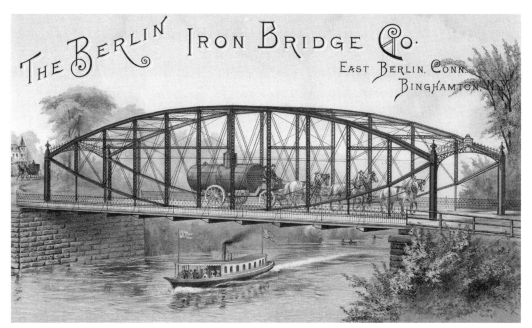

Lenticular truss. (Courtesy of the Connecticut Historical Society, Hartford, Connecticut)

eye-shaped profile. Because the design used 10 percent less metal, the lenticular truss was a popular design for railroad (and highway) bridges in the last decades of the century. Lens-shaped bridges fabricated in Berlin were constructed throughout the Northeast and as far west as Texas.[49]

Rail lines that traversed the hills of Connecticut's eastern and western uplands, such as the New Haven & Derby Railroad from Derby to Botsford and the Air Line between Middletown and Willimantic, were often required to span valleys that were deep and wide. To do this in a cost-effective manner, builders used a trestle bridge, a triangular design in which the splayed legs of the bridge supported horizontal beams structured in layers, one atop the other, as the width of the bridge decreased from the valley floor to the railroad above. Such trestles were made of either wood or iron.

Two notable railroad trestles in Connecticut were the Rapallo and Lyman viaducts, built to carry the Air Line over Flat Brook ravine in East Hampton and Dickerson Ravine in Colchester. The Rapallo viaduct was the longer of the two, measuring 1,380 feet, while the Lyman viaduct, more than 1,100 feet long, was the highest, reaching 137 feet. The two structures were designed by Edward W. Serrell, a Civil War general turned engineer, using hollow wrought-iron columns developed by the Phoenix Iron Works of Phila-

Lyman Viaduct, Conn.

delphia. Riveting the hollow columns together with flanges and using tie rods to brace the interior created a lightweight frame strong enough to support heavy trains yet flexible enough to withstand high winds.[50]

An overlooked aspect of railroad bridge construction was the introduction of many at-grade crossings of rail lines and public highways throughout Connecticut in the nineteenth century, bringing delays for travelers, as well as the potential for deadly collisions. With the state's rail network at its peak, a General Railroad Commission survey in 1889 noted that there were then fifteen hundred railroad crossings in Connecticut, of which twelve hundred, or 80 percent, were at-grade ones. Nearly half these crossings were along the routes of the state's three major railroads: the New York, New Haven & Hartford; the New York and New England; and the Housatonic. To deal with the problem, the legislature banned the building of any new at-grade crossings and made provisions for railroads to gradually remove existing ones.[51]

Connecticut's rail network included two important railroad ferries along the shoreline route between New Haven and Providence. A ferry across the Connecticut River from Old Saybrook to Lyme began operation with the opening of the Shore Line in 1852. A second ferry opened six years later across the Thames River from Groton to New London when the New York, Boston & Providence was extended from Groton to Stonington. The two crossings were made by steam-powered ferries specifically built to accommodate railcars. The larger of the two boats, capable of carrying up to eight railcars, was stationed at the Thames River. Once railcars were loaded onto the ferry, the steam locomotive stayed behind, while another engine was ready to remove the cars from the ferry on the opposite shore. With the transfers came excitement, as noted by Charles Dickens, who rode the Shore Line Railroad on a trip through Connecticut in 1868:

> two rivers had to be crossed, and each time the whole train is banged aboard a steamer. The steamer rises and falls with the river which the railroad don't do, and the train is banged uphill or banged downhill. In coming off the steamer at one of these crossings yesterday, we were banged up to such a height that the rope broke and the carriage rushed back with a run downhill into the boat again. I whisked out in a moment, and two or three others after me, but nobody else seemed to care about it.[52]

The same year, the Shore Line Railroad received permission from the legislature to build a bridge across the Connecticut River. The single-track bridge was a Howe truss of six sections, with one section designed to swing open to accommodate river traffic. Steamboat operators and barge owners on the river opposed the bridge. On several occasions during construction, barges laden with stone quarried in Portland, Connecticut, were purposefully crashed into the bridge, tearing the piers from their moorings. Nonetheless, the bridge was completed in 1870. But as the first train was set to cross the span, the crew, concerned for their safety, abandoned their posts. While spectators looked on, the supervisor of construction boarded the train and drove it across the bridge without incident.[53]

In 1889, a double-tracked steel bridge was erected to carry Shore Line trains over the Thames River, replacing the ferry at that location. At the same time, the Connecticut River span was rebuilt as a double-tracked drawbridge. Construction of the two bridges allowed travelers for the first time to ride the shoreline on a double-tracked railroad from New York to Boston without being interrupted by time-consuming ferry crossings, thereby making the lower post route via Providence an alternative to the upper post road route of Boston-bound trains, and completing Connecticut's overland rail network.[54]

THE CONSOLIDATED

At the same time that Connecticut's policy of town aid was promoting new construction as a way to encourage competition among the state's rail lines, existing railroads entered into a period of consolidation, as financially stronger roads looked to ensure their continued success by exerting a measure of control over weaker lines. This was accomplished in a variety of ways, including majority stock control, where one road owned enough securities of another road to control its traffic policies; pooling agreements, where two roads were operated as one and revenues shared according to a predetermined formula; leases, where one road operated another for a period of years in return for an annual rent; and merger, where the capital stock issued by two existing roads was combined to form a new corporation.[55] By the use of these measures, individual rail lines were consolidated into rail systems, first within each state and later across state lines.

The Connecticut railroad in the best position geographically and financially to benefit from consolidation was the New York & New Haven, the road that controlled the stem line common to all traffic into and out of New York City from Connecticut. No sooner had the road opened in 1849 than it negotiated traffic-sharing agreements with the Housatonic and Naugatuck railroads to extend its control. The main target of the New York & New Haven, however, was the Hartford & New Haven, the north-south link on the upper rail route to Boston. But when the New York & New Haven opened, the Hartford & New Haven also operated a steamboat line to New York, so it declined an offer to combine the two railroads. Its independent stance, however, did not last long.[56]

When Joseph Sheffield, president of the New Haven & Northampton (Canal Line) Railroad, became a large shareholder in the New York & New Haven, he negotiated a lease between the two railroads. The New York & New Haven now had the same leverage over the Hartford & New Haven that the Farmington Canal had had on the Connecticut River Company a generation earlier. By threatening to extend the New Haven & Northampton into Massachusetts, the New York & New Haven was able to intimidate the Hartford & New Haven into an agreement. Realizing the benefit of being part of an all-rail route between New York and Boston, Hartford businessmen executed a twenty-year contract with the New York & New Haven without legislative approval that required the Hartford & New Haven to exchange passenger traffic with the New York & New Haven railroad and to pay it $12,000 a year to guarantee that Sheffield's parallel road would not be extended any farther north than Granby.

For several years all was well, until a new railroad, the Hampshire & Hamden, was chartered to run from Granby to Northampton, Massachusetts. While the Hampshire & Hamden was not under the direct control of

Sheffield or the New York & New Haven, both would benefit from its construction. The railroad was completed in 1857, and when the New York & New Haven began diverting traffic from the upper river valley to the New Haven & Northampton, attorneys for the Hartford & New Haven filed an injunction to stop the activity.

The suit by the Hartford & New Haven made the contractual agreement between the two roads public knowledge, which in turn prompted the state's attorney to sue the Hartford & New Haven. In its suit, the state asserted that by directing its passenger traffic to the New York & New Haven, the Hartford railroad had violated its state charter, which said that the road was to operate from Hartford "to the navigable waters of New Haven harbor," where passengers had access to steamer service to New York. In their defense, the Hartford & New Haven note that nothing in their charter "requires them to run their trains over any particular part of their road, or indeed to operate their road at all," and therefore their agreement with the New York & New Haven was "a valid one."[57]

In *State v. The Hartford & New Haven Railroad Company* (1861), the Connecticut Supreme Court of Errors unanimously upheld the state's position. At the heart of the ruling, the court said, was the obligation of both railroads to operate according to their charters, thereby providing the public with the option of traveling to New York by either steamboat or railroad. The decision is significant for the strong language the court used to express its attitude toward monopoly:

> What right have they to covenant with that corporation that they will not run cars to tide water, as the charter provides that they shall, and as the public accommodation requires, especially when they enter into that covenant to secure to that corporation a monopoly of the public travel to and from New York, and, as an equivalent, to secure to themselves a like monopoly of all the travel in the Connecticut valley, to the prejudice of every other corporation that might have an interest in those routes? The whole proceeding, from first to last, seems to us to be in contravention of the charter obligations of both these companies, and to present a case of odious monopoly, if not of positive oppression and wrong, which can receive no countenance from an impartial tribunal.[58]

Following the decision, the Hartford & New Haven reopened steamboat service from New Haven, and passengers were given the option of traveling to New York via either steamer or the New York & New Haven. More important, the court's decision in this case illustrated the judicial attitude against monopoly that prevailed in 1861.

In 1867, the Massachusetts legislature created that state's largest railroad corporation by approving the consolidation of its trunk line railroads, the Boston & Worcester and the Western, into the Boston & Albany Railroad. A few months later, the New York & New Haven and the Hartford & New Haven likewise petitioned their legislature for permission to merge into one corporation. While small mergers had taken place in Connecticut during the canal and early railroad periods, state legislators and citizens were suspicious of mergers of this magnitude, as noted by the General Railroad Commission:

> the tendency which is everywhere manifesting itself to *consolidate* lines, threatens injurious consequences. The sense of individual interest and responsibility is thereby not only greatly weakened, but an extend of line and investment is often reached, which is utterly beyond the capacity of any one man, or set of men, to properly manage. There can be no doubt that a road 100 miles in length, with a capital of five or six millions, is quite up to the capacity likely to be employed in the management of these works. There are hundreds capable of managing a work of this magnitude to one capable of properly conducting a road 500 miles in length. The tendency to consolidation, which in almost every instance is prompted by personal or selfish motives on the part of the chief managers, is a great evil, and unless speedily checked will materially impair the value of railroad property.[59]

While debate continued through two legislative sessions, the petition to merge the state's two largest and most important railroads was twice defeated.

Meanwhile, legislators passed a law allowing Connecticut railroads to enter into operating contracts and leases with connecting or intersecting roads, so long as the stock of the two roads was not consolidated. Making the most of the new law, the New York & New Haven executed an agreement with the Hartford & New Haven that brought the management of the two railroads under one board of directors and shared their combined earnings according to a preset formula, all while keeping the stock of the two corporations separate.

Faced with a legal contract that was a merger in everything but name, the legislature in 1871 approved a full stock merger of the two railroads, creating the New York, New Haven & Hartford Railroad. With a capitalization of $15 million, the new railroad was Connecticut's largest rail corporation, referred to simply as the New Haven. Because the Hartford & New Haven had operated their railroad across the state line to Springfield, Massachusetts, the state legislature in Massachusetts was called on to endorse the consolidation, which it did the following year.[60]

To placate opponents of the merger and to keep the possibility of competition alive as rail lines joined together into larger, more powerful railroads, the legislature enacted a second general incorporation law concerning transportation, which allowed any twenty-five individuals to organize a railroad without obtaining a state charter, so long as the group made a financial commitment to the project of $10,000 per mile of proposed track and had the route approved by the General Railroad Commission. The law required that the corporation begin construction within one year and obtain legislative approval before any railroad bridge was built over a navigable river. While allowing competition, the provisions of the law favored the New Haven by making it difficult for competitors to mount a real challenge.[61]

Soon after the law was passed, the Harlem River & Port Chester Railroad was incorporated in New York to build a rail line in Westchester County parallel to that of the New Haven. Before the Harlem River & Port Chester could organize itself under Connecticut's general railroad law, the New Haven purchased the company, eager to show perhaps that parallel schemes would not be tolerated. Unfortunately, the action signaled potential incorporators that a scheme to parallel the New Haven might be good business, whether or not the road was ever built.[62]

In 1882, the legislature liberalized the state's general railroad incorporation law by allowing several years for a new corporation to build its road and by taking responsibility for the approval of bridges across navigable rivers away from the legislature and giving it to the General Railroad Commission.[63] Within a span of several years, more than a half dozen different railroads were organized under the revised law, all threatening the New Haven with construction of a parallel road to compete with its main line service. These threats included the New York & Boston Inland Railroad, across Connecticut on a diagonal from Greenwich to Thompson (1882); the New York, Connecticut & Boston Railroad, along the shoreline from Greenwich to Rhode Island (1882); the New York & Connecticut Airline Railroad, from Greenwich to New Haven (1882); the Hartford & Harlem Railroad, from Greenwich to Hartford via New Britain (1883); and the New York & Boston Rapid Transit Company, an express from New York to Boston that stopped only in New Haven (1887).

Unfortunately, the General Railroad Commission had no authority to choose from among the proposed roads the one or two that were in the public's best interest. Instead, the commission was forced to approve all parallel projects that met the requirements of the general incorporation law. In the end, each project was thwarted either by the New Haven, which bought out many of the companies before construction could begin, or because the project fizzled of its own accord.[64] In the interim, the New Haven acquired stock control or leases of existing railroads that might pose a threat in the future. These included the Shore Line (1870), the Connecticut Valley Railroad (1879), the Canal Line (1881), the Air Line (1882), and the Naugatuck Railroad (1887).

By 1887, with four hundred miles of Connecticut rail lines under its control, the New Haven, now referred to as the Consolidated, had become the state's dominant railroad system. It had also improved its own main line from the road's junction with the Harlem Railroad at Williams Bridge in New York to New Haven, and on to Springfield, Massachusetts, prompting the General Railroad Commission to comment: "The whole has now become a thoroughly equipped, double tracked road, second in efficiency to none in the country, laid throughout with steel rail, with a great part of the original perishable timber bridges replaced either by structures of iron or substantial stone arches."[65] To the credit of the road's directors, the Consolidated accomplished it all in a fiscally responsible manner, without either increasing the company's $15 million capitalization, or denying stockholders the 10 percent annual dividend they came to expect.[66]

It was true that the majority of Consolidated stock was owned out of state, mainly in New York, but the majority of the railroad's shareholders were Connecticut residents, and the company worked hard to nurture its image as Connecticut's premier railroad. When Hartford was chosen as the permanent capital of Connecticut in 1875, stone blocks and other construction material for the new capitol building were hauled by the Consolidated free of charge. In addition, the railroad issued free travel passes to all state legislators. Thus, the Consolidated's influence extended literally to the seats in the state Capitol and the legislators who sat in them. As the Consolidated was acutely aware, when the next phase of railroad consolidation got under way and state systems were pitted against one another, the political influence exerted by Connecticut's largest railroad corporation might well be the deciding factor in its continued success.[67]

In the 1870s, a new wave of technological innovation swept the nation, centered on the development of electrical power and large-scale technological systems. As the industrial economy continued to expand, railroading became the nation's first big business and a forerunner of managerial capitalism. By the end of the century, with the state's population approaching one million persons, the Connecticut landscape had become predominantly urban and industrial. While industrialization brought increased railroad and steamboat traffic, congested urban areas and electrical power combined to create a new mode of travel: the street railway. With the support of the Connecticut legislature, and with little objection from the public, the Consolidated expanded its operation in size and scope until it established control over all major rail systems in southern New England. Under the direction of J. P. Morgan and Charles S. Mellen, the Consolidated went on to acquire railroad systems in northern New England, as well as steamship and street railway lines throughout the region, converting the New York, New Haven & Hartford from a railroad giant into a transportation monopoly. Public distrust of the Consolidated's growing power led to outcries from Boston lawyer and progressive reformer, Louis D. Brandeis. In 1915, after two anti-trust investigations by the Federal Interstate Commerce Commission and much protest over the road's questionable financial practices, the New Haven was forced to divest itself of its more controversial assets. While the Consolidated continued operations for another two decades, the road finally slipped into bankruptcy in 1935 as a result of the debt accumulated during the Morgan and Mellen era.

Connecticut Becomes an Urban-Industrial State

After more than a century of technological change and economic growth, Connecticut was transformed into an urban-industrial landscape of more than one million persons, as large-scale technological systems became an essential component of modern American life.

With the completion of the first transcontinental railroad in 1869, a true national economy began to develop around the powerful transportation and communication links provided by a coast-to-coast railroad and telegraph system. Over the next fifty years, the economies of the South and West grew and merged with the established manufacturing base of the Northeast.

Following the Civil War, the dominance of the textile and footwear manufacturing centered in Connecticut's highlands gave way to expanding metal-work industries located in lowland valleys, close to railroad access. Items manufactured included typewriters, sewing machines, and farm implements, as well as the products of machine tool making common to all metal industries, epitomized by the Pratt & Whitney Company of Hartford. Because working with industrial metals involved similar skills regardless of the product manufactured, the state where Simeon North and Eli Whitney pioneered the American System of Manufactures was known by the end of the century for its workforce of skilled machinists ready to apply their inventiveness to many different industrial processes.[1]

As the national wave of industrialization broke over Connecticut in the decades after the Civil War, it brought factory work sufficient to support a much larger population. As a result, the population of the state grew threefold in a sixty-year period: from 460,000 in 1860 to 1,380,000 by 1920. Ninety percent of this increase took place in towns within the central valley, the southwest hills, and the coastal slope of western Connecticut, regions that constituted the state's industrial core. These three regions, which cut across the state from Greenwich to New Haven and Hartford, and through the Naugatuck Valley from Bridgeport to Torrington, grew one and a half times faster than the state as a whole.[2]

At the same time, Connecticut became increasingly more urbanized. Ten more cities were incorporated, bringing the total number of cities in the state to seventeen. All but four of these were now located within the state's industrial core. Whereas the seven cities that had existed in Connecticut in 1860 had contained 30 percent of the state's population at that time, the seventeen cities of 1920 held nearly two-thirds of Connecticut's total popula-

These two murals
in the Bridgeport
Post Office,
painted by the
Works Progress
Administration in
the 1930s, depict
the heavy
industrialization
of Connecticut
during the second
half of the
nineteenth
century.
*(By permission of
the U.S. Postal
Service. All rights
reserved)*

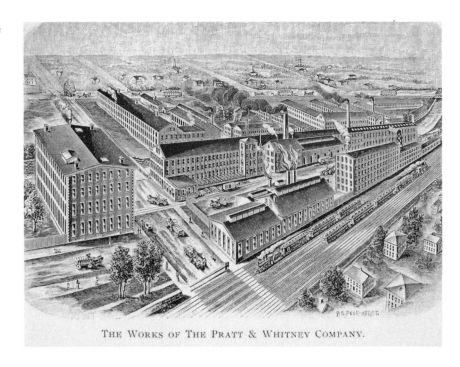

THE WORKS OF THE PRATT & WHITNEY COMPANY.

tion. And a full one-third of the population, or 450,000 persons, lived in the
state's three largest cities: New Haven, Bridgeport, and Hartford.[3]

Not only did Connecticut become more urbanized, but the composition of
its population changed dramatically. In 1870, Connecticut was predominantly a Yankee state, and three-quarters of Connecticut residents were born
in the state. By 1910, a steady influx of European immigrants attracted to the
state by the demand for industrial workers reduced the portion of native-
born persons to one-third of the population. In absolute terms, during this
forty-year period the number of native-born persons in Connecticut remained constant at four hundred thousand, while the increase in total population came from a fivefold increase in the number of foreign-born persons.[4]

The increase in industrial production, the population growth sustained by
that production, and the mass distribution of goods made possible by the
railroad were a triad of interdependent causes and effects that redefined the
culture of nineteenth-century America. As the consolidation of railroads
continued, the rivalry of cities for access to a rail line, once an important
factor in railroad-building, became less important as entire rail systems competed with one another for regional dominance. However, with the growth

of regional systems, railroad corporations came up against an unexpected obstacle: time.

In Massachusetts, most railroads operated their trains by the local time in Boston, provided to the railroads (for a fee) over telegraph lines by scientists working at the observatory of Harvard College. On crossing into Connecticut, trains were required to adjust their schedules to the standard used by the Consolidated, the local time in New York City. Since time-telling in each city was based on its longitude, local time in Boston was twelve minutes ahead of local time in New York City. With many railroads still operating single-track lines, coordinating schedules was vital in avoiding collisions of trains moving in opposite directions. One railroad, the New York & New England, adapted to the time difference by running its trains on Boston time east of Hartford and on New York time west of Hartford. But as rail systems became more complex, uniform scheduling became an urgent matter.

As early as 1870, Charles Dowd of Madison, Connecticut, had devised a plan to divide the entire country into four time zones, each zone one hour earlier than the one to the east. In this way, Dowd believed the problem of railroad time scheduling could be simplified nationwide. But Dowd's idea was ahead of *its* time. Consolidation was only beginning, and scheduling difficulties were not yet critical, so railroad owners had disregarded Dowd's proposal.

Selling the time to railroads, cities, and individuals was a popular business made possible by the telegraph. In 1880, Leonard Waldo, head of the Harvard observatory, petitioned the City Council of Hartford to convert local time in Hartford to Boston time, with the hope that as Hartford went so would the rest of Connecticut, thereby expanding observatory business. Unfortunately Waldo's proposal backfired. His proposition was strongly opposed by the Consolidated, and as a result Hartford chose to adopt as its new local time the standard of New York City.

To unify railroading within the state, the Connecticut legislature the following year passed An Act Establishing a Standard of Time, which defined "time for the meridian of the city hall in the city of New York" as the standard for all of Connecticut. The time signal was to be sent via telegraph at least once each day (except Sunday) from the observatory of the state's own Yale College to the New Haven depot of the New York, New Haven & Hartford Railroad for a sum not to exceed $1,000 a year. The Consolidated was to transmit this time "over its entire line and to all other railroad companies in the state connecting to said railroad." Railroads outside the state that ran on time other than that of New York were required to convert their schedules and advertisements to the Connecticut standard when operating within Connecticut.

The time situation in the New York–Boston corridor was hardly unique. Similar situations were repeated in dozens of cities across the nation and affected dozens of other railroads. In April 1883, at a convention of railroad executives, managers, and agents in St. Louis, Missouri, a resolution was passed to divide the country into four longitudinal time zones as Dowd had first proposed a decade earlier. The width of each zone was fifteen minutes of longitude, with Eastern Standard Time defined as the local time at the seventy-fifth meridian, near New York City. General Standard or Railroad Time was introduced on the nation's railroads at noon on Sunday, November 18, 1883.[5] Fourteen years after the first transcontinental railroad united the country physically, Railroad Time united the country temporally.

Railroad consolidation was not the only form of system-building going on in the last decades of the nineteenth century. The invention of the telephone in 1876 continued the communication revolution begun by the telegraph, making communication at a distance readily available to the general public. Connecticut companies pioneered the spread of the new technology, and local telephone exchanges were soon in operation within New Haven and Hartford. By 1883, one of the first city-to-city telephone links was established between New York and Boston, and from this beginning, two centuries after the first post rider, a network of interconnected telephone exchanges grew around the region.

The transformation of Connecticut into an urban-industrial state was accompanied by a second wave of technological change that was based in large part on the development of electricity as a power source for homes, factories, and businesses. Electric power came to Connecticut with the incorporation of electric lighting companies in Hartford (1881), Bridgeport (1881), and New Haven (1883). Similar corporations were organized in other parts of the state, and by the turn of the century many local electric companies were consolidated into a handful of generating and distribution systems: the United Illuminating Company in the shoreline communities from Bridgeport to New Haven; the Connecticut Light and Power Company in the Housatonic and Naugatuck valleys; the Hartford Electric Light Company in the Hartford area; the Eastern Connecticut Power Company in portions of the state east of the Connecticut River; and the Willimantic Electric Company in Willimantic.[6]

The building of railroad, telephone, and electrical systems in the latter half of the nineteenth century was a significant expression of the role technology had assumed in American society. As a nation, we became enmeshed in the complex infrastructures of transportation, communication and electronic systems.[7] But system-building was only part of the change. The way business was conducted also changed, as market capitalism gave way to a new form of commercial interaction called managerial capitalism, where large corporations came to dominate particular sectors of the economy. Railroads led the way in this development as they had in that of technological systems.

As individual railroads combined into rail systems, the internal structure of the parent corporation changed to accommodate expanding operations. Individual rail lines were now managed as separate divisions of a larger corporation, with the operations and workers of each division overseen by a hierarchy of professional managers. This meant that the success of the company as a whole fell to a group of hired hands, specialized executives who were perhaps not even stockholders of the corporation. Whereas market capitalism relied on the invisible forces of the marketplace to determine a company's fate, large, multiunit railroad corporations like the Consolidated were now steered toward success or failure by the visible hand of professional managers.[8]

By 1887, the Consolidated had grown tenfold from its beginning as the fifty-mile New York & New Haven Railroad to a statewide rail system of five hundred track miles. As a result, the company was reorganized into seven divisions, with about forty managers directing a workforce of seven thousand employees. The corporation itself was managed by six executives: a general manager, general accountant, and general counsel, in addition to a president, secretary, and treasurer. By the turn of the century, as expansion continued and the number of divisions increased, it took 150 divisional managers and a workforce of twenty-six thousand employees to keep the Consolidated system running.[9]

The size and complexity of managerial railroads made their regulation ever more difficult. This was especially true in the area of finance, where new entities such as the holding company and the interlocking directorate made subterfuge easier to commit and more difficult to detect as the capitalization and bonded debt of parent railroads grew. As managerial capitalism spread to other sectors of the economy, including investment banking, the concentration of wealth and power in the hands of a few became an issue of national importance. The resulting oligarchy, not unlike the Standing Order of colonial Connecticut, was a ready target for progressive reformers.

Competition from Other Modes

By the end of the nineteenth century, steamboats and electric street railways had emerged as effective competitors to the Consolidated railroad monopoly.

THE RAILROAD AND THE STEAMBOAT: AN UNEASY PARTNERSHIP

The geography of Long Island Sound divided the steamboat services that plied its waters into two groups: one that traveled the inner reaches of the sound to Bridgeport, New Haven, and Hartford, serving the valleys of western and central Connecticut; and another that traveled the outer reaches of the sound to Norwich, New London, and Stonington in Connecticut, Providence in Rhode Island, and Fall River in Massachusetts. In addition to providing steamboat access for cities at the eastern end of Long Island Sound, the outer routes, particularly those to Providence and Fall River, were important steamer-railroad routes between New York and Boston.

Before the coming of the railroad in the late 1830s, steamboat service was well established on both the inner and outer reaches of Long Island Sound. As the railroad network in Connecticut and southern New England grew, rail travel did not supplant the steamboat or even lessen its importance. Instead, the two modes developed a symbiotic relationship in which the steamboat remained an important link in the region's transportation network. There were several reasons for this. First, passenger travel by steamboat was more comfortable than rail, especially for the long journey from New York to Boston, where it was possible to traverse three-quarters of the distance by steamer. For manufacturers, steamboat docks in lower Manhattan gave convenient access to the city's commercial center, whereas the Consolidated's uptown railroad terminal did not. Steamboat travel in the outer reaches of the sound bypassed the two rail-ferry crossings that existed on the shoreline route until 1889. Steamer schedules were also passenger-friendly. After leaving New York City in the early evening for Providence or Fall River, steamboat travelers arrived in Boston early the following morning, well rested and ready for a full day of activity. As a vice-president of the Consolidated once acknowledged he "never saw any sleeping car yet that was comfortable." Even after the two shoreline rail ferries were eliminated and overland trains were able to reach Boston in six hours flat, the convenience of steamboat

The steamboat City of Hartford. *(Courtesy of the Connecticut Historical Society, Hartford, Connecticut)*

schedules was so attractive that many Boston-bound travelers still preferred the comfort of an overnight steamer.[10]

This combination of geography and travel preference allowed the railroad and the steamboat to coexist, but competition on the water between steamboat operators made the partnership an uneasy one. First, there was the competition at individual ports for passengers and freight traveling a particular route. Later, as a regional rail network evolved, steamboat companies vied for the upper hand on one or another of the outer routes from New York to Boston. The result was a series of rate wars in the 1850s, 1860s, and 1870s that drove fares for travel to Boston down from $5 to $1, and cargo rates to less than one-half their usual amount. While passengers and shippers benefited from the lower fares, rate wars added a degree of uncertainty and mistrust to the transportation services that many came to depend on.[11]

To the good, competition stimulated steamboat design, as operators sought a competitive edge by running larger, faster, more luxurious vessels. By the 1880s, as traffic increased and a new tourist trade headed for the summer resorts of Rhode Island and beyond, a generation of large steamers appeared on Long Island Sound, including the *Pilgrim* (1882), the *Puritan* (1889), the *Plymouth* (1890), and the *Priscilla* (1894), all built for the Fall River line.

Best described as floating hotels, these larger boats measured three to four hundred feet in length and cruised at fifteen to twenty knots. The *Priscilla,* the largest steamer to run on Long Island Sound, had a grand salon one hundred feet long and two decks high and as elegantly decorated as a Victorian parlor. With more than three hundred staterooms, the *Priscilla* accommodated one thousand passengers. To keep such a large vessel functioning required a crew of up to one hundred persons, including pursers, stewards, engineers, coal passers, firemen, watchmen, oilers, water tenders, waiters, deckhands, and porters, as well as chambermaids and stewardesses to attend to female passengers. Though steamers on other routes were neither as large nor as glamorous as those of the Fall River line, they remained competitive, with a state-of-the-art design suitable to the market they served.[12]

Powering these larger vessels required substantial advances in the technology of the steamboat's engine and drive train. Because Long Island Sound steamers used low-pressure engines, the easiest way to increase power was to make the elements of the engine bigger. Whereas the engine designed by John Fitch in the 1780s had used a cylinder twelve inches in diameter, the walking beam engines built for the *Pilgrim* and *Puritan* had cylinders nine *feet* in diameter, an opening large enough to drive a horse and carriage through. Other engine designs were developed as well, including a compound engine, in which steam passed through two cylinders, a smaller one at high pressure and a larger one at a lower pressure. This allowed for greater power with a smaller engine. In the 1890s came the inclined engine, whose cylinders were slanted to allow a direct linkage to the shaft that turned the paddle wheel. The result was a more efficient engine that consumed fewer tons of coal. The *Priscilla* was powered by one of the first inclined engines put to use on Long Island Sound.[13]

Two other design innovations appeared on Long Island Sound steamers in the 1880s: steam-assisted power steering and feathered paddle wheels. Whereas the manual steering of larger steamboats required two or more wheels and up to six helmsmen to hold the vessel on course, power steering required only a slight touch of a single wheel attached to a steam cylinder to position the boat's rudder. Once set, the rudder was held in place by two auxiliary cylinders filled with glycerin. To propel large steamers such as the *Pilgrim,* designers employed paddle wheels with a mechanical linkage that changed the angle of the bucket as it entered and exited the water, reducing water resistance. This allowed designers to achieve the same thrust with a wheel of smaller diameter. These innovations, together with iron hulls and screw propellers, made it possible to build the larger steamers needed to accommodate increasing steamboat traffic while maintaining the level of speed and comfort that customers expected.[14]

Railroads used several strategies to cope with the impact of the Long Island Sound steamboats on their revenues. One strategy was to contract with a particular steamboat company to provide the railroad's connecting service to New York City. The contract detailed scheduling and transfer arrangements for passengers and cargo, as well as the division of receipts between the two companies. A second strategy was to have railroad directors, who were typically large investors in their railroad company, invest also in the steamboat company with which the railroad was affiliated. With an interlocking relationship, the railroad company was in a better position to influence steamer fares and service. But best of all was for the railroad to own a controlling interest in its steamboat partner. While this did not preclude a second operator from entering a particular market and competing for revenues, it did protect the continuity of service for the railroad in question.[15]

As the New York, New Haven & Hartford brought individual rail lines under its control, whether by lease, stock control, or outright purchase, it acquired with the transaction whatever steamboat assets the subsidiary railroad owned or had under contract. In this way, as the Consolidated grew, steamer service on Long Island Sound became more stable. In addition, with a large railroad corporation behind them, steamboat lines controlled by the Consolidated were better able to finance the construction of larger, more modern steamers.[16]

By the 1880s, between ten and twenty steamers were making daily trips from New York City to ports on the inner and outer reaches of Long Island Sound. Both day boats and overnight service were commonplace to Hartford and to the outer ports of the sound, where a combination of distance and speed made an overnight schedule practical. Attaining speeds that could only be imagined in the early days, steamers such as the *Bristol* and the *Providence* routinely made their way from New York to Providence in twelve hours or less, half the time required by the *Fulton* sixty years earlier.[17]

Comparable traffic statistics with regard to Long Island Sound steamboats are difficult to find, but data from the u.s. Census of 1880 indicate that steamers on the Sound carried a total of about one million passengers, and one and one-half million tons of cargo, that year. Traffic on the three outer routes between New York and Boston carried 250,000 passengers, while all-rail routes in the corridor carried 200,000 persons. Likewise, for freight, the three steamer lines carried some 200,000 tons of cargo between New York and Boston, while Consolidated rail lines carried only one-third as much.[18] Even though steamboat passengers and freight still relied on the rail network for the final leg of their journey from New York to Boston, statistics show that Long Island Sound steamers were a significant link in the regional rail system, one the Consolidated could not ignore.

HORSE RAILROADS, STREET RAILWAYS, AND INTERURBANS

The growth of Connecticut cities during the nineteenth century brought with it a need for more efficient transportation within cities' limits to link outlying homes and factory villages to stores and services in the center. As early as 1848, public transportation was available in some cities, as is evidenced by a state law that allowed a city's common council to "make such orders, rules and ordinances as they may deem necessary for the regulation of the public hacks or other public carriages for the conveyance of passengers . . . [and] establish the rates of fare for the conveyance of any passengers to or from any steamboat landing or railroad station, or other place or places within the limits of such city."[19]

A popular vehicle for transporting the public was the omnibus, an elongated stagecoach-style vehicle in which six or eight passengers sitting lengthwise were drawn over unpaved city streets by one or two horses. In the 1860s, for example, an omnibus ran along Main Street in Hartford between the South Green and Spring Grove Cemetery. The flat fare for traveling any distance along the route was 5 cents, and the coaches left both ends of the line at half-hour intervals.[20]

As railroad tracks became commonplace and iron rails more readily available, the idea arose to install iron rails along city streets, allowing one horse to pull a railcar carrying twice the load of an omnibus on a dirt roadway. The result was a horse railroad. The first horse railroad vehicle was a standard omnibus whose body was fitted with flanged wheels and attached to the wheeled chassis by a kingpin that allowed the upper body of the vehicle to be reversed at the end of the line without the need to construct a turnaround. Later, this omnibus design was replaced by a longer streetcar with entrances at both ends and a transverse arrangement of seats. With the aid of reduced

This stage-style omnibus operated between Hartford and West Hartford as late as 1900. (Courtesy of the Connecticut Valley Chapter, National Railway Historical Society)

friction, one or two horses could pull a streetcar containing twelve to sixteen passengers, at a speed equal to or greater than that of a rail omnibus.

The first two horse railroads in Connecticut were the Hartford & Wethersfield Horse Railway, chartered in 1859 to operate between Hartford and Wethersfield, and the Fairhaven & Westville Horse Railway, chartered in 1860 to run between New Haven and Westville. By 1863, both lines were open for business.[21] As with its steam-powered counterpart, the horse-drawn railroad was first seen as an intrusion on an otherwise contented community, though opinions changed once the benefits of a horse railroad were apparent. The following evaluation by the *Hartford Courant* noted the public's change of view toward the Hartford & Wethersfield line after one year of operation:

> Here, as in other cities where such roads have been built, serious opposition was made to the laying of railway tracks through prominent thoroughfares, because they formed an obstacle to pleasure driving in carriages, etc., but now that the road is in successful operation, and its cheap and convenient mode of travel appreciated by all classes of people, the wonder is that Hartford did not accept the improvement long before it did. Aside from the conveniences afforded the public, the road has been a source of great profit to property owners in the north, south and west sections of the city, as the price of real estate in those sections will show by comparison. Altogether we accept the road as an established institution which we could hardly do without.[22]

Over the next three decades more than thirty horse railroad corporations were chartered in Connecticut in two dozen more communities, including Danbury, Bridgeport, Stamford, Waterbury, Meriden, Middletown, Norwich, and New London. Though these urban railroads were chartered by the state legislature, the laying out of individual routes and other regulatory issues was under the control of the city council or board of selectmen where the lines operated.

While horse railroads provided the public with convenience and enhanced property values, the operation of a horsecar line was an expensive proposition. Each car in service required a company to own five to eight horses at a purchase price of $150 each, and these horses could be used no more than five hours per day for perhaps four years before replacements were necessary. Feeding and stabling these horses, and employing hostlers, blacksmiths, veterinarians, and other workmen to care for them added to a horse railroad's ongoing costs.

And the animals were subject to illness. When horse flu struck America in the Great Epizootic Epidemic of 1872, this debilitating respiratory illness spread quickly to horse railroad stock around the nation. In Connecticut, the first case appeared in March 1872, and by that fall the epidemic had forced the closure of nearly all horse railway lines in the state. Even after the illness had passed its peak, many services ran at a reduced level for a month or more. As one Hartford newspaper noted in November 1872: "People no longer wait for the cars but trudge home on foot, realizing for once the inestimable value of the road and the great annoyance of the pesky disease which has stopped the traffic. In this life there are very many things which we do not appreciate until we are deprived of them; a horse railroad is one."[23]

After the epidemic a search began for a more reliable and less costly source of power for transportation within city limits. Prompted by several of the state's horse railroad companies, the Connecticut legislature in 1873 passed a law allowing the use of steam power on street railways. While there was much talk of testing a steam-propelled streetcar in Hartford, the experiment never materialized. The cable car system provided another option. First developed for the hilly streets of San Francisco, a cable car was pulled along by a moving underground cable connected to a steam-powered engine housed somewhere along the route. In New England, cable car technology was put to use only in Providence, on the hilly streets near Brown College. Battery-powered cars were a third possibility, and in 1891 a battery-powered streetcar was operated in Hartford on a trial basis. But the battery lasted only fifty miles before needing to be recharged, which meant that a railway company needed two battery-powered cars to provide the same level of service as one horse-powered car, making the cost prohibitive.[24]

The one power source with true potential for streetcar application was electricity. By 1880 the know-how to adapt electrical power to streetcar operation was available, but producing an electric motor that could propel a streetcar and withstand the shock and strain of continued use remained an obstacle. By the end of the decade the problem had been solved by Frank Sprague (1857–1934) of Milford, Connecticut. Sprague had been educated at the United States Naval Academy, where he pursued an interest in the science of electricity. He then joined the Edison Company and developed an improved electric motor. Convinced that his motor could be applied to a street railway, Sprague left the Edison group to form the Sprague Electric Railway & Motor Company, where he perfected a five-hundred-volt motor and a mounting mechanism that enabled the motor to propel the streetcar with minimal shock to the motor.

Using his technology, Sprague designed a citywide transit system for Richmond, Virginia, that opened to much acclaim in 1888. In addition to its functionality, it was discovered that the cost of Sprague's railway was only 40 percent that of a horse railroad. The next year Sprague's system was chosen for the West End Railway in Boston, the nation's largest street railway. After this, orders came in from cities across the country. Within three years, 90 percent of the two hundred street railway systems built or under contract in the United States used the Sprague system. Meanwhile, Sprague invented an electric motor system to power multiple-car trains that made possible Chicago's elevated railway and the subways of New York City.[25]

The first electric street railway to operate in Connecticut was the Derby Horse Railway, whose company converted its existing horsecar line to electric power on April 30, 1888. The local newspaper described a late-night trip of the state's first electric railway:

It was a handsome, cream colored four wheeled car, sixteen feet in length and handsomely upholstered. About four feet of the forward end of the car is partitioned off and in the compartment is situated the motor, of about three or four horse power. Besides the [thirty or so] elect who were invited to take a ride on the new vehicle were about 250 men and boys, many of whom doubted whether the machine was going to make a successful trip down to Derby and back. The car was lighted by four incandescent lights in the interior and one in the rear end. . . . [The boys] ran after the car as it went bowling along the track. They shouted

and laughed and cheered in high glee. . . . The boys were very proud of the new road and fired fire crackers to show their goodwill towards the new enterprise.

With a top speed of twelve miles per hour, the streetcar's one-way trip to Derby took about twenty minutes.[26]

Between 1887 and 1925 Connecticut chartered about 150 street railway companies, half of which produced operating railways. Charters peaked in 1893, when thirty-five railway corporations were created in that year alone. By 1918, the state's street railway system had reached its maximum extent, with eleven hundred miles of track and three thousand streetcars in operation. Because street railways did not require locomotives and their cars were lighter than railroad cars, construction costs were lower, averaging $10,000 per mile.[27]

Connecticut's electric street railways were regulated as a cooperative effort between local governments that maintained control of the layout and scheduling of railway lines within their jurisdictions and the state's General Railroad Commission, to whom trolley companies were required to submit annual reports beginning in 1895. As with Connecticut's railroads, the main concern of the commission was safety. However, streetcar accidents happened. The worst took place on August 6, 1899, in Bridgeport, when a streetcar derailed while crossing a bridge. The car fell, top down, into a dry

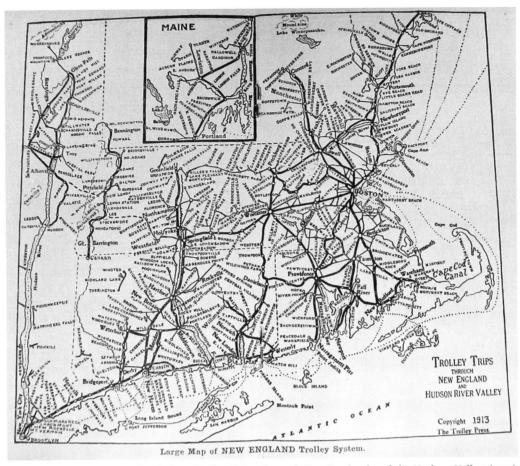

Street railways in New England, from Trolley Trips through New England and the Hudson Valley *(1913).*

streambed forty feet below, killing twenty-nine of the thirty-five passengers on board.[28]

Initially, the range of electric streetcar service was limited by the use of low voltage direct current, which could not be transmitted effectively over long distances. The development of a three-phase distribution system in 1893 made intercity electrical transmission practical. As a result, street railway lines were extended from one urban center to another, creating an interurban network throughout New England. In 1913, a trolley guide to the region noted that it was possible to travel from New York to Boston along the upper post road by street railway for little more than $3. The trip covered 250 miles, required thirteen line changes, and took eighteen and one-half hours!

For $2 (and ten hours) more, the truly adventurous could continue on an-other one hundred–plus miles to Portland, Maine.[29]

In a state where rail passenger traffic was largely local in nature, a parallel system of street railways served many passengers who might otherwise have traveled on the New York, New Haven & Hartford Railroad. In addition, once the Connecticut street railway network was tied into railway systems in Rhode Island and Massachusetts, many companies began to transport freight during their off-peak hours, bringing it to steamboat ports on Long Island Sound for shipment to New York or Boston. Along with the independent steamboat operators, New England's street railway system posed a challenge the Consolidated could not let stand.

From Consolidation to Monopoly

The reckless and unethical attempt by the Consolidated to create a New England transportation monopoly brought public scrutiny and antitrust investigations that led to its corporate downfall.

THE NEW YORK & NEW ENGLAND

In the autumn of 1889, Agnes Watson traveled with her husband and daugh-ter from Scotland to visit her uncle, Henry Affleck, a tobacco grower who lived in Glastonbury, Connecticut. Writing to her family back in Scotland, Mrs. Watson described the last leg of their transatlantic journey, a twelve-hour, 180-mile trip from New York City to Glastonbury. Her record of that trip illustrates the multimodal nature of transportation in the New York–Boston corridor in the late 1880s:

> We stepped from off our ship at 8 A.M. on Wednesday. What a vast and magnificent city New York is! . . . After having had our boxes examined, and no fault being found, we had them fixed up again (poor father had an awful time of it, no help being given).
>
> We posted our letters, and after infinite labour we gathered information about Glastonbury, which seemed to be a place that no one knew anything about. According to directions given we walked to a line of steam cars, where we were told to ride to 42nd Street. We went up three very high stairs to reach the cars. They run on rails laid upon iron pillars as high as the tops of the houses. The carriages and carts do their work on the street below. At 42nd Street we got into a horse-car, and were taken to the "Great Central Station," to which place our luggage

had been sent. We were just in time to get a train to Newhaven. The railway cars are a treat. You go in at one end, and can walk right through. They are fitted up like drawing-rooms, and contain smoking and luncheon rooms. From Newhaven we had to find our way to the air line for Middletown. That journey occupied two hours. Arrived there, we found we had to wait till 4:30 for a train to Rockiehill. We consoled ourselves by hiring a carriage and driving around Middletown, a good-sized town, whose handsome villas would put to shame all we have in the old country. They cost little money, being built of wood with brick foundations.

On reaching Rockiehill we were handed over to the mail-gig. The driver chanced to be a right good fellow, and, joy of joys, he knew Henry Affleck, who, he said, was one of the good sort. We then got into the mail-gig, the boxes being strapped on behind. Fixed thus we drove a little way, then crossed a ferry. The road again for six miles seemed to us to cut through the back-woods. It was now 8 o'clock. In all we had done 180 miles. Our feelings by this time were down to zero. It seemed so strange that no one was meeting us. Uncle's house was reached at last; all was still and quiet. Our driver went in first to break the news of our arrival.

The Watsons' journey from New York might have been made more quickly and in much greater comfort by steamboat direct to Rocky Hill except for a missed communication. It seemed the letter announcing the date and time of the family's arrival did not reach Mr. Affleck, who "was quite sorry, as he meant to meet us in New York, and bring us here by the river."[30]

In the train portion of their trip from New York to Glastonbury, the Watsons traveled on three divisions of the Consolidated: the New Haven, Air Line, and Valley divisions. Their patronage was not as much a matter of choice as it was the Consolidated's dominance in the region, which included access via the Harlem division of the New York Central to the newly constructed Grand Central Terminal in New York City. However, the Consolidated soon had a formidable challenger in the New York & New England, a Boston-based railroad that was about to reveal a devious plan of its own to dominate transportation in the New York–Boston corridor.

The New York & New England had cobbled together an impressive rail system of several hundred track miles from the remnants of two partially built Connecticut railroads, the Hartford, Providence & Fishkill and the Southbridge & Blackstone. In doing so, the New York & New England obtained control of a main line that ran across central Connecticut from Danbury to Willimantic, where it split into two segments, one headed to Boston, the other to Providence. The New York & New England system also included the Norwich & Worcester, which gave the company access to steamer service on Long Island Sound; and the Connecticut Central Railroad, which provided a rail connection to Springfield, Massachusetts. What the New York & New England did not have was access of its own into New York City.[31]

The president of the New York & New England was experienced rail manager and investor Charles P. Clark. Clark viewed the New York & New England as a local railroad and managed the system in cooperation with the Consolidated, on which he depended for long-distance freight connections and entrance into New York City. In the 1880s, Clark used his amiable relationship with the Consolidated to initiate two important services in the region: the Washington Express, from Washington, D.C., to Boston via Hartford, and Connecticut's most famous train service, the New England Limited, an express train from New York to Boston that ran over the New Haven's Air Line and covered the route in only six hours.[32]

In 1886, however, control of the New York & New England's board of directors passed from conservative Boston businessmen to a group of New York railroad speculators who were determined to challenge the supremacy of the Consolidated. When Clark proposed that the new board lease the New York & New England to the Consolidated to ensure the railroad's financial stability, he was ousted instead, after which the New York & New England began an aggressive bid to challenge the supremacy of the New Haven by gaining its own entrance into New York City.

The railroad's first move was to take financial control of Connecticut's Housatonic Railroad. It then initiated the Long Island & Eastern States Express, a service from Boston to Wilson's Point on Long Island Sound in Norwalk over the tracks of the two systems. At Wilson's Point freight was forwarded to Manhattan by barge, while passenger cars were ferried across the sound to Oyster Point, Long Island, and reassembled for the final leg of the trip to New York via the Long Island Railroad. The arrangement was cumbersome, but it was an aggressive first step in freeing the New York & New England from its dependence on the Consolidated.[33]

Next came an attempt by the New York & New England to build its own parallel road from New Haven into New York City. The proposal was initiated in 1888 by the Housatonic Railroad, which sought permission from the General Railroad Commission to construct two branch lines leading from

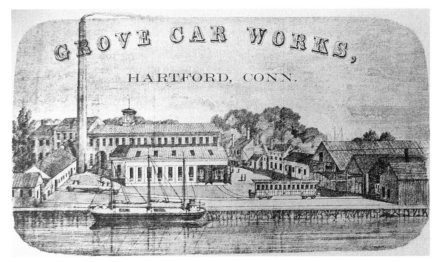

Grove Car Works in Hartford, from Henry Erving, The Connecticut River Banking Company *(1925).*

Bridgeport, one to the east and New Haven, the other to the west and the New York state line. But this devious tactic, intended to hide the New York & New England's ultimate goal, fooled no one. As the commission noted of the relationship between the Housatonic and the New York & New England, "each company is under a separate and distinct management, but the same parties own stock in both companies, and are directors of both boards, thus indicating that intimate and harmonious relations exist between the two systems."[34]

Everyone, including the Consolidated, was well aware that the Housatonic's proposal was not just another parallel road between New York and New Haven but a more substantial threat that, if successful, would turn the New York & New England into a parallel rail *system* capable of competing with the Consolidated for dominance in the region. For the Consolidated, which relied on the Boston & Providence, a Massachusetts railroad, for its entrance into Boston, such a competitor could prove fatal.

To counter the attack and deal once and for all with the threat of parallels, the Consolidated asked its new president, none other than Charles P. Clark, to submit a charter revision to the General Railroad Commission that contained two significant provisions. The first increased the company's capitalization to $50 million from $15 million; the second allowed the Consolidated to purchase any Connecticut railroad it had under lease. Lacking the authority to select which petition was in the public's best interest, the commission approved both requests and sent them on to the legislature for politics to decide the outcome.

The battle between the New York & New England and the Consolidated that occurred during the legislative session of 1889 was termed by the *New York Times* "the bitterest one in the annals of railroad warfare in Connecticut." Meanwhile, the *Bridgeport Standard,* the Housatonic's hometown paper, noted that twenty thousand businessmen along the route supported the parallel road, while the project had only one opponent: the Consolidated. "Any monopoly is dangerous in a republican government," the *Standard* said. "Is this a popular government, or has it come to be a government by the Consolidated railroad?"[35]

One opponent with the clout of the Consolidated, however, was enough. The Housatonic's petition was defeated in the legislature's Joint Railroad Committee by a vote of five to four, while the Consolidated's charter amendment easily won legislative approval, though not before each side accused the other of trying to purchase victory at $1,000 per vote. To forestall similar episodes in the future, the legislature passed a law that permitted branch lines like those proposed by the Housatonic to be built only if they are first judged to be a public necessity by the state's Superior Court. As the *New York Times* commented at the close of the session, the legislature not only endorsed the Consolidated and its request for expansion capital; it once and for all "planted itself against competing parallel lines of railway in the State."[36]

In its decision to support the New York, New Haven & Hartford as Connecticut's railroad of choice, the legislature had crossed the Rubicon on its way to creating monopoly. But its support did not end there. The charter of the Consolidated was amended again in 1893 to raise the company's total capitalization to $100 million and to allow the Consolidated to acquire railroads in adjoining states whose lines were contiguous with those of the Consolidated in Connecticut.[37]

Clark wasted little time putting the newfound funds to good use. He first made numerous physical improvements to the road in Connecticut, modernizing signals, yards, and rolling stock and widening the road's main stem from New York to New Haven from two tracks to four—in effect taking the steam out of future competitors by building his own parallel road. He then solidified the road's position in the region by leasing the shoreline route east of New London through Rhode Island to Boston, giving the Consolidated the entrance it had previously lacked. He did this through a lease of the New York, Providence & Boston and the purchase of the Old Colony system, which included the Boston & Providence and roads throughout Rhode Island and southeastern Massachusetts as far east as Cape Cod.[38]

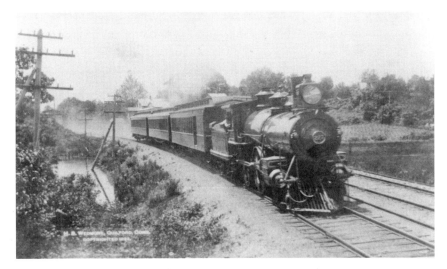

The Bay State Limited, pictured here in Guilford in 1893, traveled the shoreline route to Boston. (Courtesy of the Library of Congress)

Still, Clark had time to keep an eye on the New York & New England. When the New York speculators abandoned their financial position after their defeat, the Consolidated took control of the Housatonic system and redirected shared freight traffic away from the New York & New England, thereby depleting its revenues and driving the road into bankruptcy. Following a two-year reorganization, the New York & New England was reborn as the New England Railroad, with the Consolidated firmly in control. Several years later, a formal lease of the New England Railroad brought the one-time rival fully within the New York, New Haven & Hartford system.[39]

Under the twelve-year presidency of Clark, the Consolidated grew by leaps and bounds into the dominant railroad system in southern New England, expanding to more than two thousand track miles from four hundred in 1887. The Consolidated now owned, leased, or held a majority stock position in 80 percent of all rail mileage in Connecticut and 100 percent of railroads in Rhode Island and was a greater presence in Massachusetts than either of that state's other major systems, the Boston & Albany and the Boston & Maine.

The Clark expansion bordered on the excessive. With a capitalization of $100 million, the bonded debt of the Consolidated expanded tenfold under Clark, while gross receipts increased at only half that rate. Yet the expansion of the Consolidated after the defeat of the New York & New England from a Connecticut rail system into a southern New England railroad monopoly drew little public protest. Consolidated stock sold at $206 per share, more than twice its par value, and stockholders continued to receive the 8–10 percent annual dividend they were accustomed to. What more could a railroad desire?[40]

MORGAN, MELLEN, AND MONOPOLY

During Clark's presidency, John Pierpont Morgan (1837–1913) joined the New Haven as one of its twelve directors. Morgan had been born and raised in Hartford and had a fondness for New England that dated to his childhood. When the first train of the Hartford & New Haven Railroad had traveled to Boston in 1844, John, seven years old, had been on it, with his grandfather, Joseph Morgan, a prominent Hartford businessman and shareholder of the railroad. It was telling that throughout his life Morgan referred to the New York, New Haven & Hartford not as the New Haven, as most people did, but as the Hartford.

J. P. Morgan rose through the world of mercantile banking in New York to become one of the most influential dealmakers in American finance. As railroad construction boomed in the 1870s and 1880s, Morgan's power grew as a result of his skill in organizing the syndicates of foreign and domestic capital that the unbridled expansion required. Later, as the economy entered new areas of mass production in steel, agriculture, and electricity, Morgan brokered the financing of these new industries as well through his New York banking house. By the end of the century, he was the de facto central banker of the nation, with influence that extended from the Oval Office in Washington to the boardrooms of numerous American corporations he helped to create. But it was his relationship with the New Haven that made J. P. Morgan an exemplar of the excesses of the banker management that ruled railroading and managerial capitalism in the late nineteenth century.[41]

Following the New Haven's expansion under Charles P. Clark, Morgan used his influence to arrange a peace treaty between the Consolidated and northern New England's largest rail system, the Boston & Maine. Under pressure from Morgan, the banker of record for both systems, the two railroads agreed to divide the six-state region of New England in half along the main line of the Boston & Albany and not to expand into or interfere with rail operations in each other's territory. The agreement was a clear violation of the Sherman Anti-Trust Act passed in 1890, but Morgan was not concerned. Instead, he promised each railroad it would have the money it needed to become the dominant railroad within its territory. By using his power as the banker-director-manager of the New Haven and the Boston & Maine, Mor-

J. P. Morgan. (Courtesy of the Library of Congress)

gan not only curtailed competition in New England, he nullified the authority of the stockholders in each company.[42]

Peace agreement aside, Morgan's intent was to consolidate all of New England's railroads under one corporation, the New Haven, and to further combine all steamboats and street railways in the region into one transportation monopoly. Following Clark's retirement (and a short period of calm under his immediate successor) Morgan found in Charles S. Mellen just the man he needed to turn his vision into reality. Mellen was a confident, self-made railroad manager who had joined the New Haven management team in the 1890s. He was then appointed by Morgan to the presidency of the troubled Northern Pacific Railroad, whose net revenues and price per share Mellen dramatically increased. Having passed his baptism of fire, Mellen was brought back to head the New Haven in 1903.[43]

Mellen was a consolidator at heart, someone who despised the inefficiency of competition. On becoming president of the New Haven, Mellen told newspapers: "Railroading is a natural monopoly, and should be protected as such. In return for that protection, it should submit to reasonable regulation." There was logic in his approach, especially in New England, a fringe region whose rail connections to the rest of the nation depended on the trunk line railroads of other rail corporations, including the New York Central, the Pennsylvania, and the Grand Trunk of Canada. By creating a regional monopoly, Mellen could ensure that the New Haven obtained the best competitive rates from these trunk line railroads, while within New England a monopoly of railroad, steamboat, and electric railway operations would allow him to eliminate redundant lines, lower rates on high traffic routes, and ensure the best integrated service overall. But the question remained: could Morgan and Mellen legally form such a transportation monopoly while maintaining the financial security of the parent company and the operating safety of the system?[44]

Mellen took his first step toward monopoly by adding to the New Haven's steamboat acquisitions. The New Haven already operated steamboats from Bridgeport, New Haven, Norwich, Stonington, and Providence through its control of the railroads that owned these services. But there were other steamboat companies to be had, including the Hartford & New York Transportation Company, the Maine Steamship Company, and the Boston & Philadelphia Steamship Company. One by one, Mellen acquired these and other companies, and by 1910, after spending $25 million in steamboat purchases, the New Haven controlled 90 percent of all water transportation in New England.[45]

To accomplish this, Mellen utilized a wholly owned subsidiary of the New Haven called the New England Navigation Company, a holding company into which he placed the Consolidated's steamboat operations. But the history of the New England Navigation Company showed it to be more than a means to efficient management. The company had been incorporated in 1901—while Morgan was a New Haven director but before Mellen returned as New Haven president—under the name Colonial Commercial Company, with a capitalization of a mere $50,000. However, it was authorized by its charter to do almost anything from "manufacturing, mining, trading and mercantile business" to the operation of "public improvements and works, including steamboats and railroads." The corporation could even "buy, sell and deal in all kinds of real and personal property, including the securities and franchises of other corporations." Unlike other corporations, however, the Colonial Commercial Company was not required to make its finances public. The company remained dormant until 1904, when under Mellen it became the New England Navigation Company. The shareholders of the new company were Charles Mellen, who held 496 of the company's 500 shares, and four of his New Haven associates, who each held one of the four remaining shares.[46]

The New England Navigation Company was clearly created for the purpose of hiding from view whatever financial shenanigans Morgan and Mellen thought were necessary to finance future purchases. By trading steamboat and other holdings among its many subsidiaries and borrowing against the paper profits these transactions generated, the New Haven was able to purchase street railway companies throughout southern New England at a cost of $120 million over ten years. The purchases represented nearly all street railway operations in Connecticut and Rhode Island and street railway companies in Worcester, Springfield, and western Massachusetts amounting to 20 percent of the railway network in that state. Most railway franchises were purchased at prices far above their actual worth and were operated by the New Haven at a net loss of $2 million per year.

Mellen reserved his boldest move for the New Haven's treaty partner, the Boston & Maine. By using the New England Navigation Company, Mellen was able to acquire shares in northern New England's biggest railroad system with little notice until he had attained majority control of the Boston & Maine in 1907. By 1913, having purchased half interest in the Boston & Albany and several smaller railroads in the region, Mellen had brought the New Haven's monopoly of New England transportation to its peak. However, the rapid expansion cost the New Haven plenty. Beginning with an effective capitalization of $93 million in 1903, Mellen spent an additional $204 million on expansion purchases, as well as $120 million on legitimate improvements to the system, for a total capitalization of $417 million by 1913.[47]

Much of this expansion was accomplished by means of financial slight of hand, yet Mellen could not have done what he did without the ongoing support of the Connecticut legislature. At each step in the process, Connecticut lawmakers endorsed charter amendments for the parent railroad that gave the New Haven the authority it needed to move forward. This included an amendment in 1905 that made the New Haven a holding company with authority to buy and sell securities in railroads in other states and that in one broad stroke increased the New Haven's capital "to such amount as it shall find necessary" to accomplish such acquisitions. Two years later, another amendment was enacted allowing the New Haven to "merge, consolidate,

*Union Station,
New Haven.
(Courtesy of
the Thomas J.
Dodd Research
Center,
University of
Connecticut
Libraries)*

and make common stock with any or all corporations engaged in transportation, wherever organized."[48]

At noon on October 25, 1911, President Charles S. Mellen called to order the two hundred people gathered in the General Offices of the New York, New Haven & Hartford Railroad in New Haven for that year's annual shareholders meeting. After an overview of the annual report, in which Mellen noted a net deficit of $1,300,000 for the prior twelve months, one stockholder dared to ask what most were thinking: Why was the price of his stock falling? And was it true that the New Haven would for the first time in its history declare no dividend that year?

Mellen calmly reminded the questioner that the New Haven was currently in the midst of a substantial transaction with the Boston & Maine and that this purchase had produced the short-term deficit he reported. However, he assured his audience that this investment would pay great returns in just a few years, after which profits and the price of New Haven stock would rise. In the interim, Mellen declared, "The dividend won't be reduced unless something unforeseen should occur."[49] With that explanation, the stockholders accepted the annual report and elected the recommended slate of directors, all by unanimous vote, and the meeting was adjourned less than fifty minutes after it began. But for those who did not have blind faith in the infallibility of Mellen and the New Haven, the "unforeseen" was already visible.

AN EMPIRE ON TRIAL

The New Haven's move into northern New England did not go unnoticed. With the purchase of the Boston & Maine, public scrutiny of the transportation monopoly intensified. The focus for protest over the New Haven's actions was Louis D. Brandeis (1856–1941), a wealthy Boston lawyer known as the people's attorney for work he performed *pro bono publico* on behalf of organized labor, women's rights, and consumer banking. His battle against the New Haven, however, turned Brandeis into a national figure.[50]

Following the New Haven's purchase of the Boston & Maine, Brandeis published his first attack on the transportation monopoly: a seventy-seven-page report that used public documents concerning the finances of the two railroads to show that the New Haven was not the unflagging investment everyone thought it was. Despite the limitations of the study (the public documents included little or no information on subsidiary corporations) the findings were stunning. Brandeis discovered that the New Haven had recorded a $10 million purchase of locomotives as a loss instead of an operating expense. The railroad had then exchanged enough stock with a subsidiary to cover the loss *and* generate a paper profit sufficient to cover that year's dividend. With other examples, the report went on to show just how overextended the New Haven really was, and concluded: "If solvency is to be maintained a large reduction in the dividend is inevitable."[51]

The impact of the Brandeis report was amplified the following spring when the Supreme Court of Massachusetts ruled that the New Haven's acquisition of street railways in that state had been illegal, since the purchases had been made without legislative approval. The ruling cast a legal shadow on the New Haven's subsequent purchase of the Boston & Maine, which was likewise executed without the legislature's consent. The ruling and its implications for the Boston & Maine purchase finally piqued the interest of the Interstate Commerce Commission in Washington, which promised to look into the matter.[52]

What followed was one of the more bizarre episodes in the history of the New Haven: the Billard affair. While the Interstate Commerce Commission debated the propriety of the New Haven's Boston & Maine purchase, Mellen quietly sold the controversial stock to a Connecticut coal merchant named John L. Billard. Although Billard was worth barely $30,000, he borrowed

Louis Brandeis.
(Courtesy of the Library
of Congress)

the $14 million needed to purchase the stock with little difficulty from a Morgan bank in New York City. Meanwhile, the Massachusetts legislature contrived with its governor to create the Boston Railroad Holding Company, a paper corporation in which Mellen and the New Haven, through a subsidiary, held majority control. Billard then resold the stock to the Boston Railroad Holding Company (for a profit of $2 million), and the issue of legality concerning the New Haven's purchase of the Boston & Maine was cleverly circumvented. Since the politicians and the two railroads appeared satisfied with the outcome, the Interstate Commerce Commission halted its investigation, content to leave New England railroaders to their own devices, for the moment at least.[53]

As extensive as the New Haven's monopoly was, it was not total. One railroad, the Central Vermont, remained beyond the New Haven's reach. The Central Vermont was a descendant of Connecticut's New London, Willimantic & Palmer Railroad and ran from New London, Connecticut, to Palmer, Massachusetts, and on to northern Vermont, where it became part of its parent railroad, the Grand Trunk of Canada. The threat that the Central

Vermont and Grand Trunk systems posed to the New Haven created another bizarre episode in the history of the New Haven, one that precipitated the monopoly's fall from grace.

The Grand Trunk of Canada was headed by Charles M. Hayes, a seasoned veteran who, like Mellen, had worked his way up through the railroading ranks to become president of Canada's largest rail system. The Central Vermont was important to the Grand Trunk network because it provided access to year-round steamboat service to New York City from New London, the only ice-free port in the Grand Trunk system. A segment of this route between Windsor and Brattleboro in Vermont, however, was controlled by the Boston & Maine. The New Haven's takeover of the Boston & Maine created a threatening situation for the Central Vermont that Hayes, who had a personal dislike for Mellen and his methods, could not abide.

To make the Grand Trunk independent of Mellen and at the same time a competitor of the New Haven in its home territory, Hayes obtained the necessary charters for the Central Vermont to build a parallel line from Windsor to Brattleboro and to construct the Southern New England Railroad from Palmer, Massachusetts, to Providence, Rhode Island, a warm-water port beyond the control of the Connecticut legislature. Mellen considered the ploy an empty threat until construction began in earnest along the Southern New England right-of-way and Hayes ordered the construction of two Long Island Sound steamers for the run from Providence to New York.

With construction of the Southern New England well under way, fate intervened. Returning from a meeting in London in 1912, Hayes booked passage home on the maiden voyage of the *Titanic* and perished when the unsinkable ship sank. Hayes's replacement as president of the Grand Trunk Railroad was Edson J. Chamberlin, a longtime friend of Mellen and a man of a more cooperative bent. Later that year, with the railroad's right-of-way cleared and graded and many bridges already built, construction on the Southern New England stopped abruptly. Soon the newspapers revealed a secret agreement between the Grand Trunk and the New Haven roads that affirmed trackage rights for the Vermont Central from Windsor to Brattleboro, as well as access to the port of New London.[54]

The Grand Trunk incident was the last straw for critics of the New Haven. Rate complaints by Boston shippers who were organized by Brandeis brought on the first of two investigations of the New Haven's finances by the Interstate Commerce Commission. Meanwhile, a federal grand jury voted to indict both Mellen and Chamberlin for actions in restraint of trade, a violation of the

PUCK

ELISHA ROOSEVELT SICKETH THE BEARS UPON THE BAD BOYS OF WALL STREET.

This political cartoon shows the Theodore Roosevelt administration's efforts to use the Interstate Commerce Commission and the federal courts to rein in Wall Street bulls like Morgan and Rockefeller. (Courtesy of the Library of Congress)

Sherman Anti-Trust Act. At the same time, cutbacks authorized by Mellen to help counter the road's bonded debt were blamed for a series of accidents in which dozens of passengers and crew lost their lives, making the New Haven a target of public outrage.[55] In an effort to divert attention, Mellen used a Boston publication under his control to cast anti-Semitic aspersions on Brandeis, calling his attacks against the New Haven part of the "age-long struggle between Jew and Gentile."[56]

In the midst of this turmoil, the worst in the history of the New Haven, J. P. Morgan died on March 31, 1913, at age seventy-six. Following services in New York City, the body was brought by private train to his hometown of Hartford, where a funeral cortege made its way along the three-mile route from the Asylum Street station to the Morgan family tomb at Cedar Hill Cemetery. To mark the occasion, the Hartford fire bell tolled seventy-six times, as schools, businesses, and government offices closed for the afternoon.[57]

With Morgan gone, Mellen lost his best ally. When Morgan's son and heir took charge of the family's financial empire, the reign of Charles Mellen came to an abrupt end. With New Haven stock trading at a forty-year low of $106 per share (from a high of more than $200 per share a few years earlier). Mellen was forced to resign as president of the New York, New Haven & Hartford Railroad in July 1913. Later, directors of the New Haven who together with Morgan and Mellen had executed the costly expansion were charged with criminal conspiracy for their complicity in the whole antitrust affair, but in the end none were found guilty. In an attempt to exact a measure of justice, some New Haven shareholders filed a civil suit against the directors for $150 million, but settled out of court for $2.5 million, $1 million of which was paid to their attorneys.[58]

When the final results of the Interstate Commerce Commission investigation were released in July 1914, many of the insidious transactions of the New Haven monopoly under Morgan and Mellen became public for the first time. On the use of subsidiaries and interlocking directorates, first uncovered by Brandeis seven years earlier, the commission noted:

> The New Haven system has more than 300 subsidiary corporations, in a web of entangling alliances with each other, many of which were seemingly planned, created, and manipulated by lawyers expressly retained for the purpose of concealment or deception. . . . The accounts of the company are replete with instances in which profits have been declared to be earned by the transfer of stocks, bonds, debentures, and securities of one of the subordinate and subsidiary companies of the New Haven system to another such subsidiary, and such profits are solemnly recorded as real profits in making up the accounts of the system as a whole.[59]

Such "reckless and profligate financing," the commission concluded, represented "one of the most glaring instances of maladministration revealed in all the history of American railroading."[60]

One month later, as the New Haven revealed that for the first time in its history it was unable to pay a dividend, the U.S. attorney general initiated antitrust proceedings against the monopoly. Recognizing that it reached the end of the line, the New Haven negotiated a settlement with the Justice Department by which it agreed to divest itself of the Boston & Maine and Boston & Albany railroads, as well as street railways in Massachusetts. To further reduce the reach of its once favored monopoly, the Connecticut legislature required the New Haven to "sell, pledge or otherwise dispose of " its interests in the Boston & Providence and Old Colony railroad systems and rescinded the corporation's blanket authority to buy and sell the securities of other transportation corporations and to merge with such corporations at will.[61]

The railroad also disposed of its street railways in Rhode Island, while railway operations in Connecticut continued under a subsidiary called the Connecticut Company. Despite a federal law that forbade railroads to own steamboat services, however, the Interstate Commerce Commission allowed the New Haven to maintain steamboat operations on Long Island Sound, a concession that resulted from a strong outpouring of customer support for the well-used services. However, the New England Navigation Company, the marine corporation at the heart of many of the New Haven's misdeeds, was dissolved.[62]

Within a few short years, the New Haven returned to being a Connecticut railroad whose extent was approximately that of the Consolidated following its takeover of the New York & New England a generation before. Unfortunately, the $250 million in long-term debt the company had accumulated during the Morgan-Mellen era was not as easily gotten rid of. Payments on the debt burdened the truncated New Haven for decades before what had been New England's most powerful railroad corporation slipped into bankruptcy in 1935.[63]

EPILOGUE

The investigation of the New Haven empire by the Interstate Commerce Commission finally unveiled the corporate mess that Morgan and Mellen had created in their pursuit of a transportation monopoly in New England. In the words of the commission:

> The investigation has demonstrated that the monopoly theory of those controlling the New Haven was unsound and mischievous in its effects. To achieve such monopoly meant the reckless and scandalous expenditure of money; it meant the attempt to control public opinion, corruption of government, the attempt to pervert the political and economic instincts of the people in insolent defiance of law. Through exposure of the methods of this monopoly, the invisible government which has gone far in its efforts to dominate New England has been made visible.[64]

Much ink has been spent discussing the relative guilt of J. P. Morgan and Charles S. Mellen in the fall of the New Haven empire. In reality the two men were of one mind, each contributing one-half of what was needed to bring their vision of monopoly to life: Morgan the unquestioning finance; Mellen the unrelenting execution. But as Brandeis noted shortly after Mellen's resignation, the real problem was larger than either man:

> The issue is not Mellen, but the policy which Mellen has been carrying out at the instance of those who have employed him. We shall never have good transportation conditions in New England unless the policy of monopoly is abandoned, and unless we also reduce the size of our units so that they can be properly managed; and this proper management means not merely management of operation, but financial management, and the ability to raise money.[65]

In fact, the more he looked into the activities of J. P. Morgan, the more Brandeis was convinced that the underlying problem was even larger than the New Haven. "The decline of the New Haven is of more than local significance. It teaches a lesson of national importance. . . . The story of the New Haven should be an object lesson to those . . . who believe that the business thinking and financial guidance of the great enterprises of all the country can safely be committed to a few men."[66]

Brandeis believed the underlying problem was the freewheeling influence exerted in all major sectors of the economy by investment bankers such as Morgan, for whom the New Haven was but one piece of a larger financial empire known as the Money Trust. The actions of men like Morgan, with their blind belief in bigness and a penchant for shady arithmetic, created a concentration of wealth and power that threatened the economic freedom of the working man. Brandeis formulated this lesson from his experience with the New Haven, and he presented his views on the matter in a collection of essays published in 1914 under the title *Other People's Money and How Bankers Use It.* His conclusion was simple: "We must break the Money Trust or the Money Trust will break us."[67]

Despite a congressional investigation of the banking industry in 1912 and the subsequent creation of the Federal Reserve System, investment bankers continued to promote consolidation and speculation in all segments of the economy. The unregulated frenzy prompted Brandeis to write to his brother in 1926 saying how amazed he was that the bubble had not yet burst. "These consolidations and security floatations, plus the building boom, beat my comprehension—unless there is to be a breakdown within a year."[68] The collapse Brandeis long anticipated took another three years to arrive, and when it did, the nation and the world slid into the Great Depression of the 1930s.

In 1932, the U.S. Senate Committee on Banking and Currency conducted an in-depth investigation into the causes of the stock market crash of 1929. The investigation was headed by the committee's chief counsel, Ferdinand Pecora, the son of an Italian immigrant. Through pointed cross-examination of Wall Street bankers, including J. P. Morgan, Jr., Pecora uncovered the many illicit activities that had contributed to the crash of 1929, including the practice of underwriting unsound securities as a way to pay for bad bank loans. Regarding the impact of these activities, Pecora concluded:

> The prestige of these institutions was enormous. They stood in the minds of the unsophisticated public for safety, strength, prudence and high-mindedness, and they were supposed to be captained by men of unimpeachable integrity, possessing almost mythical genius and foresight. Yet from the very mouths of these trusted leaders, there came forth an amazing recital of practices to which the catastrophic collapse of the entire banking structure of the country seemed but the natural climax.[69]

Recognizing the connection between his probe and the work of Louis Brandeis, then a sitting justice on the U.S. Supreme Court, Pecora noted: "even in 1914, Mr. Justice Brandeis had noted the beginning of this process. But its proportions then were embryonic compared with the growth that came in ensuing years."[70] Pecora's investigation led to landmark congressional legislation, including the Banking Act of 1933, which for the first time separated the commercial and investment banking functions serving the economy; and the Securities and Exchange Act of 1934, which created the Securities and Exchange Commission to oversee trading in the nation's stock markets, actions that helped stabilize financial markets in the Unites States for decades.

By the turn of the twentieth century a new transportation technology and a new transportation policy were
poised to challenge the dominance of the New Haven's steam-powered monopoly and redirect Connecticut's transportation history.

During the course of the nineteenth century, Connecticut acquired an impressive array of transportation improvements. From the turnpike era, the
state inherited a highway network that included sixteen hundred miles of
intertown highways and numerous river-spanning bridges, all but a few
bridges having reverted to public ownership by the end of the century. Construction of the state's last rail line in 1902 (a short extension of the Central
New England Railway from Tariffville to Springfield, Massachusetts) completed a network of steam railroads that extended to one thousand track
miles, accompanied by an equally large system of electric street railways that
provided local service within and between Connecticut cities. In outlying
areas of the western and eastern highlands, where electricity and street
railways had yet to intrude, a small number of stagecoach lines were still
active, keeping even these more remote areas connected to the whole state
through regular stage service. And on the water, multiple steamboat operators provided daytime and overnight service to New York City from port
towns along the Connecticut River and Long Island Sound.

Compared to the crude network of unimproved dirt roads, man-powered
ferries, and limited packet boat service that had existed at the end of the
colonial period, transportation in Connecticut had come a long way indeed.
Yet this listing of modes and mileages, impressive though it is, does not give
the full picture. To this must be added an equally dramatic improvement in
speed and comfort. In general, transportation improvements reduced travel
times within the state by at least half, and long-distance travel between New
York and Boston even more. Whereas early post riders required two weeks
for the one-way trip from lower Manhattan to Boston Common, stage service

over an improved upper post road in the 1820s dropped the time to thirty-six hours. By the 1880s, a combined steamboat and railroad journey between New York and Boston took just twelve hours, and was made on a convenient overnight schedule in a luxurious hotel-style steamer. If time were of the essence, one could travel the direct route of Connecticut's Air Line railroad, in which case the trip took only six hours. A century of steam-powered innovation had turned the intimidating 250-mile journey from New York to Boston into a routine undertaking.

All of these improvements (including the attempt to extend steamboat and canal services to the upper Connecticut River) were made to serve a state economy that expanded in scope and volume several times during the century: from an essentially colonial economy at the start in which agricultural subsistence was mixed with limited market capitalism to a regional economy by midcentury in which mass production and market capitalism had become the norm, and to an integrated national economy by century's end in which managerial capitalism played a significant role in many large-scale industries, including transportation, as exemplified in New England by the exploits of the New York, New Haven & Hartford Railroad.

This hundred-year-long flurry of boom and bust market activity transformed Connecticut from a land of family farms into one of the most industrialized and urbanized states in the nation. As industrial output grew, the number of persons living in the state increased as well, from 250,000 in 1800 to one million by the end of the century. So concentrated was this largely industrial workforce that more than half of these one million persons lived in fourteen cities on less than 10 percent of the state's total land area. This created an average urban density of 1,650 persons per square mile, and concentrations of twice that amount in the state's three most populous cities: Hartford, New Haven, and Bridgeport. Meanwhile, the remaining residents of Connecticut lived in a rural landscape at an average density of less than one hundred persons per square mile.[1]

In response to technological change, Connecticut's population had redistributed itself on the landscape in an interesting and dynamic way. Beginning with the incursion of the first English settlers into the broad central valley and coastal slopes of colonial Connecticut, population first spread out across the western and eastern highlands, displacing native Ninnimissinuwock people as the hunt for farmable land continued. With Connecticut resettled to new manmade borders and reorganized as an outpost of European culture, excess population then moved inward to the water-powered factory villages that sprang up in the early decades of the nineteenth century, and inward again, in even higher concentrations, during the era of the steamboat and the railroad, as steam power transformed lowland towns into industrial centers and transportation hubs, with raw materials and manufactured goods flowing in and out of an independent state highly dependent on a thriving national economy.[2]

By 1900 high population densities made it difficult for city governments to provide adequate public services for their populace, and the state's cities became increasingly overcrowded, noisy, and unsanitary. Those who could lived outside the urban center, along railroad and railway lines that put them within a reasonable commute to jobs in the city. Yet while there was plenty of land available for home building in these areas, transportation access was restricted to fixed, straight-line rail corridors and was typically clustered in areas around railroad stations and railway stops.

At the same time, while steam power and electricity evolved to dominate rail transportation over land, highway travelers had yet to partake in the technological revolution. As toll roads reverted to public use in the second half of the century, little beyond normal maintenance was done to modernize these important intertown routes. In effect, highway travel in Connecticut at the turn of the twentieth century was still mired in the era of the horse and buggy and the rutted dirt road. Conditions were ripe for a transportation technology that could relieve congestion by making lands adjacent to the state's cities easily accessible as a living area for urban workers.

In retrospect, the two decades from 1895 to 1915 were a period of transition for highway travel. As Morgan and Mellen worked to expand their control of the mass transportation of people and goods, history was at work on behalf of individualized travel. In 1895, Frank and Charles Duryea drove America's first commercial automobile on the streets of Springfield, Massachusetts. The engine they used derived its power from the combustion of gasoline vapor within the engine's cylinders. The result was a lightweight source of power able to propel their carriage-like vehicle to speeds of twenty miles per hour or more. By 1915, experimentation and the leadership of Henry Ford had turned the automobile from a luxury item for the wealthy into a mass-produced commodity whose cost was within the reach of many working-class families.[3]

Unlike a fixed rail line, the new horseless carriage (and wagon) provided a flexible means of transporting people and goods directly from their point of origin to their final destination. What was needed to realize the full

Hop River Turnpike, Andover, c. 1900.
(Courtesy of the Thomas J. Dodd Research Center, University of Connecticut Libraries)

potential of the horseless carriage was a network of highways that were smoother and more impervious to rain and snow than the state's existing dirt turnpikes and could be used year round. In 1895, the Connecticut legislature created a highway commission to investigate the growing need for good roads, and before long the state entered into a joint effort with town and city governments to resurface public highways around the state. It was the first time in the state's history that its central government assumed direct and ongoing responsibility for the funding of transportation improvements.[4] In 1913, as Hartford residents mourned the passing of J. P. Morgan and the New York, New Haven & Hartford empire teetered on the brink of collapse, the Connecticut legislature adopted the state's first system of trunk line highways, fourteen cross-state routes totaling one thousand miles in length, whose improvement would be paid for in large part with state funds administered by a permanent state agency, the Connecticut Highway Department.

For the first time since the appearance of the factory village and the continued congregation of people and industry in urban centers, Connecticut's population was poised to again move outward over the landscape, with gasoline-powered carriages and trucks available to transport factory-made goods and agricultural products throughout Connecticut and New England, cargo that had previously been shipped on a railroad or steamboat controlled by the New York, New Haven & Hartford Railroad. Connecticut was about to enter a new transportation era, one dominated by the internal combustion engine and the public financing of highways, a new technology and a new policy that together would significantly alter the direction of Connecticut's history yet again.

Appendix A **Population by Geomorphic Region, 1800–1920**

The grouping of Connecticut towns into the six geomorphic regions used in this book is based on the regional plan promoted by the Connecticut Historical Commission in *Historic Preservation: A Cultural Resource Management Plan for Connecticut* (1990). These regions have been delineated to reflect the geological and ecological divisions of the state's natural history. The six regions correspond more closely to the human activities that underlie the history of Connecticut than administrative divisions such as counties and planning regions imposed on the landscape from above. Moreover, the use and awareness of these six geomorphic regions reminds us of the importance of the land and its natural history in the telling of the human story.

All the population figures in the following tables are taken from u.s. census data. The land areas of individual towns are listed in the 2003 edition of the *Connecticut State Register and Manual*. All population statistics cited in the text are based on these data.

Connecticut Towns' Populations by Geomorphic Region, 1800–1920

Region 1: Central Lowland

	Land Area	1800	1820	1840	1860	1880	1900	1920
Avon	23.1	0	0	1001	1059	1057	1302	1534
Berlin	26.5	2702	2877	3411	2146	2385	3448	4298
Bloomfield	26.0	0	0	986	1401	1346	1513	2394
Cheshire	32.9	2288	2281	1529	2407	2284	1989	2855
Cromwell	12.4	0	0	0	1617	1640	2031	2454
Durham	23.6	1029	1210	1095	1130	990	884	959
East Granby	17.5	0	0	0	833	754	684	1056
East Hartford	18.0	3057	3373	2389	2951	3500	6406	11648
East Haven	12.3	1004	1237	1382	2292	3057	1167	3520
East Windsor	26.3	2766	3400	3600	2580	3019	3158	3741
Ellington	34.1	1209	1196	1356	1510	1569	1829	2127
Enfield	33.4	1761	2065	2648	4997	6755	6699	11719
Farmington	28.1	2809	3042	2041	3144	3017	3331	3844
Glastonbury	51.4	2718	3114	3077	3363	3580	4260	5592
Granby	40.7	2735	3012	2611	1720	1340	1299	1342
Hamden	32.8	1482	1687	1797	2725	3408	4662	8611
Hartford (1784)	*17.3*	*5347*	*6901*	*12793*	*29152*	*42551*	*79850*	*138036*
Manchester	27.3	0	0	1695	3294	6462	10601	18370
Meriden (1867)	*23.8*	*0*	*1309*	*1880*	*7426*	*18340*	*28659*	*34764*
Middlefield	12.7	0	0	0	0	928	845	1047
Middletown (1784)	*40.9*	*5001*	*6479*	*7210*	*8620*	*11732*	*17486*	*22129*
New Britain (1870)	*13.3*	*0*	*0*	*0*	*5212*	*13979*	*28202*	*59316*
New Haven (1784)	*18.9*	*5157*	*8327*	*14390*	*39267*	*62882*	*108027*	*162537*
Newington	13.2	0	0	0	0	934	1041	2381
North Branford	24.9	0	0	1016	1050	1025	814	1110
North Haven	20.8	1157	1298	1349	1499	1763	2164	1968
Plainville	9.7	0	0	0	0	1930	2189	4114
Portland	23.4	0	0	0	3657	4157	3856	3644
Rocky Hill	13.5	0	0	0	1102	1108	1026	1633
Simsbury	33.9	2956	1954	1895	2410	1830	2094	2958
Somers	28.3	1353	1306	1621	1517	1242	1593	1673
Southington	36.0	1804	1875	1887	3315	5411	5890	8440
South Windsor	28.0	0	0	0	1789	1902	2014	2142
Suffield	42.2	2686	2681	2669	3260	3225	3521	4070
Vernon	17.7	0	966	1430	3838	6915	8483	8898
Wallingford	39.0	3214	2237	2204	3206	4686	9001	12010
West Hartford	22.0	0	0	0	1296	1828	3186	8854
West Haven (1961)	*10.8*	*0*	*0*	*0*	*0*	*0*	*0*	*0*
Wethersfield	12.4	3992	3825	3824	2705	2173	2637	4342
Windsor	29.6	2773	3008	2283	3865	3058	3614	5620

Connecticut Towns' Populations by Geomorphic Region, 1800–1920 (*Continued*)

Region 1: Central Lowland (*Continued*)

	Land Area	1800	1820	1840	1860	1880	1900	1920
Windsor Locks	9.0	0	0	0	0	2332	3062	3554
Region 1: Total	1007.7	61000	70660	87069	163355	242094	374517	581304

Region 2: Western Coast

	Land Area	1800	1820	1840	1860	1880	1900	1920
Bridgeport (1836)	*16.0*	*0*	*0*	*4570*	*13299*	*29148*	*70996*	*143555*
Darien	12.9	0	1126	1080	1705	1949	3116	4184
Fairfield	30.0	3735	4151	3654	4379	3748	4489	11475
Greenwich	47.8	3047	3790	3921	6522	7892	12172	22123
Milford (1959)	*22.6*	*2417*	*2785*	*2455*	*2828*	*3347*	*3783*	*10193*
New Canaan	22.1	0	1689	2217	2771	2673	2968	3895
Norwalk (1893)	*22.8*	*5146*	*3004*	*3863*	*7582*	*13956*	*19932*	*27743*
Orange	17.2	0	0	1329	1974	3341	6995	16614
Stamford (1893)	*37.8*	*4352*	*3284*	*3516*	*7185*	*11297*	*18839*	*40067*
Stratford	17.6	2650	3438	1808	2294	4251	3657	12347
Westport	20.0	0	0	1803	3293	3477	4017	5114
Region 2: Total	266.8	21347	23267	30216	53832	85079	150964	297310

Region 3: Eastern Coast

	Land Area	1800	1820	1840	1860	1880	1900	1920
Branford	22.0	2156	2230	1322	2123	3047	5706	6627
Chester	16.0	0	0	974	1015	1177	1328	1675
Clinton	16.3	0	0	1239	1427	1402	1429	1217
Deep River/Saybrook	13.6	3363	4165	3417	1213	1362	1634	2325
East Lyme	34.0	0	0	1412	1506	1731	1836	2291
Essex	10.4	0	0	0	1764	1855	2530	2815
Groton (1964)	*31.3*	*4302*	*4664*	*2963*	*4450*	*5128*	*5962*	*9227*
Guilford	47.1	3597	4131	2421	2624	2782	2785	2803
Killingworth	35.3	2047	2342	1130	1126	748	651	531
Ledyard	38.1	0	0	1871	1615	1373	1236	1161
Lyme	31.9	4380	4069	2856	1246	1025	750	674
Madison	36.2	0	0	1788	1865	1672	1518	1857
New London (1784)	*5.5*	*5150*	*3330*	*5519*	*10115*	*10537*	*17548*	*25688*
Old Lyme	23.1	0	0	0	1304	1387	1180	946
Old Saybrook	15.0	0	0	0	1105	1302	1431	1463
Stonington	38.7	5437	3056	3898	5827	7355	8540	10236
Waterford	32.8	0	2239	2329	2555	2701	2904	3935
Westbrook	15.7	0	0	1182	1056	878	884	849
Region 3: Total	463.0	30432	30226	34321	43936	47462	59852	76320

(*continued*)

Connecticut Towns' Populations by Geomorphic Region, 1800–1920 (*Continued*)

Region 4: Southwest Hills

	Land Area	1800	1820	1840	1860	1880	1900	1920
Ansonia (1893)	6.0	*0*	*0*	*0*	*0*	*0*	*12681*	*17643*
Beacon Falls	9.8	0	0	0	0	379	623	1593
Bethany	21.0	0	0	1170	974	637	517	411
Bethel	16.8	0	0	0	1711	2727	3327	3201
Bethlehem	19.4	1138	932	776	815	655	576	536
Bridgewater	16.2	0	0	0	1048	708	649	481
Bristol (1911)	26.5	*2723*	*1362*	*2109*	*3436*	*5347*	*9643*	*20620*
Brookfield	19.8	1010	1159	1255	1224	1152	1046	896
Derby (1893)	5.0	*1878*	*2088*	*2851*	*5443*	*11650*	*7930*	*11238*
Easton	27.4	0	0	0	1350	1145	960	1017
Middlebury	17.8	0	838	761	664	687	736	1067
Monroe	26.1	0	0	1351	1382	1157	1043	1161
Morris	17.2	0	0	0	769	627	535	499
Naugatuck	16.4	0	0	0	2590	4274	10541	15051
Newtown	57.8	2903	2879	3189	3578	4013	3276	2751
Oxford	32.9	1410	1683	1626	1269	1120	952	998
Plymouth	21.7	1791	1758	2205	3244	2350	2828	5942
Prospect	14.3	0	0	548	574	492	562	266
Redding	31.5	1632	1678	1674	1652	1540	1426	1315
Roxbury	26.2	1121	1124	971	992	950	1087	647
Seymour	14.6	0	0	0	1749	2318	3541	6781
Shelton (1915)	30.6	*2792*	*2805*	*1326*	*1477*	*2499*	*5572*	*9475*
Southbury	39.1	1757	1662	1542	1346	1740	1238	1093
Thomaston	12.0	0	0	0	0	3225	3300	3993
Trumbull	23.3	1291	1232	1204	1474	1323	1587	2597
Washington	38.2	1568	1487	1622	1659	1590	1820	1619
Waterbury (1853)	28.6	*3256*	*2882*	*3668*	*10004*	*20270*	*51139*	*91715*
Watertown	29.2	1622	1439	1442	1587	1897	3100	6050
Weston	19.8	2680	2767	2561	1117	918	840	703
Wilton	27.0	0	1818	2053	2208	1864	1598	1284
Wolcott	20.4	948	943	633	574	493	581	719
Woodbridge	18.8	2198	1998	958	872	829	852	1170
Woodbury	36.5	1944	1885	1948	2037	2149	1988	1698
Region 4: Total	767.9	35662	36419	39443	58819	82725	138094	216230

Connecticut Towns' Populations by Geomorphic Region, 1800–1920 (*Continued*)

Region 5: Eastern Hills

	Land Area	1800	1820	1840	1860	1880	1900	1920
Andover	15.5	0	0	0	517	428	385	389
Ashford	38.8	2445	2778	2651	1231	1041	757	673
Bolton	14.4	1452	731	739	683	512	457	448
Bozrah	20.0	934	1083	1067	1216	1155	799	858
Brooklyn	29.0	1202	1264	1488	2136	2308	2358	1655
Canterbury	39.9	1812	1984	1791	1591	1272	876	896
Chaplin	19.4	0	0	794	781	627	529	385
Colchester	49.1	3163	2152	2101	2862	2974	1991	2050
Columbia	21.4	0	941	842	832	757	655	706
Coventry	37.7	2021	2058	2018	2085	2043	1632	1582
Eastford	28.9	0	0	0	1005	855	523	496
East Haddam	54.3	2805	2572	2620	3056	3032	2485	2312
East Hampton	35.6	3295	3159	3413	1766	1967	2271	2394
Franklin	19.5	1210	1161	1000	2358	686	546	552
Griswold	35.0	0	1869	2165	2217	2745	3490	4220
Haddam	44.0	2307	2478	2599	2307	2419	2015	1736
Hampton	25.0	1379	1313	1166	936	827	629	475
Hebron	36.9	2256	2094	1726	1425	1243	1016	915
Killingly	48.5	2279	2803	3685	4926	6921	6835	8178
Lebanon	54.1	3652	2719	2194	2174	1845	1521	1343
Lisbon	16.3	1158	1159	1052	1262	630	697	867
Mansfield	44.5	2560	2993	2276	1697	2154	1827	2574
Marlborough	23.3	0	839	713	682	391	322	303
Montville	42.0	2233	1951	1990	2141	2664	2395	3411
North Stonington	54.3	0	2624	2269	1913	1769	1240	1144
Norwich (1784)	*28.3*	*3476*	*3634*	*7239*	*14048*	*21143*	*24637*	*29685*
Plainfield	42.3	1619	2097	2383	3665	4021	4821	7926
Pomfret	40.3	1799	2042	1868	1673	1470	1831	1454
Preston	30.9	3440	1899	1727	2092	2523	2807	2743
Putnam	20.3	0	0	0	2722	5827	7348	8397
Salem	29.0	0	1053	811	830	574	468	424
Scotland	18.6	0	0	0	720	590	471	391
Sprague	13.2	0	0	0	0	3207	1339	2500
Stafford	58.0	2345	2369	2469	3397	4455	4297	5407
Sterling	27.2	908	1200	1099	1051	957	1209	1266
Thompson	46.9	2341	2928	3535	3259	5051	6442	5055
Tolland	39.7	1638	1607	1566	1310	1169	1036	1040
Union	28.7	767	757	669	732	539	428	257
Voluntown	38.9	1119	1116	1185	1055	1186	872	656

(*continued*)

Connecticut Towns' Populations by Geomorphic Region, 1800–1920 (*Continued*)

Region 5: Eastern Hills (*Continued*)

	Land Area	1800	1820	1840	1860	1880	1900	1920
Willington	33.3	1278	1246	1268	1166	1086	885	1200
Windham	27.1	2644	2489	3382	4711	8264	10137	13801
Woodstock	60.5	2463	3017	3053	3285	2639	2095	1767
Region 5: Total	1430.6	64000	70179	74613	89515	107966	109374	124531

Region 6: Northwest Highlands

	Land Area	1800	1820	1840	1860	1880	1900	1920
Barkhamsted	36.2	1437	1592	1571	1272	1297	864	719
Burlington	29.8	0	1360	1201	1031	1224	1218	1109
Canaan	33.0	2137	2332	2166	2834	1157	820	561
Canton	24.6	0	1322	1736	2373	2301	2678	2549
Colebrook	31.5	1119	1274	1232	1375	1148	684	492
Cornwall	46.0	1614	1662	1703	1953	1583	1175	834
Danbury (1889)	*42.1*	*3180*	*3873*	*4504*	*7234*	*11666*	*19474*	*22325*
Goshen	43.7	1493	1586	1529	1381	1093	835	675
Hartland	33.0	1318	1254	1060	846	643	592	448
Harwinton	30.8	1481	1500	1201	1044	1016	1213	2020
Kent	48.5	1607	1956	1759	1855	1622	1220	1086
Litchfield	56.1	4285	4610	4038	3200	3410	3214	3180
New Fairfield	20.5	1665	788	956	915	791	584	468
New Hartford	37.0	1753	1685	1703	2758	3302	3424	1781
New Milford	61.6	3221	3830	3974	3535	3907	4804	4781
Norfolk	45.3	1649	1422	1393	1803	1418	1614	1229
North Canaan	19.5	0	0	0	0	1537	1803	1933
Ridgefield	34.4	2025	2301	2474	2213	2028	2626	2707
Salisbury	57.3	2266	2695	2562	3100	3715	3489	2497
Sharon	58.7	2340	2573	2407	2556	2580	1982	1585
Sherman	21.8	0	957	938	911	828	658	533
Torrington (1923)	*39.8*	*1417*	*1449*	*1707*	*2278*	*3327*	*12453*	*22055*
Warren	26.3	1083	875	872	710	639	432	350
Winsted/Winchester (1917)	*32.3*	*1371*	*1601*	*1667*	*3513*	*5142*	*7763*	*9019*
Region 6: Total	909.8	38461	44497	44353	50690	57374	75619	84936
State Total	4845.8	250902	275248	310015	460147	622700	908420	1380631

Cities in italics, with the year formed.

Connecticut Cities' Populations by Geomorphic Region, 1800–1920

Region 1: Central Lowland

	Year	Area	1800	1820	1840	1860	1880	1900	1920
Hartford	1784	17.3	5347	6901	12793	29152	42551	79850	138036
Middletown	1784	40.9	5001	6479	7210	8620	11732	17486	22129
New Haven	1784	18.9	5157	8327	14390	39267	62882	108027	162537
Meriden	1867	23.8					18340	28659	34764
New Britain	1870	13.3					13979	28202	59316
West Haven	1961	10.8							
Region 1: Total City		125.0	15505	21707	34393	77039	149484	262224	416782
Region 1: Total Region			61000	70660	87069	163355	242094	374517	581304
Region 1: Percentage in Cities		12%	25%	31%	40%	47%	62%	70%	72%

Region 2: Western Coast

	Year	Area	1800	1820	1840	1860	1880	1900	1920
Bridgeport	1836	16			4570	13299	29148	70996	143555
Norwalk	1893	22.8						19932	27743
Stamford	1893	37.8						18839	40067
Milford	1959	22.6							
Region 2: Total City		99.2	0	0	4570	13299	29148	109767	211365
Region 2: Total Region			21347	23267	30216	53832	85079	150964	297310
Region 2: Percentage in Cities		37%	0	0	15%	25%	34%	73%	71%

Region 3: Eastern Coast

	Year	Area	1800	1820	1840	1860	1880	1900	1920
New London	1784	5.5	5150	3330	5519	10115	10537	17548	25688
Groton	1964	31.3							
Region 3: Total City		36.8	5150	3330	5519	10115	10537	17548	25688
Region 3: Total Region			30432	30226	34321	43936	47462	59852	76320
Region 3: Percentage in Cities		8%	17%	11%	16%	23%	22%	29%	34%

Region 4: Southwest Hills

	Year	Area	1800	1820	1840	1860	1880	1900	1920
Waterbury	1853	28.6				10004	20270	51139	91715
Ansonia	1893	6						12681	17643
Derby	1893	5						7930	11238
Bristol	1911	26.5							20620
Shelton	1915	30.6							9475
Region 4: Total City		96.7	0	0	0	10004	20270	71750	150691
Region 4: Total Region			35662	36419	39443	58819	82725	138094	216230
Region 4: Percentage in Cities		13%	0%	0%	0%	17%	25%	52%	70%

(continued)

Region 5: Eastern Hills

	Year	Area	1800	1820	1840	1860	1880	1900	1920
Norwich	1784	28.3	3476	3634	7239	14048	21143	24637	29685
Region 5: Total City		28.3	3476	3634	7239	14048	21143	24637	29685
Region 5: Total Region			64000	70179	74613	89515	107966	109374	124531
Region 5: Percentage in Cities		2%	5%	5%	10%	16%	20%	23%	24%

Region 6: Northwest Highlands

	Year	Area	1800	1820	1840	1860	1880	1900	1920
Danbury	1889	42.1						19474	22325
Winsted/Winchester	1917	32.3							9019
Torrington	1923	39.8							
Region 6: Total City		114.2	0	0	0	0	0	19474	31344
Region 6: Total Region			38461	44497	44353	50690	57374	75619	84936
Region 6: Percentage in Cities		13%	0%	0%	0%	0%	0%	26%	37%

		Area	1800	1820	1840	1860	1880	1900	1920
Total Cities		500.2	24131	28671	51721	124505	230582	505400	865555
Total State		4845.8	250902	275248	310015	460147	622700	908420	1380631
Cities as Percentage of State		10.3%	10%	10%	17%	27%	37%	56%	63%

Connecticut Population Summary by Geomorphic Region, 1800–1920

	1800	1820	1840	1860	1880	1900	1920
Region 1: Central Lowland							
Population	61000	70660	87069	163355	242094	374517	581304
Percentage of State	24.3%	25.7%	28.1%	35.5%	38.9%	41.2%	42.1%
Persons per square mile of land area	61	70	86	162	240	372	577
Region 2: Western Coast							
Population	21347	23267	30216	53832	85079	150964	297310
Percentage of State	8.5%	8.5%	9.7%	11.7%	13.7%	16.6%	21.5%
Persons per square mile of land area	80	87	113	202	319	566	1114
Region 3: Eastern Coast							
Population	30432	30226	34321	43936	47462	59852	76320
Percentage of State	12.1%	11.0%	11.1%	9.5%	7.6%	6.6%	5.5%
Persons per square mile of land area	66	65	74	95	103	129	165
Region 4: Southwest Hills							
Population	35662	36419	39443	58819	82725	138094	216230
Percentage of State	14.2%	13.2%	12.7%	12.8%	13.3%	15.2%	15.7%
Persons per square mile of land area	46	47	51	77	108	180	282
Region 5: Eastern Hills							
Population	64000	70179	74613	89515	107966	109374	124531
Percentage of State	25.5%	25.5%	24.1%	19.5%	17.3%	12.0%	9.0%
Persons per square mile of land area	45	49	52	63	75	76	87
Region 6: Northwest Highlands							
Population	38461	44497	44353	50690	57374	75619	84936
Percentage of State	15.3%	16.2%	14.3%	11.0%	9.2%	8.3%	6.2%
Persons per square mile of land area	42	49	49	56	63	83	93
State Total	250902	275248	310015	460147	622700	908420	1380631
Persons per square mile of land area	52	57	64	95	129	187	285

Appendix B Corporation Charters

This appendix contains the names of the privately owned joint-stock corporations that were chartered by the state of Connecticut to provide transportation services from the 1790s to the 1920s. During this time Connecticut chartered nearly five hundred transportation corporations. Included in the following lists are turnpike, toll bridge, plank road, railroad, horse railroad, street railway, ferry, canal, steamboat, and harbor and river improvement companies. The tables were compiled using the "Incorporations" section of *A General Index to the Private Laws and Special Acts of the State of Connecticut,* published by the Connecticut General Assembly (Special Act 541) in 1943.

Transportation charters fall into three categories: highway, rail, and maritime. Within each category, companies are listed chronologically by the year of their original charter, with a reference to the volume and page of the *Private Laws of the State of Connecticut* where the charter can be found. To make each list as complete as possible, corporations named in the *General Index* were checked against similar lists published by others—in particular, turnpike corporations with Frederic J. Wood's *Turnpikes of New England*; railroad corporations with Ronald D. Karr's *Rail Lines of Southern New England*; and horse railroad and street railway corporations with the Connecticut Valley Chapter of the National Railway Historical Society's *Street Railways of Connecticut.*

A word of caution: company names changed often as a result of a reorganization or combination (rail corporations in particular) and at times these name changes resulted in a new charter, whereas at other times they did not. In addition, rail corporations formed under the general rail incorporation law of 1872 required no legislative charter, though some of these companies later secured one. None of these qualifications affect a large number of corporations, so the corporations listed in this appendix represent perhaps 90 percent or more of the transportation charters issued in Connecticut. Still, no one list should be considered definitive.

Highway Charters: Turnpikes, Toll Bridges, and Plank Roads

Connecticut Turnpike Charters, 1795–1839

Turnpike Company	Chartered	Private Laws
New London & Windham County Society	1795	I, 1380
Oxford	1795	I, 1415
Hartford, New London, Windham & Tolland County Society	1795	I, 1309
Norwalk & Danbury	1795	I, 1400
Fairfield, Weston & Reading	1797	I, 1266
Saugatuck (Saquituck)*	1797	I, 1437
Stratfield & Weston*	1797	I, 1460
Striat's	1797	I, 1456
New Milford & Litchfield	1797	I, 1383
Boston	1797	I, 1202
Talcott Mountain	1798	I, 1465
Ousatonic	1798	I, 1411
Derby	1798	I, 1251
Green Woods	1798	I, 1282
Hartford & New Haven	1798	I, 1297
Litchfield & Harwinton	1798	I, 1337
Windham	1799	I, 1492
Canaan & Litchfield	1799	I, 1217
Farmington River	1800	I, 1273
Windham & Manfield Society	1800	I, 1499
Cheshire	1800	I, 1223
Granby	1800	I, 1277
Hartford & New London	1800	I, 1303
Farmington & Bristol	1801	I, 1271
Danbury & Ridgefield	1801	I, 1249
Torrington	1801	I, 1476
Norwich & Woodstock	1801	I, 1406
Salisbury (& Canaan)	1801	I, 1435
Bridgeport & Newtown	1801	I, 1212
Waterbury River	1801	I, 1482
Hartford & Tolland	1801	I, 1312
Pomfret & Killingly	1802	I, 1426
Hebron & Middle Haddam	1802	I, 1319
Middlesex	1802	I, 1350
New Preston	1802	I, 1393
New Haven & Milford	1802	I, 1374
Rimmon's Falls	1802	I, 1428
Greenwich & Ridgefield*	1802	I, 1280
Goshen & Sharon	1803	I, 1286

(continued)

Connecticut Turnpike Charters, 1795–1839 (*Continued*)

Turnpike Company	Chartered	Private Laws
Stafford Pool (Stafford Mineral Springs)	1803	I, 1449
Washington	1803	I, 1481
Thompson	1803	I, 1471
Middle Road	1803	I, 1346
Colchester & Norwich	1803	I, 1237
Cornwall & Washington	1805	I, 1249
Connecticut	1806	I, 1242
Connecticut & Rhode Island	1806	I, 1247
Hartland	1806	I, 1318
Warren	1806	I, 1479
New London & Lyme	1807	I, 1378
Woodstock & Thompson	1808	I, 1510
Middletown & Berlin	1808	I, 1354
Woodstock & Somers	1808	I, 1510
Colchester & Chatham	1808	I, 1232
Columbia	1808	I, 1241
Tolland County	1809	I, 1473
Sharon & Cornwall	1809	I, 1439
Chatham & Marlborough	1809	I, 1221
Middletown & Meriden	1809	I, 1360
East Haddam & Colchester	1809	I, 1256
Durham & East Guilford	1811	I, 1254
Southington & Waterbury	1812	I, 1447
Farmington & Harwinton*	1812	I, 1271
Killingworth & Haddam	1813	I, 1332
Middletown, Durham & New Haven	1813	I, 1357
Litchfield & Cornwall	1814	I, 1335
Haddam & Durham	1815	I, 1294
Still River	1815	I, 1454
Chester & North Killingworth	1816	I, 1227
Dragon*	1817	I, 1252
New Milford & Sherman	1818	I, 1388
Granby & Barkhamsted*	1818	I, 1279
Wolcott & Hamden*	1818	I, 1504
Petipauge & Guilford	1818	I, 1417
Groton & Stonington	1818	I, 1289
Pleasant Valley*	1820	I, 1425
Essex	1822	I, 1259
Woodbridge & Waterbury*	1823	I, 1508
New Milford & Woodbury*	1823	I, 1391
East Middle Road	1823	I, 1258
West Middle Road	1823	I, 1258

Connecticut Turnpike Charters, 1795–1839 (*Continued*)

Turnpike Company	Chartered	Private Laws
Salem & Hamburg	1824	I, 1432
Pine's Bridge	1824	I, 1422
Guilford & Durham	1824	I, 1291
Fair Haven	1824	I, 1269
Providence	1825	I, 1426
Sandy Brook	1825	I, 1435
Humphreysville & Salem	1825	I, 1323
Center	1826	I, 1219
Northfield	1826	I, 1397
Windham & Brooklyn	1826	I, 1496
Monroe & Zoar Bridge	1826	I, 1369
Zoar Bridge*	1826	I, 1510
Wolcottville*	1826	I, 1506
Norwich & Salem	1827	I, 1404
New Milford & Roxbury	1827	I, 1386
Tolland & Mansfield	1828	I, 1474
Huntington	1828	I, 1326
Weston	1828	I, 1489
Sugar Hollow	1829	I, 1461
Newtown & Norwalk	1829	I, 1394
Shetucket	1829	I, 1441
Wells' Hollow	1830	I, 1486
Moosup*	1830	I, 1372
Branch	1831	I, 1208
Black Rock & Weston	1832	I, 1200
Simpaug*	1832	I, 1445
Monroe & Newtown	1833	I, 1367
Fairfield County	1834	I, 1262
Hadlyme	1834	I, 1295
Chester & North Killingworth Second	1834	I, 1229
Sherman & Redding	1834	I, 1439
Kent & Warren*	1834	I, 1330
River	1834	I, 1431
Hartford & Worcester Railroad*	1834	I, 1316
Madison & North Killingworth	1835	I, 1344
Hop River	1835	I, 1321
Litchfield & Plymouth*	1836	I, 1342
Millington*	1839	IV, 1322

* According to Frederic J. Wood, *Turnpikes of New England: A New Edition of the 1919 Classic* (Pepperell, Mass.: Branch Line Press, 1997), the turnpikes associated with these charters were never built.

Connecticut Toll Bridge Charters, 1796–1895

Toll Bridge Company	Chartered	Private Laws
Company to . . . New Haven–East Haven Toll Bridge	1796	I, 241
Niantic Toll Bridge	1797	I, 279
Company to . . . Enfield to Suffield Toll Bridge	1798	I, 249
Enfield to Suffield Toll Bridge	1798	I, 249
Milford & Stratford Bridge	1802	I, 288
Bennett's Toll Bridge	1803	I, 234
Hawley's Toll Bridge	1803	I, 261
Warner's Toll Bridge	1803	I, 287
Leavenworth's Bridge	1804	I, 244
Bull's Falls Toll Bridge	1807	I, 239
Mitchell's Bridge	1807	I, 271
Zoar Bridge	1807	I, 292
Hartford Bridge	1808	I, 254
Bridgeport Bridge	1810	I, 237
Norwich & Preston Bridge	1816	I, 280
Kent Toll Bridge	1816	I, 263
Mystic Bridge	1819	I, 274
Union Bridge	1828	I, 285
Gaylord's Bridge Toll Bridge	1832	I, 252
Derby Bridge & Ferry	1833	I, 244
Mill Cove Bridge	1835	I, 272
New Milford Toll Bridge	1835	I, 276
East Bridgeport Bridge	1836	I, 247
Company to Rebuild Zoar Bridge	1840	III, 284
Bridgewater & Brookfield Toll Bridge	1849	III, 268
Crescent Foot Bridge Company of Bridgeport	1850	III, 273
Center Bridge Company of Bridgeport	1852	III, 271
Laurel Hill Bridge	1853	III, 281
Saugatuck Bridge Company of Westport	1866	VI, 14
Mitchell's Bridge	1875	VII, 983
Warehouse Point & Windsor Locks Bridge	1883	IX, 813
Suffield & Thompsonville Bridge	1889	X, 1206
Middletown & Portland Bridge	1893	XI, 903

Connecticut Plank Road Charters, 1851–1853

Plank Road Company	Chartered	Private Laws
Danbury, Redding, Weston & Westport*	1851	IV, 851
Stamford, New Canaan & Ridgefield*	1851	IV, 861
New Haven & Seymour*	1852	IV, 855
Waterbury & Cheshire	1852	IV, 867
Woodbury & Seymour*	1852	IV, 869
Salisbury*	1853	IV, 858
Wallingford, North Haven & New Haven*	1853	IV, 864

* According to Frederic J. Wood, *Turnpikes of New England: A New Edition of the 1919 Classic* (Pepperell, Mass.: Branch Line Press, 1997), the plank roads associated with these charters were never built.

Rail Charters: Railroads, Horse Railroads, and Street Railways

Connecticut Railroad Charters, 1832–1911

Railroad Company	Chartered	Private Laws
Boston, Norwich & New London	1832	I, 992
New York & Stonington (New York, Providence & Boston)	1832	I, 1019
Sharon & Salisbury	1832	I, 1030
Hartford & New Haven (New Haven, Hartford & Springfield)	1833	I, 1002
Manchester	1833	I, 1014
Fairfield County (Danbury & Norwalk)	1835	I, 998
Hartford & Springfield	1835	I, 1006
Worcester & Hartford	1835	I, 1010
Housatonic	1836	I, 1025
Norwich & Worcester	1836	I, 996
Norwich & Lyme	1841	IV, 1034
Middletown	1844	IV, 934
New York & New Haven	1844	IV, 1020
Branch	1845	IV, 874
Naugatuck	1845	IV, 944
New Britain & Plymouth	1845	IV, 957
New York & Hartford	1845	IV, 1012
Farmington Canal (New Haven & Northampton)	1846	IV, 888
New York & Boston	1846	IV, 999
New London, Willimantic & Springfield (Palmer)	1847	IV, 990
Hartford & Providence (Hartford, Providence & Fishkill)	1848	IV, 904
New Haven & New London	1848	IV, 967
New Haven, Danbury & Erie	1848	IV, 961

(continued)

Connecticut Railroad Charters, 1832–1911 *(Continued)*

Railroad Company	Chartered	Private Laws
Danbury & New York	1849	IV, 879
Willimantic & Thompson	1849	IV, 1067
Stamford & Danbury	1850	IV, 1063
Windsor & Tariffville	1850	IV, 1071
Killingly	1851	IV, 929
Norwich & Westbrook	1851	IV, 1038
Farmington Valley (Hampshire & Hamden)	1852	IV, 893
Meriden	1852	IV, 931
Middlesex & Hartford County	1852	IV, 939
New Britain & Middletown	1852	IV, 954
New London & Stonington	1852	IV, 975
Salem & Lisbon	1852	IV, 1055
East Thompson	1853	IV, 884
Granby	1854	IV, 896
Westbrook & Deep River	1855	IV, 1065
Union Branch	1856	IV, 1073
Middletown Extension	1857	V, 36
Rockville Branch (Rockville)	1857	V, 139
Thompson & Willimantic	1857	V, 76
New London Northern	1859	V, 261
Litchfield County Branch	1860	V, 382
Boston, Hartford & Erie	1863	V, 543
New Haven & Derby	1864	V, 653
Shore Line Railway	1864	V, 590
Shetucket	1865	V, 725
Connecticut Western	1866	VI, 94
New Canaan	1866	VI, 22
Rockville & Springfield	1866	VI, 32
Salisbury	1866	VI, 48
Shepaug Valley	1866	VI, 96
South Manchester	1866	VI, 24
Suffield & Windsor Locks (Windsor Locks & Suffield)	1866	VI, 29
New Haven, Middletown & Willimantic	1867	VI, 286
Ridgefield & New York	1867	VI, 177
Connecticut Valley	1868	VI, 398
Middletown Wharf	1868	VI, 463
New England & Erie	1868	VI, 391
Pachaug River	1868	VI, 457
Saugatuck Valley	1868	VI, 465
Derby & Woodbury	1869	VI, 637
Meriden & Cheshire	1869	VI, 583

Connecticut Railroad Charters, 1832–1911 (*Continued*)

Railroad Company	Chartered	Private Laws
Stafford & Springfield	1869	VI, 608
Watertown & Waterbury	1869	VI, 647
Whitestone	1869	VI, 735
Waterbury & Cheshire	1870	VI, 842
Connecticut Central	1871	VII, 46
Hartford & Farmington	1871	1871, 249
Hazardville & Thompsonville	1871	VII, 18
New York, New Haven & Hartford	1871	VII, 252
Norwich & Colchester	1871	1871, 60
Brooklyn & Killingly	1872	1872, 143
Lyme & Colchester	1872	1872, 117
Middletown, Meriden & Cheshire	1872	1872, 71
New York & New England	1873	VII, 466
Putnam & Stafford	1873	1873, 184
Shepaug	1873	VII, 463
East Haven	1874	VII, 789
Boston & New York Air Line	1875	VII, 885
Providence, Ponagansett & Springfield	1875	VII, 953
Colchester	1876	VIII, 34
Hartford & Connecticut Valley	1879	VIII, 348
Hartford & Connecticut Western	1881	IX, 169
Providence, Danielsonville & Willimantic	1883	IX, 840
Shepaug, Litchfield & Northern	1887	X, 478
Mystic Valley	1889	X, 1294
Westerly & Jewett City	1893	XI, 870
Branford Steam	1903	XIV, 16
Damascus	1905	XIV, 1081
Westchester Northern	1911	XVI, 647

Connecticut also chartered several railroad companies that maintained offices in the state but whose railroads were located in Illinois and Mexico.

Chicago & St. Louis (Illinois, with an office in New Haven)	1859	V, 249
Mexican International (Mexico, with an office in New Haven)	1882	IX, 668
Chiapax (Mexico, with an office in Hartford)	1887	X, 438
Peninsular of Lower California (Mexico, with office in Hartford)	1887	X, 435
Mexican Eastern (Mexico, with office in Hartford)	1893	XI, 186

Connecticut Horse Railroad Charters, 1859–1889

Horse Railroad Company	Chartered	Private Laws
Hartford & Wethersfield	1859	V, 306
Fair Haven & Westville	1860	V, 370
Norwalk	1862	V, 487
Hartford & West Hartford	1863	V, 306
Bridgeport	1864	V, 607
Norwich	1864	V, 575
Rocky Hill & Wethersfield	1864	V, 587
East Haven & Morris Point	1865	V, 763
New Haven & Centerville	1865	V, 701
New Haven & West Haven	1865	V, 741
East Hartford & Glastonbury	1866	VI, 85
State Street	1868	VI, 344
Hartford & Cedar Hill	1869	VI, 661
Meriden & Hanover	1869	VI, 580
Gregory's Point (Norwalk Harbor)	1870	VI, 904
Mystic	1870	VI, 917
Stamford	1870	VI, 886
Edgewood	1871	VII, 63
Middletown	1871	VII, 26
Whitney Avenue	1871	VII, 143
New Haven & Allingtown	1872	VII, 316
New Haven, Hamden & North Haven	1872	VII, 366
New London	1873	VII, 565
New Haven & Mount Carmel	1874	VII, 801
Birmingham & Ansonia	1876	VIII, 49
Meriden	1876	VIII, 29
Westport & Saugatuck	1876	VIII, 7
Waterbury	1884	IX, 941
Bridgeport & West Stratford	1885	X, 168
Danbury & Bethel	1885	X, 81
Derby	1885	X, 55
Bucks Hill	1889	X, 1041
Montville	1889	X, 1135

Connecticut Street Railway Charters, 1886–1925

Street Railway Company	Chartered	Private Laws
New Britain Tramway	1886	X, 233
Southington & Plantsville Tramway	1887	X, 655
Naugatuck & Waterbury Tramway	1889	X, 1281
New Haven & Morris Cove Rail Road	1889	X, 1040
Norwalk Tramway	1889	X, 1067
Winchester Avenue Rail Road	1889	X, 1024
Hartford & West Hartford	1893	XI, 1077
Bridgeport	1893	XI, 872
Bristol & Plainville Tramway	1893	XI, 730
Derby & New Haven Electric	1893	XI, 1159
Dixwell Avenue Electric	1893	XI, 1073
East Haven & Morris Cove	1893	XI, 902
Enfield & Longmeadow Electric	1893	XI, 838
Enfield & Somers Tramway	1893	XI, 890
Greenwich Tramway	1893	XI, 888
Groton Bank	1893	XI, 1032
Hartford	1893	XI, 1082
Hartford & Middletown Electric	1893	XI, 1025
Hartford, Manchester & Rockville Tramway	1893	XI, 968
Hartford Suburban	1893	XI, 766
Lake Saltonstall	1893	XI, 886
Lisbon, Griswold & Voluntown	1893	XI, 928
Mad River Rapid Transit	1893	XI, 772
Manufacturers' Street Railway of New Haven	1893	XI, 861
Moodus, Marlborough & Glastonbury	1893	XI, 859
Mystic	1893	XI, 781
New Haven & Centerville	1893	XI, 1027
New Haven & North Haven	1893	XI, 848
New Haven	1893	XI, 843
New Milford & Lake Waramaug	1893	XI, 733
Newington Tramway	1893	XI, 1035
People's Tramway	1893	XI, 1045
Portchester & Glenville Tramway	1893	XI, 786
Portland	1893	XI, 865
Putnam & Thompson	1893	XI, 746
Quinebaug Valley Traction	1893	XI, 1148
Rockville & Ellington	1893	XI, 997
Rockville, Stafford & Southbridge Tramway	1893	XI, 1079
Shelton	1893	XI, 830
South Manchester Light, Power & Tramway Co.	1893	XI, 752

(continued)

Connecticut Street Railway Charters, 1886–1925 (*Continued*)

Street Railway Company	Chartered	Private Laws
Stonington Borough	1893	XI, 788
West Shore	1893	XI, 1067
West Side	1893	XI, 778
Willimantic	1893	XI, 726
Windsor & Suffield Tramway	1893	XI, 783
Winsted	1893	XI, 1075
Woodbury & Southbury Electric	1893	XI, 720
Cheshire #1	1895	XII, 422
Milford	1895	XII, 387
Bloomfield, Tariffville & East Granby Tramway	1897	XII, 859
Branford Electric	1897	XII, 1012
Danbury & Golden's Bridge	1897	XII, 793
Danbury & Sherman	1897	XII, 808
Duluth-Superior Traction	1897	XII, 1003
East Windsor, Broad Brook & Rockville	1897	XII, 810
East Windsor Electric	1897	XII, 791
Hartford & Torrington Tramway	1897	XII, 879
Meriden, Southington & Compounce Tramway	1897	XII, 863
Mountain View	1897	XII, 902
New Haven & East River	1897	XII, 1015
Springfield & Southwestern	1897	XII, 826
Suffield & East Granby	1897	XII, 889
Torrington & Winchester	1897	XII, 676
Watertown & Litchfield Tramway	1897	XII, 1069
Woodbridge	1897	XII, 1194
Canaan & Berkshire Tramway	1899	XIII, 344
Columbia Traction	1899	XIII, 517
East Lyme	1899	XIII, 189
Somers & Enfield Electric	1899	XIII, 205
Cheshire #2	1901	XIII, 1181
Danielson & Norwich	1901	XIII, 800
East Windsor	1901	XIII, 711
Litchfield & Torrington Tramway	1901	XIII, 990
Middletown & Meriden Traction	1901	XIII, 927
Norwalk, Bridgeport & Bethel Traction	1901	XIII, 978
Rockville, Broad Brook & East Windsor	1901	XIII, 1119
Stafford Springs	1901	XIII, 916
Suffield	1901	XIII, 1093
Thomaston & Watertown Electric	1901	XIII, 741
Thompson Tramway	1901	XIII, 747
Willimantic & Southbridge	1901	XIII, 1126

Connecticut Street Railway Charters, 1886–1925 (*Continued*)

Street Railway Company	Chartered	Private Laws
Willimantic Traction	1901	XIII, 1099
Windsor Locks & Rainbow	1901	XIII, 1160
Groton & Stonington	1903	XIV, 151
Middletown & Middlefield Traction	1903	XIV, 412
Moodus & East Hampton Tramway	1903	XIV, 190
Naugatuck Valley Electric	1903	XIV, 26
Norwich, Mystic & Westerly	1903	XIV, 158
Pawcatuck	1903	XIV, 278
Plainville & Farmington Tramway	1903	XIV, 425
Voluntown & Jewett City	1903	XIV, 402
Wallingford Tramway	1903	XIV, 239
Woodbury & Seymour	1903	XIV, 187
Woodbury & Waterbury	1903	XIV, 315
Crystal Lake	1905	XIV, 246
Hartford & Middletown	1905	XIV, 997
Lebanon	1905	XIV, 1057
New Canaan	1905	XIV, 1049
Norwich, Jewett City & Voluntown	1905	XIV, 878
Shore Line Electric Railway	1905	XIV, 719
Thomaston Tramway	1905	XIV, 1077
Willimantic & Stafford	1905	XIV, 1096
Bridgeport & Danbury Electric	1907	XV, 184
Danbury & New Milford	1907	XV, 472
Danbury & Northern Electric	1907	XV, 325
Highland Street	1907	XV, 404
Meriden, Middletown & Guilford Electric	1907	XV, 412
Norwich, Colchester & Hartford Traction	1907	XV, 368
Orange	1907	XV, 486
Oxoboxo Valley	1907	XV, 415
Putnam & Rhode Island	1907	XV, 366
Thomaston & Plymouth Tramway	1907	XV, 397
Waterbury & Milldale Tramway	1907	XV, 180
Windsor Locks & Western	1907	XV, 340
Windsorville & East Hartford	1907	XV, 170
Attawaugan	1909	XV, 957
Berlin	1909	XV, 1099
Tolland County	1909	XV, 809
Tolland	1909	XV, 778
West Peak	1909	XV, 782
Moodus & East Hampton Electric	1911	XVI, 404

(*continued*)

Connecticut Street Railway Charters, 1886–1925 (*Continued*)

Street Railway Company	Chartered	Private Laws
Mount Carmel	1911	XVI, 630
New Britain, Kensington & Meriden	1911	XVI, 597
Norwalk & New Canaan	1911	XVI, 635
Willimantic & Stafford Traction	1911	XVI, 333
Stafford & Monson	1913	XVI, 825
Willimantic & Manchester	1915	XVII, 519
Meriden, New Britain & Hartford	1915	XVII, 339
Middletown & Chester	1915	XVII, 377
Torrington Traction	1915	XVII, 472
Danielson & Willimantic	1917	XVII, 1086
Lordship	1917	XVII, 1065
Stanley	1917	XVII, 1138
Waterbury & Bristol Tramway	1917	XVII, 926
Danbury & Bethel Traction	1919	XVIII, 305
East Lyme Traction	1921	XVIII, 446
Eastern Connecticut	1921	XVIII, 521
Groton & Stonington Traction	1921	XVIII, 522
Shore Line Traction	1921	XVIII, 1008
Woodbridge Railway	1921	XVIII, 682
New Haven & Shore Line	1923	XIX, 165
Norwich & Hallville	1923	XIX, 84
Silica Railway & Transportation Co.	1923	XIX, 324
Hartford & Springfield Transportation Co.	1925	XIX, 736

Maritime Charters: Steamboats, Canals, Ferries, and River and Harbor Improvements

Connecticut Steamboat Charters, 1818–1893

Steamboat Company	Chartered	Private Laws
Connecticut Steamboat	1818	I, 1110
Connecticut River Steamboat #1	1823	I, 1108
Bridgeport Steamboat #1	1824	I, 1106
Hartford Steamboat	1824	I, 1112
New Haven Steamboat	1824	I, 1115
Norwalk & New York Steamboat Assn	1824	I, 1119
Stamford Steamboat	1825	I, 1125
Steam Navigation (Middletown)	1825	I, 1126
Norwich Steamboat	1826	I, 1121
New London & Norwich Steamboat	1832	I, 1117
Ousatonic Steamboat (Derby-Bridgeport)	1835	I, 1123
Hartford & New York Steamboat	1854	IV, 1207
Bridgeport Steamboat #2	1866	VI, 3
New Haven Steam Transportation	1866	VI, 45
American Navigation (New Haven)	1869	VI, 695
Connecticut River Steamboat #2	1882	IX, 462
New London Steamboat	1882	IX, 506
People's Steamboat (Bridgeport)	1889	X, 811
South Eastern Steamship (New Haven)	1893	XI, 841

Connecticut Canal Charters, 1822–1829

Canal Company	Chartered	Private Laws
Farmington Canal (New Haven & Northampton)	1822	I, 300
Ousatonic Canal	1822	I, 311
Quinebaug Canal	1824	I, 311
Enfield Canal (Connecticut River Company)	1824	I, 73
Sharon Canal	1826	I, 318
Saugatuck & New Milford Canal	1829	I, 311

Connecticut Ferry Charters, 1857–1901

Ferry Company	Chartered	Private Laws
Middletown Ferry	1852	*
Union Ferry	1857	V, 132
Pleasure Beach Ferry	1893	XI, 499
East & West Shore Ferry & Transportation	1901	XIII, 815

* This company does not appear in the private laws, but can be found in the General Statutes of 1854, p. 547.

Connecticut River Improvement Charters, 1795–1873

River Company	Chartered	Private Laws
Ousatonic River Channel	1795	I, 517
Union	1800	I, 517
Norwich Channel	1805	I, 512
Proprietors of the Enfield Locks & Channels	1818	I, 507
Connecticut River	1824	I, 73
Eight Mile River	1827	I, 502
Proprietors of the Madison Channel	1828	I, 510
Naugatuck River	1833	I, 511
Norwalk River Protection	1854	III, 477
Mad River	1873	VII, 528

Connecticut Harbor Improvement Charters, 1801–1897

Harbor Company	Chartered	Private Laws
Union Wharf Company in New Haven	1801	I, 523
Contractors to Rebuild Union Wharf in New Haven	1810	I, 497
Fair Haven Wharf	1833	I, 504
Madison Union Wharf	1834	I, 506
East Wharf Company of Madison	1849	IV, 1378
Salt Island Wharf	1854	IV, 1385
Norwalk Harbor Improvement	1867	VI, 199
Firmill River Dock	1870	VI, 913
Sargent Wharf	1871	VII, 107
Bridgeport Dock & Building	1887	X, 654
Hammock Meadow Dike & Imp. Co. of Clinton	1893	XI, 382
Madison Wharf	1897	XII, 803

This appendix lists the nineteen railroad lines that operated in Connecticut according to the naming and numbering used by Karr in *The Rail Lines of Southern New England: A Handbook of Railroad History*. The list includes the rail corporations that operated each line during its history, and the names of charters that were issued in connection with each line, whether or not they resulted in actual construction. Charters and mileage include branch lines. Note that the final operator of each line, with the exception of the New London Northern (Central Vermont) was the New York, New Haven & Hartford Railroad.

Connecticut Railroads and Operators

Line	Miles	Railroad Name	Route in Connecticut	Opened	Operators	Dates	Associated Charters
1	52	New York & New Haven	Greenwich to New Haven	1849	New York & New Haven New York, New Haven & Hartford	1849–1872 1872–1968	New York & New Haven New Canaan Stamford & New Canaan
2	37	Danbury & Norwalk	Danbury to Norwalk	1852	Danbury & Norwalk Housatonic New York, New Haven & Hartford	1852–1886 1886–1892 1892–1968	Fairfield County Danbury & Norwalk
3	86	Housatonic	Bridgeport to state line in Canaan	1840–1842	Housatonic New York, New Haven & Hartford	1840–1892 1892–1968	Housatonic Housatonic Valley
4	32	Shepaug	Hawleyville to Litchfield	1872	Shepaug Valley Shepaug Shepaug, Litchfield & Northern New York, New Haven & Hartford	1872–1873 1873–1887 1887–1898 1898–1948	Shepaug Valley Shepaug Shepaug, Litchfield & Northern
5	61	Naugatuck	Devon to Winsted	1849	Naugatuck New York, New Haven & Hartford	1849–1887 1887–1968	Naugatuck Watertown & Waterbury
6	13	New Haven & Derby	New Haven to Derby Junction	1871	New Haven & Derby Housatonic New York, New Haven & Hartford	1871–1889 1889–1892 1892–1968	New Haven & Derby

7	67	New Haven & Northampton	New Haven to state line in Granby	1848–1855	New York & New Haven New Haven & Northampton New York, New Haven & Hartford	1848–1869 1869–1887 1887–1968	New Haven & Northampton Granby Farmington Valley
8	72	Hartford & New Haven	Hartford to New Haven	1838–1844	Hartford & New Haven New York, New Haven & Hartford	1838–1872 1872–1968	Hartford & New Haven Hartford & Springfield Branch Middletown New Britain & Middletown Windsor Locks & Suffield
9	31	Meriden, Waterbury & Connecticut River	Cromwell to Waterbury	1885–1888	Meriden & Cromwell Meriden, Waterbury & Connecticut River New York & New England New England New York, New Haven & Hartford	1885–1888 1888–1892 1892–1895 1895–1898 1898–1968	Meriden & Cromwell Meriden & Waterbury Meriden, Waterbury & Connecticut River Middletown, Meriden & Waterbury Waterbury
10	137	Hartford, Providence & Fishkill	State line in Plainfield to Danbury	1849–1855, 1881	Hartford, Providence & Fishkill New York & New England New England New York, New Haven & Hartford	1849–1878 1878–1895 1895–1898	Manchester Hartford & Providence New York & Hartford

(continued)

Connecticut Railroads and Operators (*Continued*)

Line	Miles	Railroad Name	Route in Connecticut	Opened	Operators	Dates	Associated Charters
					New York, New Haven & Hartford	1898–1968	Hartford, Providence & Fishkill Rockville South Manchester
11	55	Air Line	New Haven to Willimantic	1870–1873	New Haven, Middletown & Willimantic	1870–1875	New York & Boston
					Boston & New York Air Line	1875–1882	New Haven, Middletown & Willimantic
					New York, New Haven & Hartford	1882–1968	Colchester
							Boston & New York Air Line
12	49	Shore Line	New Haven to state line in Stonington	1852–1858	New Haven & New London	1852–1857	New Haven & New London
					New Haven, New London & Stonington	1857–1858	New London & Stonington
					New York, Providence & Boston	1858–1862	New Haven, New London & Stonington
					New Haven, New London & Stonington	1862–1864	Shore Line
					Shore Line	1864–1870	
					New York & New Haven	1870–1872	
					New York, New Haven & Hartford	1872–1968	
13	47	Connecticut Valley	Hartford to Saybrook	1871	Connecticut Valley	1871–1880	Hartford & Middlesex County

No.	Miles	Railroad	Route	Date built	Company	Dates	Name
					Hartford & Connecticut Valley	1880–1887	Connecticut Valley
					New York, New Haven & Hartford	1887–1968	Hartford & Connecticut Valley
14	60	New London Northern	New London to state line in Stafford	1849–1850	New London, Willimantic & Palmer	1849–1861	New London, Willimantic & Springfield
					New London Northern	1861–1871	New London, Willimantic & Palmer
					Vermont Central	1871–1873	New London Northern
					Central Vermont	1873–1895	
					New England Central	1895	
15	52	Norwich & Worcester	Norwich to state line in Thompson	1840	Norwich & Worcester	1840–1869	Boston, Norwich & New London
					Boston, Hartford & Erie	1869	Norwich & Worcester
					New York & New England	1869–1895	
					New England	1895–1898	
					New York, New Haven & Hartford	1898–1968	
16	35	Southbridge & Blackstone	State line in Thompson to Willimantic	1854, 1872	Boston & New York Central	1854–1855	East Thompson
					East Thompson	1857–1858	Willimantic & Thompson
					Boston, Hartford & Erie	1867–1875	Thompson & Willimantic
					New York & New England	1875–1895	Boston & New York Central

(continued)

Connecticut Railroads and Operators (Continued)

Line	Miles	Railroad Name	Route in Connecticut	Opened	Operators	Dates	Associated Charters
17	75	Connecticut Western	Hartford to state line in Canaan	1871	New England	1895–1898	Boston, Hartford & Erie
					New York, New Haven & Hartford	1898–1968	
					Connecticut Western	1871–1881	Connecticut Western
					Hartford & Connecticut Western	1881–1889	Hartford & Connecticut Western
					Central New England & Western	1889–1892	East Granby & Suffield
					Philadelphia, Reading & New England	1892–1898	
					Central New England	1898–1927	
					New York, New Haven & Hartford	1927–1968	
18	28	Connecticut Central	East Hartford to state line in Enfield	1876	Connecticut Central	1876–1880	Connecticut Central
					New York & New England	1880–1895	
					New England	1895–1898	
					New York, New Haven & Hartford	1898–1968	
19	19	New York, Providence & Boston	Stonington to Rhode Island line	1837	New York, Providence & Boston	1837–1892	New York & Stonington
					New York, New Haven & Hartford	1898–1968	New York, Providence & Boston

Introduction

1. Bell, "Connecticut's Historic Contexts," 101–19. The geomorphic regions used in this book, and on which the population statistics in the appendix are based, are those developed in 1990 by the Connecticut Historical Commission. The regions reflect a combination of bedrock geology and surface ecology, and are considered to correspond more closely to subsequent human activity than manmade divisions such as counties or planning regions, imposed on the landscape. See Connecticut Historical Commission, *Historic Preservation*, 63.

2. Bell, *Face of Connecticut*, 145–70.

3. Keegan, *Archaeology of Connecticut*, 2–6; Moeller, "Indian Lifeways," 257.

4. Oberg, *Uncas*, 25; Bragdon, *Native People*, 55–79.

5. Precontact population estimates for New England vary considerably. However, sources agree that the large majority of this population lived in the coastal regions of southern New England from the Merrimac basin to the Connecticut shore.

6. Bragdon, *Native People*, 25; Oberg, *Uncas*, 19. The spelling of Ninnimissinuwock is taken from Oberg.

7. Johnson, *Ninnuock*, 52–69.

8. Spiess, *Connecticut circa 1625*.

9. Johnson, *Ninnuock*, 52–70.

10. Bragdon, *Native People*, 92; Oberg, *Uncas*, 137.

11. Cronon, *Changes in the Land*, 85–86.

12. Ibid., 90.

13. Ibid.

14. Bradford, *Bradford's History*, 387.

15. Ibid., 388.

16. Gradie, *Connecticut Path*, 25; Salisbury, *Manitou and Providence*, 218.

17. Cronon, *Changes in the Land*, 162.

18. Ibid., 56.

19. Ibid., 56–57.

1. Colonial Connecticut

1. Daniels, *Connecticut Town*, 18.

2. Ibid., 10–34. Connecticut today contains 169 incorporated towns. The latest incorporation was the town of West Haven in 1921.

3. U.S. Department of Commerce, *Historical Statistics*, Z1–23.

4. For details on the governance of the Connecticut colony, see Daniels, *Connecticut Town*, 74–90, and Taylor, *Colonial Connecticut*, 20–48.

5. Daniels, *Connecticut Town,* 41. For a discussion of the economic and spiritual requirements of Puritan society that produced this pattern of town founding see Martin, *Profits in the Wilderness.*

6. Mitchell, *Roads and Road Making,* 7–8.

7. Ibid., 6–7; Gordon, "Travel," 171.

8. Garvan, *Architecture and Town Planning,* 67.

9. *Records of the Colony,* 14:80 (1773).

10. Mitchell, *Roads and Road Making,* 8–9.

11. Ibid., 20.

12. Ibid., 11.

13. Ibid., 10.

14. Friends of the Office of State Archaeology, member newsletter, spring 2009, 7–8.

15. *Records of the Colony,* 1:71 (1641), 1:174 (1648); *Records of New Haven,* 1:165.

16. Mitchell, *Roads and Road Making,* 17–18.

17. Whittlesey, *Crossing and Recrossing,* 42, 39.

18. *Records of the Colony,* 1:174 (1648), 1:281 (1656), 1:310 (1658) and 1:394 (1663); Whittlesey, *Crossing and Recrossing,* 47.

19. *Records of the Colony,* 4:155 (1695), 4:248 (1698); Mitchell, *Roads and Road Making,* 18–19.

20. Mitchell, *Roads and Road Making,* 14; *Records of New Haven,* 1:61; Gordon, "Travel," 1; *Records of the Colony* 1:164 (1648), 1:225 (1651), 1:417 (1663), 3:50 (1680), 4:80 (1692).

21. Clouette and Roth, *Connecticut Historic Highway Bridges,* 3.

22. Jaffe, *The King's Best Highway: The Lost History of the Boston Post Road, the Route That Made America* 12, 16–17; Jenkins, *Old Boston Post Road,* 1–2.

23. Jenkins, *Old Boston Post Road,* 3.

24. Robbins, "On the Boston Post Road," 22; *Records of the Colony,* 2:242–44 (1674).

25. Postal History Society of Connecticut, *Journal,* spring 1975, 16.

26. Jenkins, *Old Boston Post Road,* 7–8. The shoreline route was preferred since the Winthrop family, including the current governor of Connecticut, Fitz Winthrop, had moved from Hartford to New London. See Jaffe, *King's Best Highway,* 35.

27. Gradie, *Connecticut Path,* 28; Spencer, *Journey of Benjamin Wadsworth,* 16.

28. *Records of the Colony,* 4:246 (1698).

29. Knight, *Journal,* 26–29, 30–33.

30. Ibid., 61.

31. Daniels, *Connecticut Town,* chap. 6; Rosenbury, *Migrations from Connecticut Prior to 1800.*

32. Daniels, *Connecticut Town,* chap. 7.

33. Mitchell, *Roads and Road Making,* 20, 23–24.

34. Ibid., 20; Warren, "Clearing the Trail," 197.

35. "New London c. 1812," 1:364.

36. Prager, *Autobiography of John Fitch,* 28–29.

37. Mitchell, *Roads and Road Making,* 29; *Acts and Laws,* 1796, 198; *Records of the*

Colony, 12:236 (1764). Rates varied from ferry to ferry, and at each crossing depending on the load carried. See *Acts & Laws of the State of Connecticut in America,* 1791, 198.

38. *Acts & Laws of the State of Connecticut in America,* 1791, 413; 1794, 479–81; 1805, 692; *Public Statutes,* 1812:108.

39. Mitchell, *Roads and Road Making,* 15; Gordon, "Travel," 6; number of bridges from author's review of the *Colonial Records.*

40. Edwards, *Record of the History and Evolution of Early American Bridges,* 29–30.

41. *Records of the Colony,* 6:239 (1721), 6:364 (1722), 11:283 (1759).

42. *Records of the Colony,* 4:229 (1697), 7:156 (1728), 11:32 (1757).

43. *Records of the Colony,* 7:361 (1731), 7:500 (1734), 8:152 (1737), 8:405 (1741), 11:88 (1757), 8:125 (1737); 11:110 (1758).

44. Taylor, "Turnpike Era," 66; Saladino, "Economic Revolution," 406.

45. *Records of the Colony,* 11:570 (1761), 13:605 (1772).

46. Wood, *Turnpikes,* 273; Mitchell, *Roads and Road Making,* 21.

47. Robbins, "On the Boston Post Road," 28; *Records of the Colony,* 12:334 (1767).

48. Finlay, *Hugh Finlay Journal,* 34, 38.

49. *Records of the Colony,* 6:37 (1717).

50. Wood, *Turnpikes,* 278; Mitchell, *Roads and Road Making,* 26.

51. Earle, *Stage-Coach and Tavern Days,* 271; Jenkins, *Old Boston Post Road,* 22–42.

52. Jenkins, *Old Boston Post Road,* 23.

53. Saladino, "Economic Revolution," 45–46, 68.

54. National Park Service, *Washington–Rochambeau Revolutionary Route,* 12–14, 22.

55. Saladino, "Economic Revolution," 44–45.

56. Ibid., 401.

57. Smith and Clark, "Connecticut's Changing Landscape," 2:197–214.

58. Bradford, *Bradford's History,* 95.

59. Bell, *Face of Connecticut,* 9.

60. *Records of the State,* 5:viii.

2. Turnpikes and Stagecoaches

1. Albert, *Turnpike Road System,* 17–22.

2. Ibid., 93–100.

3. *Private Laws,* 1790:229; 1792:394, 531, and 536.

4. Parks, *Roads and Travel,* 21. For the pre-turnpike effort to keep the Mohegan Road in good repair through reservation lands see *Records of the Colony,* 1757:36; 1759:276; 1762:36.

5. Kirkorian and Zeranski, "Investigations of a Colonial New England Roadway," 4.

6. Wood, *Turnpikes,* 321.

7. *Private Laws,* 1795:287.

8. Wood, *Turnpikes,* 274.

9. See the list of turnpike corporation charters in appendix B.

10. The following discussion of the phases of turnpike construction is drawn from my analysis of turnpike charters. The number of Connecticut turnpikes increases to

121 when the state's two publicly operated roads, the Mohegan and Greenwich turnpikes, are included.

11. In the late 1790s, Middletown businessmen lost significant sums in land speculation schemes and were apparently in no position to take part in turnpike-building at an early date. See Saladino, "Economic Revolution," 285, 348.

12. Taylor, "Turnpike Era," 347.

13. Parks, *Roads and Travel*, 17.

14. Ibid., 18.

15. Ibid., 19.

16. Wood, *Turnpikes,* 13–14; Parks, *Roads and Travel,* 10; Warren, "Thoroughfares," 723–24.

17. *Private Laws,* 1789–1836: 241–44, 279–80, 249–50; toll bridge corporations listed in appendix B.

18. DeVito, *Connecticut's Old Timbered Crossings,* 4–5; Allen, "Covered Bridges in Connecticut," 16–18.

19. Shank, *Historic Bridges,* 8–12.

20. Ibid., 17; Town, "Ithiel Town's Bridge," 207–14.

21. Field, "Statistical Account," 179.

22. See the brief account of Carthage Bridge, 1819, and the illustration of it at the website Vintage Views, available at vintageviews.org; brief account is in the list entitled "Bridges at Lower Falls," at www.vintageviews.org/vv-r/river/bridges.html; illustration at www.vintageviews.org (last visited March 17, 2011).

23. Wright, *Crossing the Connecticut,* 10–12; Trumbull, *Memorial History,* vol. 1, 367–69.

24. *Private Laws,* 1796:198; *Public Statutes,* 1821:219, 1866:456. With construction of the first Hartford bridge in 1810, no provision was made in the bridge charter to halt the ferry that the town of East Hartford operated nearby. When the first bridge was destroyed, the company had its charter revised to require that the ferry be discontinued when the bridge was rebuilt. When the second bridge was completed in 1818, ferry service ceased, and for two decades all was well. In 1836, political pressure from East Hartford had the no-ferry provision of the charter repealed by the legislature, and the town reinstituted a ferry in competition with the toll bridge. In 1841, the bridge company regained the political upper hand and had the no-ferry provision reinstated. But after another reversal the following year, the bridge company sought relief in the courts, where their no-ferry charter was upheld, and the company was awarded a judgment of $12,000, the equivalent of six years of ferry revenue. East Hartford appealed, but the Connecticut Supreme Court of Errors affirmed the ruling in 1844. To pay the judgment, East Hartford then sold its shares of bridge company stock. *Hartford Bridge Company v. Town of East Hartford,* 16 Conn.149 (1844).

25. *Public Statutes,* 1821:219–27; 1847:30–31.

26. Wood, *Turnpikes,* 391; *Public Statutes,* 1821:219–27; 1854:547.

27. Hall, "Organizational Values," 70; appendix B; *Public Statutes,* 1839:107.

28. Garraty, *Quarrels,* 21–35.

29. *Middletown Bank v. Magill* (5 Conn. 28) 1823; Horton, *History of the Connecti-*

cut Supreme Court, 31. Morse, *Neglected Period,* 249, cites two earlier banking cases: *Southmayd & Hubbard v. Russ et al.* (3 Conn. 52) and *President, Directors & Company of the Middletown Bank v. Russ et al.* (3 Conn. 135) both decided in 1819.

30. *Perrin v. Sikes,* 1 Day's 19 (1802).

31. *Enfield Toll Bridge Company v. Connecticut River Company,* 7 Conn. 28 (1828), quotation from 51. Horton, *History of the Connecticut Supreme Court,* 36, notes that the decision questions the constitutionality of the legislature's action in granting the river company charter in the first place, and therefore "the precedential value of Enfield is a bit murky." However, the decision confirmed that in 1809 the legislature "on the petition of the [bridge] company, resolved that the building of the locks be suspended, and the company discharged from the obligation to build the same, until the further order of the General Assembly." The decision, therefore, rests on the fact that the repeal of the portion of the bridge company's charter dealing with the improvement of the river (made at the company's request in 1819, a decade before *Dartmouth College v. Woodward*) cleared the way for the river company charter in 1824, and the construction of the Enfield Canal.

32. Garraty, *Quarrels,* 71–85.

33. See the list of turnpike corporation charters in appendix B. Sources often claim, incorrectly, that the legislature gave turnpike companies (as well as canal and railroad corporations) the right of eminent domain in the acquisition of their property. The right of eminent domain resides in the legislative branch of the government as representatives of the people, and is a paramount right attached to every person's land; it cannot be delegated to a private corporation or public agency. The right of eminent domain, however, is limited in the constitution of Connecticut (and almost every state) by the requirement of just compensation, and even here, Connecticut at first used a legislative committee to assess damages, and a charter provision to require payment before work could begin. As time went on, charters became somewhat more lenient, with corporations allowed to deal directly with property owners, and only contested offers being referred to a county court or committee for adjudication. Therefore, nineteenth-century court actions regarding eminent domain focused not on whether a corporation had the right but on questions such as What is public use? What constitutes a taking? and What is just compensation? See Lewis, *Treatise.*

34. Ibid. Toll rates, as well as the number and location of gates on a turnpike, were set in each company charter. Typical tolls were 4 cents for a horse and rider, 12½ cents for a two-wheel chaise, and 25 cents for a four-wheel pleasure carriage. A toll of 1 cent was charged for each sheep, ox, or other animal passing a gate.

35. *Records of the State,* 11:357 (1802–3).

36. *Acts & Laws of the State of Connecticut in America,* 1803: 648; 1806: 717–20.

37. Turnpike charters after 1808 are shown in appendix B.

38. Compare, for example, the charters of the Bridgeport & Newtown, Waterbury River, Colchester & Norwich, and New London & Lyme turnpike companies (see appendix B).

39. Clouette and Roth, *Connecticut Historic Highway Bridges,* 4.

40. *Acts & Laws of the State of Connecticut in America,* 1760:302; 1771:365.

41. Cooper, "Building an Industrial District," 46; Grant, *Yankee Dreamers and Doers,* 170.

42. Cooper, "Building an Industrial District," 47.

43. Ibid. Osborn, *History of Connecticut,* 206.

44. Osborn, *History of Connecticut,* 207–8; Grant, *Yankee Dreamers and Doers,*244.

45. John, *Spreading the News.*

46. Holmes, *Stagecoach East,* 18.

47. Holmes, "Levi Pease," 241–45. The English pound was replaced by the u.s. dollar as the monetary standard of America in 1792, but it took years for the new system to take hold fully.

48. Ibid., 247, 256–58.

49. Ibid., 254.

50. Jenkins, *Old Boston Post Road,* 24.

51. DeWarville, *New Travels,* 121. Kirkorian and Zeranski, "Investigations of a Colonial New England Roadway," 3, note that a traveler named John Cutler more accurately described the height when he said: "The road ascends a precipice by different windings, which appears to me to be nearly 60 feet high and almost perpendicular."

52. Holmes, *Stagecoach East,* 47.

53. Badger and Porter, *Stage Register,* 1827.

54. Holmes, *Stagecoach East,* 67–68, 145.

55. Ibid., 162.

56. *Federalism Triumphant,* 1.

57. Ibid., 10.

58. Parks, *Roads and Travel,* 19.

59. Taylor, "Turnpike Era," 201.

60. Parks, *Roads and Travel,* 21.

61. Hartley, *History of Hamden,* 134; *Salem & Hamburg Turnpike v. Town of Lyme,* 18 Conn. 451 (1847).

62. *Public Statutes,* 1835:585–86.

63. *Public Statutes,* 1837:82–84; 1841:65; 1844:40; 1853:119–22; 1854:133; 1856:75–77; 1863:9.

64. Wood, *Turnpikes,* 317–20.

65. Basset, "Derby Turnpike," 108, 116.

66. Silliman, *Remarks,* 2, 35.

67. Holmes, *Stagecoach East,* 33–34.

3. Steamboats and Canals

1. Cooper, "Technology in Transition," 163–64.

2. Grant, *Dreamers and Doers,* 33–34, 74–76.

3. Ibid., app.

4. Cooper, "Technology in Transition," 150.

5. Cooper, "Building an Industrial District," 50.

6. See appendix A.

7. Ibid.

8. Morse, *Neglected Period,* 243.

9. DeLuca, "Against the Tide."

10. Ibid., 29 (n. 59).

11. Ibid., 2.

12. Ibid., 16.

13. Carter, *Samuel Morey,* 11.

14. Samuel Morey to William A. Duer, Esq., October 31, 1818, [photocopy], file of material on Samuel Morey, historical collections of the Orford Public Library, Orford, New Hampshire, quotation from 2. Several sources interpret Morey's reference to Greenwich as Greenwich, Connecticut, but given the low horsepower of Morey's boat and the swift tides at the north entrance to the East River, it is more likely that he is referring to a much shorter trip to Greenwich Street on the west side of Manhattan.

15. Sutcliffe, *Steam,* 62–64.

16. Ibid., 179–80.

17. Turnbull, *John Stevens,* 340.

18. *Hartford Courant,* August 17, 1813, 2; August 24, 1813, 4; September 7, 1813, 1; November 10, 1813, 1.

19. Jacobus, *Connecticut River Steamboat Story,* 34; Kirkland, *Men, Cities and Transportation,* 20–24.

20. Roberts, *Middlesex Canal,* 145

21. *Hartford Courant,* February 17, 1818; Jacobus, *Connecticut River Steamboat Story,* chap. 5.

22. *Private Laws,* 1789–1818:507–10.

23. Ibid., 1818:1111; *Enfield Bridge Company v. Connecticut River Company,* 7 Conn. 28 (1828).

24. *General Statutes,* 1822, 9; Kirkland, *Men, Cities and Transportation,* 20–24.

25. Foster, *Splendor,* 22; Morrison, *History of American Steam Navigation,* 339.

26. Garraty, *Quarrels,* 57–69.

27. Foster, *Splendor,* 22, 52.

28. *Private Laws,* 1789–1836:1106–28.

29. Buel and McNulty, *Connecticut Observed,* 105.

30. Dickens, *American Notes,* chap. 5.

31. *General Statutes,* 1839:586–88. The regulation of stationary steam engines took a more convoluted course in which Connecticut men played an important role. Following a deadly explosion at the Fales & Gray Car Company in Hartford in 1854 that killed twenty-one employees, a group of Connecticut businessmen from industries that relied on steam power, including Edward Reed, superintendent of the Hartford & New Haven Railroad, formed the Polytechnic Club to investigate the safe use of steam power. In 1866, Reed and executives of the insurance industry formed the Hartford Steam Boiler Inspection and Insurance Company, which offered a range of services to manufacturers of steam boilers, including supervision of boiler construction and installation and advice to policy holders on how to design their steam systems. In 1864, Connecticut passed its first law concerning the inspection of stationary steam engines. Thereafter, the governor appointed one inspector for each of

the state's congressional districts, with each engine in each district to be inspected once per year. Unsafe boilers could not be used until defects noted by the state inspector had been corrected. The law did not apply to engines in those towns that had their own inspection system, an indication that some towns had already taken on this issue. Soon inspections by the Hartford Steam Boiler Inspection and Insurance Company were accepted in Connecticut and elsewhere as fulfilling state law, with the company's expertise functioning as the steam industry's de facto standard until 1917, when it was superseded by the Boiler and Pressure Vessel Code of the American Society of Mechanical Engineers, founded in Hartford. This code is used to this day in the construction of steam and nuclear power plants. See Weaver and McNulty, *An Evolving Concern.*

32. *Oliver Ellsworth* ad, March 1826, *Victory* ad, June 1830, both in Stevens Collection, Connecticut River Museum, Essex, Connecticut; Jacobus, *Connecticut River Steamboat Story,* chap. 6.

33. Petroski, "Harnessing Steam," 121.

34. *United States Statutes At Large,* August 30, 1852, 61–75.

35. Shaw, *Canals,* 21–22.

36. Ibid., 23–24; U.S. Senate, "Roads and Canals," 724–41.

37. Shaw, *Canals,* 26; U.S. House of Representatives, "Veto of the Internal Improvement Bill," 1061.

38. Shaw, *Canals,* chap. 2.

39. Ibid., 228.

40. Harte, "Connecticut's Canals," 53–64.

41. Ibid., 10–11.

42. The influx of Irish canal workers into Connecticut in the 1820s brought a fair amount of cultural tension, though with little large-scale violence. Tension resulted from the low wages paid to immigrant workers, the crowded shanty camps in which they lived, and their Catholic religion. However, many Irish workers settled in Connecticut after the canal was completed, introducing this Protestant state to the cultural diversity that would overtake Connecticut by the end of the century. See Bender, "Uneasy Peace."

43. Harte, "Some Engineering Features," 21–49.

44. *Private Laws,* 1789–1836:300–306.

45. Harte, "Connecticut's Canals," 13–14.

46. Ibid., 8.

47. Erving, *Connecticut River Banking Company,* 21; Love, *Navigation,* 20.

48. Love, *Navigation,* 22–33.

49. *Private Laws,* 1789–1818:73–78.

50. Directors of the Association For Improving the Navigation of the Connecticut River Above Hartford, *Two Reports,* 16–17.

51. *United States Statutes,* chap. 46, April 30, 1824.

52. *Hartford Courant,* January 18, 1825; *Journal of the Proceedings of the Convention Holden at Windsor, Vermont,* February 1825; U.S. House, "Report of a Survey," 1826.

53. *Private Laws,* 1789–1818:78–82.

54. Erving, *Connecticut River Banking Company,* 101–26; Harte, "Connecticut's Canals," 49–50.

55. Erving, *Connecticut River Banking Company,* 139–49; Harte, "Connecticut's Canals," 50–52.

56. "Vermont Act of Incorporation," November 9, 1825, in Alfred Smith, comp., bound volume of 27 pamphlets, pamphlet 9, Connecticut River Company Papers, Connecticut Historical Society, Hartford.

57. U.S. House, "Surveys," 9–11.

58. Love, *Navigation,* 39.

59. Ibid., 47–48; *Journal of the Convention at Windsor, Vermont, September 1830.*

60. Stone, *Vermont,* 208.

61. Love, *Navigation,* 45. Because the river bottom was ever-changing, wooden planks were kept on board each steamer for the crew to use in prying a boat loose should it get stuck on a sandbar.

62. Lanati, *Brief Account,* 6–9. For additional revenue, the river company in the 1840s proposed the construction of an aqueduct to bring canal water to Hartford manufacturers at an estimated cost of $750,000. The project never materialized. See Anderson, *Report of the Committee,* 1847.

63. Harte, "Connecticut's Canals," 20–22.

64. Ibid., 23.

65. U.S. House, "Answer to the Remonstrance," 2; "Petition of the Farmington," 5. Alfred Smith, president of the Connecticut River Company, followed Hillhouse to Washington to object to federal funding for the canal company. This unending conflict between Hartford riverites and New Haven canalers likely contributed to the demise of the Farmington Canal legislation. See U.S. House, "Statement of the Connecticut River Company."

66. U.S. House, "Statement of the Connecticut River Company," 4; U.S. House, "Answer to the Remonstrance," 2.

67. Harte, "Connecticut's Canals," 27–30.

68. Trout, *Story of the Farmington Canal,* 11.

69. *Account of the Farmington Canal Company,* 11–13.

70. Harte, "Connecticut's Canals," 34. To encourage canal use, in 1835 directors offered one year of free tolls to the first steam-powered packet boat that operated at eight miles per hour or more "without injury to the banks of the Canal" (30). The inventor Benjamin Dutton, of Cheshire, built a screw-propelled steamboat that he and several friends rode for a short distance between West Cheshire and Milldale before the steamboat broke down. Dutton built a second boat, which was tested successfully on the Erie Canal, but he could not get financial backing for his canal steamboat. See Kingsbury, "Ericsson Propeller on the Farmington Canal."

71. *Account of the Farmington Canal Company,* 14–15. (On p. 13, the amount of capital paid in should read $266,112.39, not $216,112.39. This $50,000 typo brings the losses of the New Haven & Northampton Company to $288,114.92, not $238,114.92 as stated on p. 14, and the combined losses for all three Farmington Canal corporations to $1,327,156.54.)

4. The Railroad, Part I

1. Burpee, *History of Hartford County,* 527. Soon afterward, Kinsley began working with steamboat inventor John Stevens in Hoboken, New Jersey. See Turnbull, *John Stevens,* 151.

2. Sutcliffe, *Steam,* 224.

3. Erving, *Connecticut River Banking Company,* 134–40.

4. For an account of the Railhill Trials see McGowan, *Rail, Steam and Speed.*

5. Kirkland, *Men, Cities and Transportation,* 92–124.

6. Ibid., 223–27.

7. *Private Laws,* 1836–57:1019, 1030; Kirkland, *Men, Cities and Transportation,* 231.

8. Kirkland, *Men, Cities and Transportation,* 125–57; Warmsley, *Connecticut Post Offices,* 18.

9. Withington, *First Twenty Years,* 8–9, 11.

10. Turner and Jacobus, *Connecticut Railroads,* 22.

11. Withington, *First Twenty Years,* 6–7, 10; *Private Laws,* 1836–57:1212.

12. The names of the nineteen rail lines built in Connecticut, as given by Karr in *The Rail Lines of Southern New England,* are italicized the first time they are mentioned in the text.

13. Fischler, *Long Island Rail Road,* 14–17.

14. Farnham, *Quickest Route,* 4.

15. Connecticut General Assembly, *Report of the Joint Select Committee on Railroads*; Kirkland, *Men, Cities and Transportation,* chap. 8.

16. The charter of 1836 gave the Housatonic leeway in the construction of its road by authorizing three different routings between Brookfield and Long Island Sound. (*Private Laws,* 1837:1025.)

17. 15 Conn. 475 (1843) and 16 Conn. 367 (1844); Heckman, "Establishing the Basis for Local Financing," 241–47.

18. Kirkland, *Men, Cities and Transportation,* chap. 10.

19. Ibid., 284; Withington, *First Twenty Years,* 13.

20. Turner and Jacobus, *Connecticut Railroads,* 27–28.

21. Gordon, *Passage to Union,* 60–61; 15 Conn. 124 (1842); 19 Conn. 285 (1849).

22. Turner and Jacobus, *Connecticut Railroads,* 51.

23. *Private Laws,* 1837:992–96; *General Statutes,* 1854:751–52.

24. Mittlemann, "Dr. Russell's Account," 294–95.

25. Turner and Jacobus, *Connecticut Railroads,* 30.

26. *General Statutes,* 1854:758–62; General Railroad Commission of Connecticut, *1877 Annual Report,* 373.

27. Withington, "Strange Case of Robert Schuyler," 32–35.

28. Ibid., 42.

29. Klein, *Plank Road Fever,* 39, 41, 45, 47. Klein estimates one thousand plank road companies were chartered nationwide.

30. *Private Laws,* 1836–57:851–72. Wood, *Turnpikes,* 410, notes that a portion of the Woodbury & Seymour Plank Road may have been constructed, but evidence is inconclusive. Planking was also sometimes used on public roads where sandy soil or

road conditions made wagon travel difficult. Plank Hill Road in Simsbury (1869) was one such public road. See Woolacott, *Gavel and Book*.

31. Smith, *Map of New Haven County, 1856; Private Laws,* 1836–57:867.

32. *Hartford Courant,* March 12, 1853, 3.

33. Klein, *Plank Road Fever,* 42–43.

34. *General Statutes,* 1866:179.

35. Klein, *Plank Road Fever,* 44, 45, 63.

36. *Private Laws,* 1875:918.

37. General Railroad Commission of Connecticut, 1868.

38. Niven, *Connecticut for the Union,* 397–99.

39. Kirkland, *Men, Cities and Transportation,* 350–51.

40. Ibid., 350.

41. Ibid., 311.

42. General Railroad Commission of Connecticut, *Annual Report,* 1877, 4, 7; *Annual Report,* 1878, 4.

43. Connecticut Constitution of 1818, as amended, Article 25, October 1877. In 1886, towns with postwar railroad debt sought payment assistance from the state, but were refused. In 1903, however, the state began to help those towns with a grand list under $2 million pay their railroad debts, as long as the towns raised an equal amount in tax assessments. From 1905 to 1931 the biannual state budget included an appropriation of $10–14,000 for town railroad aid. (See *Hartford Courant,* February 3, 1886; *Public Statutes,* revision of 1918, 189, and revision of 1930, 173; and *Private Laws* [Special Acts], 1905–31.)

44. The transition began in 1847 with Squire Whipple's *Work on Bridge Building,* the first bridge manual published in America. Whipple introduced mathematical analysis into bridge design, which allowed engineers to calculate stresses on individual truss members and size them accordingly.

45. DeVito, *Connecticut's Old Timbered Crossings,* 39–56; Turner and Jacobus, *Connecticut Railroads,* 5.

46. General Railroad Commission of Connecticut, *Annual Report,* 1867, 10.

47. Turner and Jacobus, *Connecticut Railroads,*134–42.

48. Ellis, *Description of the Iron Bridge,* 12–15, 33.

49. Darnell, *Lenticular Bridges,* 19–27.

50. Connecticut State Historic Preservation Office, *Viaducts,* 7–14; General Railroad Commission of Connecticut, *Annual Report,* 1873, 30–41, *Annual Report,* 1874, 5.

51. General Railroad Commission of Connecticut, *Annual Report,*1889; *General Statutes,* 1883, chap. 107, and 1889, chap. 220.

52. Hubbard, *Crossings,* 20.

53. Ibid., 19.

54. Turner and Jacobus, *Connecticut Railroads,*14, 144.

55. Baker, *Formations of the New England Railroad Systems,* xxv–xxviii.

56. Ibid., 75–76.

57. Turner and Jacobus, *Connecticut Railroads,* 27, 60; 29 Conn. 538 (1861).

58. 29 Conn. 546 (1861).

59. General Railroad Commission of Connecticut, *Annual Report*, 1869, 8.

60. Kirkland, *Men, Cities and Transportation,* 74–75.

61. General Railroad Commission of Connecticut, *Annual Report*, 1877, 368–71.

62. Baker, *Formations of the New England Railroad Systems*, 82.

63. *General Statutes,* 1882, chap. 140.

64. Baker, *Formations of the New England Railroad Systems*, 82–88; Kirby, "On Some Abortive Connecticut Railroads," 82–84.

65. Kirkland, *Men, Cities and Transportation,* 89–90.

66. Ibid., 85–86.

67. Ibid., 78.

5. The Railroad, Part II

1. Temin, *Engines of Enterprise*, 153–63, 167.

2. See appendix A.

3. See appendix A.

4. Andersen, *From Yankee to American,* n.p. In its state constitution of 1818, Connecticut kept its colonial tradition of equal representation in both houses of the legislature. As cities grew in the nineteenth century, the unfairness of this principle became more egregious. The town of Union, with a population of four hundred persons in 1900, had the same representation in the legislature as New Haven, the state's largest city, with a population of more than one hundred thousand. To address this problem, a constitutional convention in 1902 adopted a plan to increase a town's representation in the lower house as its population grew, but voters rejected the proposal, and the inequity of urban representation continued as a fact of political life in Connecticut until the adoption of the state's second constitution in 1965.

5. Withington, "Marking Time in 1883," 120–33; Galison, *Einstein's Clocks,* 110–11.

6. Fassett, *UI*, 14–17; "CL&P History," at the website of Connecticut Light and Power: www.cl-p.com (last visited March 17, 2011).

7. Hughes, *American Genesis*, chap. 5.

8. Chandler, *Visible Hand*, 202–8.

9. General Railroad Commission of Connecticut, *Annual Report,* 1887, 1900. The managerial structure that allowed railroads to create large rail systems presented the courts with the problem of how to delegate responsibility within such corporations. At first, courts took the position that corporate responsibility ended with the hiring of competent personnel and the provision of the resources necessary for them to do their jobs, after which individual managers were considered legally responsible for their actions. In *Darrigan v. The New York & New England Railroad Company* in 1884 (52 Conn. 285), the Connecticut Supreme Court of Errors helped to change that view. An engineer was injured when two New York & New England trains collided as a result of an order issued by one of the road's dispatchers. The court held that the New York & New England was responsible for the injury, since "the whole power of the company as to the movement of these trains being delegated to the train-dispatcher, he was to be regarded as representing the company." The decision was a precedent

for the principle of superintendence, by which modern corporations are held responsible for the work-related actions of their employees.

10. Kirkland, *Men, Cities and Transportation*, 132.

11. Ibid., 137–41.

12. Dunbaugh, *Night Boat*, 293–95, 308–10; Dunbaugh, *New England,* 33–55; Kirkland, *Men, Cities and Transportation*, 22–23.

13. Foster and Weiglin, *Splendor*, 124, 133, 143, 148.

14. Ibid., 117, 136–39.

15. Kirkland, *Men, Cities and Transportation*, 143.

16. Ibid., 144.

17. Foster and Weiglin, *Splendor,* 10; Dunbaugh, *Night Boat,* 198–200.

18. Kirkland, *Men, Cities and Transportation*, 147–48.

19. *Public Statutes,* 1848:73.

20. Connecticut Valley Chapter of the National Railway Historical Society, "Transit to Wethersfield," 2.

21. Connecticut Valley Chapter of the National Railway Historical Society, "Street Railways of Connecticut," *Transportation Bulletin,* no. 62, 2.

22. Connecticut Valley Chapter of the National Railway Historical Society, "Transit to Wethersfield," 2.

23. Ibid., 24–25.

24. Ibid., 6, 53; Claflin, "Providence Cable Tramway," 41–53.

25. Hilton and Due, *Electric Interurban Railways,* 6–7, 75; Nye, *Electrifying America*, 88–89.

26. Stevens, *Derby Horse Railway*, 57.

27. Connecticut Valley Chapter of the National Railway Historical Society, "Street Railways of Connecticut," no. 62, 2; Hilton and Due, *Electric Interurban Railways,* 8.

28. Connecticut Valley Chapter of the National Railway Historical Society, "Street Railways of Connecticut," *Transportation Bulletin,* no. 45, 8.

29. *Trolley Trips,* 49. While most interurban lines in the United States ran on a separate right-of-way and charged fares on a zone system, only one interurban railway in Connecticut met those standards: the Shore Line Electric Railway, which operated between New Haven and Saybrook beginning in 1910. In 1913, the Shore Line Electric Railway expanded its operations by leasing the New London & East Lyme Street Railway, and acquiring additional lines in New London, Norwich, Willimantic, Putnam and North Grosvenordale, thereby establishing a street railway route from New York to Boston via either Worcester or Providence. Service on all lines ended in 1919, when financial damages caused by two head-on collisions brought the Shore Line into receivership. The company's original route from New Haven to Saybrook was revived by the New Haven & Shore Line Railway Company in 1923, and service continued for six years. See Cummings and Munger, "Shore Line Electric Railway Company"; Hilton and Due, *Electric Interurban Railways,* 322.

30. Buel and McNulty, *Connecticut Observed*, 172–73.

31. Turner and Jacobus, *Connecticut Railroads,* 171.

32. Ibid., 181–88.

33. Baker, *Formations of the New England Railroad Systems*, 88–93.

34. General Railroad Commission of Connecticut, *Annual Report*, 1887, insert, 7.

35. "Railroad Commissioners Report," *Hartford Courant*, January 17, 1889.

36. "A Big Railroad Fight," *New York Times*, May 3, 1889; "The Housatonic Road," *Hartford Courant*, May 9, 1889.

37. "A Long Session Ended," *New York Times*, June 21, 1889; *Private Laws*, 1893:32; 1889:1208. This amendment is cited in many sources as turning the New Haven into a holding company, when in fact it only allowed the New Haven railroad to exchange its stock for the stock of certain other Connecticut railroads. It was the charter amendment of 1905 (*Private Laws*, 1905:869) that allowed the New Haven to "hold, use, operate, exercise, enjoy, and dispose of" the stocks, bonds, and property of other railroads, "wherever organized," which is a more accurate definition of a holding company.

38. Kirkland, *Men, Cities and Transportation*, 98–101.

39. Ibid., 101.

40. Ibid., 103–8.

41. Carosso, *Morgans*, 25; *American National Biography*.

42. Carosso, *Morgans*, 355.

43. Turner and Jacobus, *Connecticut Railroads*, 212–15. Of all secondary sources on the relationship between Morgan and Mellen, only Carosso attributes the idea of a transportation monopoly to Mellen (*Morgans*, 607). Morgan's monopolistic view toward other syndicates of his making, and the fact that the Colonial Commercial Company was incorporated before Mellen's tenure but after Morgan's arrival on the board, makes it likely that the plan originated with Morgan.

44. Carosso, *Morgans*, 216.

45. Taylor, *Productive Monopoly*, 166–69.

46. Ibid., 166–68; *Private Laws*, 1901:812.

47. Taylor, *Productive Monopoly*, 169; Van Dusen, *Connecticut*, 325.

48. *Private Laws*, 1905:869; 1907:41.

49. *Remarks By Mellen*.

50. *American National Biography*; Urofsky, *Brandeis*, 181.

51. Staples and Mason, *Fall of a Railroad Empire*, 30–35.

52. Ibid., 59–62.

53. Ibid., 66–84.

54. Lowenthal, *Titanic Railroad*, 47, 78, 90, 115–19. The *Titanic* was owned by the White Star Line, a subsidiary of International Mercantile Marine, a Morgan-controlled syndicate looking to establish a monopoly in transatlantic shipping. Morgan had a private suite and promenade deck on the *Titanic*, and was scheduled to be aboard for the ship's maiden voyage, but cancelled at the last minute. The ship's sinking was a financial disaster for Morgan and the overextended International Mercantile Marine Company.

55. Taylor, *Productive Monopoly*, 205.

56. Urofsky, *Brandeis*, 283.

57. Carosso, *Morgans*, 641–43.

58. Staples and Mason, *Fall of a Railroad Empire,* 192; Turner and Jacobus, *Connecticut Railroads,* chap. 14.

59. Interstate Commerce Commission, *Financial Transactions*, 1, 28.

60. Ibid., 2, 39.

61. Urofsky, *Brandeis*, 286; Staples and Mason, *Fall of a Railroad Empire,* 188–91; *Private Laws,* 1915:38, 365–66.

62. Foster and Weiglin, *Splendor Sailed the Sound,* 312–13.

63. Staples and Mason, *Fall of a Railroad Empire,* 192, Van Dusen, *Connecticut*, 325.

64. Staples and Mason, *Fall of a Railroad Empire,* 186.

65. Ibid., 153.

66. Ibid., 194–95.

67. Brandeis, *Other People's Money,* 200.

68. Staples and Mason, *Fall of a Railroad Empire,* 198.

69. Ibid., 199.

70. Ibid. See also Ron Chernow, "Where Is Our Ferdinand Pecora?" *New York Times,* January 6, 2009. The Banking Act of 1933 (also called the Glass-Steagall Act) helped maintain financial stability in the national markets for more than a half-century. The regulations were dismantled with the Gramm-Leach-Bliley Act of 1999, which removed the legal barrier between commercial and investment banking installed in the 1930s. As a result, the assets controlled by the nation's twenty largest financial institutions increased from 35 percent to 70 percent in less than a decade. Also, the Commodity Futures Modernization Act of 2000 allowed these same institutions to trade in complicated instruments such as subprime mortgage derivatives without the oversight of the Securities and Exchange Commission, from which it excluded such transactions. Both these actions contributed to the recession of 2008, and the federal bailout that followed. (See Jeffrey Rosen, "Why Brandeis Matters," *New Republic,* July 22, 2010, 22.)

Conclusion

1. See appendix A.

2. Daniels, *Connecticut Town,* chap. 1; Bell, *Face of Connecticut,* 66–70.

3. Connecticut State Highway Department, *Report of a Survey,* 12.

4. Connecticut General Assembly, *Report of the Special Committee Appointed by the General Assembly in 1897 to Investigate the Subject of State Road Improvement.*

An Account of the Farmington Canal Company; of the Hampshire and Hampden Canal Company; and of the New Haven and Northampton Company Until the Suspension of Its Canals in 1847. New Haven: Thomas J. Stafford, 1850.

Acts & Laws of the State of Connecticut in America, 1786–1805.

Albert, William. *The Turnpike Road System in England, 1663–1840.* Cambridge: Cambridge University Press, 1972.

Allen, Richard. "Covered Bridges in Connecticut." *Antiquarian* 2.2 (November 1950): 11–19.

Andersen, Ruth. *From Yankee to American: Connecticut 1865 to 1914.* Chester, Conn.: Pequot Press, 1975.

Anderson, Joseph. *The Town and City of Waterbury Connecticut, From the Aboriginal Period to 1895.* Vol. 1. New Haven: Price & Lee Co., 1896.

Anderson, P. *Report of the Committee and Engineer on the subject of a Canal From Enfield Falls to Hartford.* January 12, 1847.

Badger and Porter. *Stage Register: A register for stages, steamboats and canal packets in New England and New York.* No. 13. Boston: James F. Howe, 1827.

Baker, George Pierce. *The Formations of the New England Railroad Systems: A Study of Railroad Combination in the Nineteenth Century.* Cambridge, Mass.: Harvard University Press, 1937.

Bassett, George. "The Derby Turnpike." In *New Haven Colony Historical Society Papers.* Vol. 10. New Haven: New Haven Colony Historical Society, 1951, 102–8.

Bell, Michael. "Connecticut's Historic Contexts: The Hand on the Land." In *Historic Preservation: A Cultural Resource Management Plan for Connecticut.* Hartford: Connecticut Historical Commission, 1990, 101–19.

——. *The Face of Connecticut: People, Geology, and the Land.* Hartford: State Geological and Natural History Survey of Connecticut, 1985.

Bender, Daniel E. "An Uneasy Peace: Irish Labor on the Farmington Canal." *Connecticut History* 35.2 (fall 1994): 235–62.

Bradford, William. *Bradford's History "Of Plimouth Plantation."* Boston: Wright & Potter, 1898.

Bragdon, Kathleen J. *Native People of Southern New England, 1500–1650.* Norman: University of Oklahoma Press, 1996.

Brandeis, Louis D. *Other People's Money and How Bankers Use It.* New York: Stokes, 1914.

Buel, Richard, Jr., and J. Bard McNulty, eds. *Connecticut Observed: Three Centuries of Visitors' Impressions, 1676–1940.* Hartford: Acorn Club, 1999.

Burpee, Charles W. *History of Hartford County, Connecticut, 1633–1928.* Vol. 1. Chicago: S. J. Clarke, 1928.

Carosso, Vincent P. *The Morgans: Private International Bankers 1854–1913.*
Cambridge, Mass.: Harvard University Press, 1987.

Carter, George Calvin. *Samuel Morey: The Edison of His Day.* Concord, N.H.:
Rumford Press, 1945.

Chandler, Alfred D., Jr. *The Visible Hand: The Managerial Revolution in American
Business.* Cambridge, Mass.: Harvard University Press, 1977.

Claflin, Albert W. "The Providence Cable Tramway." *Rhode Island History* 4 (1945).

Clouette, Bruce, and Matthew Roth. *Connecticut Historic Highway Bridges.*
Newington, Conn.: Connecticut Department of Transportation, 1991.

Connecticut General Assembly. *A General Index to the Private Laws and Special Acts
of the State of Connecticut.* Special Act 541. 1943.

——. *Report of the Joint Select Committee on Railroads.* May 1837.

——. *Report of the Special Committee Appointed by the General Assembly in 1897 to
Investigate the Subject of State Road Improvement, 1899.*

Connecticut Historical Commission. *Historic Preservation: A Cultural Resource
Management Plan for Connecticut.* Hartford: Connecticut Historical Commission,
1990.

Connecticut State Highway Department. *Report of a Survey of Transportation on the
State Highway System of Connecticut.* Washington, D.C.: Government Printing
Office, 1926.

Connecticut State Historic Preservation Office. *Viaducts, Bridges and Ghost Trains.*
Hartford: Connecticut State Historic Preservation Office, 2004.

Connecticut State Planning Board. *Study of Transportation in Connecticut
(Preliminary Report).* Pt. 3. *Legal Digest.* Hartford: Connecticut State Planning
Board, 1935.

Connecticut Valley Chapter of the National Railway Historical Society. "Transit to
Wethersfield: The First One Hundred Years." *Transportation Bulletin* 77
(September 1969–August 1970).

——. "The Street Railways of Connecticut." *Transportation Bulletin,* vols. 44–45, 47,
52–53, 57, 60, 62 (November 1957–April 1960).

Cooper, Carolyn C. "Building an Industrial District: Carriage Manufacture in New
Haven." In *Carriages and Clocks, Corsets and Locks,* edited by Preston Maynard and
Marjorie B. Noyes, 45–72. Lebanon, N.H.: University Press of New England, 2004.

——. "Technology in Transition: Connecticut Industries 1800–1832." In *Voices of the
New Republic: Connecticut Towns 1800–1832.* Vol. 2. New Haven: Connecticut
Academy of Arts and Sciences, 2003, 149–70.

Cronon, William. *Changes in the Land: Indians, Colonists, and the Ecology of New
England.* New York: Hill & Wang, 1983.

Cummings, O. R., and Charles F. Munger, Jr. "The Shore Line Electric Railway
Company." *Transportation Bulletin* 13 (October 1960).

Daniels, Bruce C. *The Connecticut Town: Growth and Development 1635–1790.*
Middletown, Conn.: Wesleyan University Press, 1979.

Darnell, Victor. "Lenticular Bridges from East Berlin, Connecticut." *Journal of the
Society for Industrial Archeology* 5.1 (1979): 19–27.

DeLuca, Richard. "Against the Tide: The Unfortunate Life of Steamboat Inventor John Fitch." *Connecticut History* 44.1 (spring 2005): 1–31.

DeVito, Michael C. *Connecticut's Old Timbered Crossings.* Warehouse Point, Conn.: DeVito Enterprises, 1964.

DeWarville, J. P. Brissot. *New Travels in the United States of America 1788.* Cambridge, Mass.: Harvard University Press, 1964.

Dickens, Charles. *American Notes; and Pictures from Italy.* Oxford: Oxford University Press, 1987.

Directors of the Association For Improving the Navigation of the Connecticut River Above Hartford. *Two Reports.* Hartford: P. B. Goodsell, 1825.

Dunbaugh, Edwin. *New England Steamship Company: Long Island Sound Night Boats in the Twentieth Century.* Gainesville: University Press of Florida, 2005.

———. *Night Boat to New England: 1815–1900.* Westport, Conn.: Greenwood Press, 1992.

Earle, Alice Morse. *Stage-Coach and Tavern Days.* New York: Macmillan, 1900.

Edwards, L. N. *A Record of the History and Evolution of Early American Bridges.* Orono, Me.: University of Maine Press, 1959.

Ellis, Theo. *Description of the Iron Bridge Over the Connecticut River on the Hartford & New Haven R.R.* Hartford: Brown & Gross, 1866.

Erving, Henry. *The Connecticut River Banking Company: 1825–1925.* Hartford: Connecticut River Banking Company, 1925.

Farnham, Elmer. *The Quickest Route: History of the Norwich and Worcester Railroad.* Chester, Conn.: Pequot Press, 1973.

Fassett, John D. *UI: History of an Electric Company.* N.p., 1991.

Federalism Triumphant . . . or the Turnpike Road to a Fortune: A Comic Opera or Political Farce in Six Acts, 1802.

Field, David D. "A Statistical Account of the County of Middlesex in Connecticut." In *Voices of the New Republic, Connecticut Towns 1800–1832.* Vol. 1. New Haven: Connecticut Academy of Arts and Sciences, 2003.

Finlay, Hugh. *The Hugh Finlay Journal: Colonial Postal History 1773–1774.* New York: Brooklyn Mercantile Library Association, 1867.

Fischler, Stan. *Long Island Rail Road.* St. Paul, Minn.: MBI, 2007.

Foster, George H., and Peter C. Weiglin. *Splendor Sailed the Sound.* San Mateo, Ca: Potentials Group, 1989.

Friends of the Office of State Archaeology. "Corduroy Roads." *Member Newsletter,* spring 2009.

Galison, Peter. *Einstein's Clocks, Poincaré's Maps: Empires of Time.* New York: Norton, 2003.

Garraty, John A., ed. *Quarrels That Have Shaped the Constitution.* Rev. and expanded. New York: Harper and Row, 1987.

Garraty, John A., and Mark C. Carnes, eds. *American National Biography.* New York: Oxford University Press, 1999.

Garvan, Anthony N. B. *Architecture and Town Planning in Colonial Connecticut.* New Haven: Yale University Press, 1951.

General Railroad Commission of Connecticut. *Annual Reports,* 1854–1910.

General Statutes of the State of Connecticut.

Gordon, Robert B. "Travel on Connecticut's Roads, Bridges, and Ferries, 1790–1830." In *Voices of the New Republic: Connecticut Towns 1800–1832.* Vol. 2. New Haven: Connecticut Academy of Arts and Sciences, 2003, 171–82.

Gordon, Sarah H. *Passage to Union: How the Railroads Transformed American Life, 1829–1929.* Chicago: Ivan R. Dee, 1996.

Gradie, Robert. *The Connecticut Path: A Preliminary Report on Its Route and History.* Hartford: Connecticut Historical Commission, 1998.

Grant, Ellsworth. *Yankee Dreamers and Doers.* Chester, Conn.: Pequot Press, 1974.

Hall, Peter Dobkin. "Organizational Values and the Origins of the Corporation in Connecticut 1760–1860." *Connecticut History* 29 (fall 1988): 63–90.

Harte, Charles Rufus. *Connecticut's Canals.* Annual Report of the Connecticut Society of Civil Engineers. Hartford: Connecticut Society of Civil Engineers, 1938.

——. *Some Engineering Features of the Old Northampton Canal.* Annual Report of the Connecticut Society of Civil Engineers. Hartford: Connecticut Society of Civil Engineers, 1933.

Hartley, Rachael M. *The History of Hamden.* New Haven: Quinnipiac Press, 1943.

Heckman, Charles A. "Establishing the Basis for Local Financing of American Railroad Construction in the Nineteenth Century: From *City of Bridgeport v. The Housatonic Railroad Company* to *Gelpoke v. City of Dubuque.*" *American Journal of Legal History* 32.3 (July 1988):236–64.

Hilton, George W., and John F. Due. *The Electric Interurban Railways in America.* Stanford, Calif.: Stanford University Press, 1960.

Holmes, Oliver W. "Levi Pease, the Father of New England Stage-Coaching," *Journal of Economic and Business History* 3 (February 1931): 241–263.

——. *Stagecoach East: Stagecoach Days in the East from the Colonial Period to the Civil War.* Washington, D.C.: Smithsonian Institution Press, 1983.

——. "Stagecoach Travel and Some Aspects of the Staging Business in New England, 1800–1850." *Proceedings of the Massachusetts Historical Society* 85 (1973): 36–57.

Horton, Wesley W. *The History of the Connecticut Supreme Court.* [Eagan, Minn.]: Thompson/West, 2008.

Hubbard, Ian. *Crossings: Three Centuries from Ferryboats to the New Baldwin Bridge.* Lyme, Conn.: Greenwich, 1993.

Hughes, Thomas P. *American Genesis: A Century of Invention and Technological Enthusiasm, 1870–1970.* New York: Viking, 1989.

Interstate Commerce Commission. *The Financial Transactions of the New York, New Haven & Hartford Railroad Company.* Hartford, July 11, 1914.

Jacobus, Melancthon W. *The Connecticut River Steamboat Story.* Hartford: Connecticut Historical Society, 1956.

Jaffe, Eric. *The King's Best Highway: The Lost History of the Boston Post Road.* New York: Scribner, 2010.

Jenkins, Stephen. *The Old Boston Post Road.* New York: Putnam, 1913.

John, Richard R. *Spreading the News: The American Postal System from Franklin to Morse.* Cambridge, Mass.: Harvard University Press, 1995.

Johnson, Stephen F. *Ninnuock (The People): The Algonkian People of New England.* Marlborough, Mass.: Bliss, 1995.

Journal of the Convention at Windsor, Vermont. 1830.

Journal of the Proceedings of the Convention Holden at Windsor, Vermont. February 1825.

Karr, Ronald Dale. *The Rail Lines of Southern New England: A Handbook of Railroad History.* Pepperell, Mass.: Branch Line Press, 1995.

Keegan, Kristen and William, eds. *The Archaeology of Connecticut.* Storrs, Conn.: Bibliopola Press, 1999.

Kingsbury, Frederick J. "An Ericsson Propeller on the Farmington Canal." *Connecticut Magazine* 7 (December 1902): 329–33.

Kirby, Richard S. "Notes on Some Abortive Connecticut Railroads." *Proceedings of the Connecticut Society of Civil Engineers,* 10. Hartford: Connecticut Society of Civil Engineers, 1935.

Kirkland, Edward Chase. *Men, Cities and Transportation: A Study in New England History 1820–1900.* Cambridge, Mass.: Harvard University Press, 1948.

Kirkorian, Cecelia, and Joseph Zeranski. "Investigations of a Colonial New England Roadway." *Northeast Historical Archaeology* 10 (1981): 1–10.

Klein, Daniel B., and John Majewski. "Plank Road Fever in Antebellum America: New York State Origins." *New York History* 75.1 (1994): 39–65.

Knight, Sarah Kemble. *The Journal of Madam Knight.* New York: Peter Smith, 1935.

Lanati, Edward E. *A Brief Account of the Windsor Locks Canal.* Windsor Locks, Conn.: Edward E. Lanati, 1976.

Lewis, John. *A Treatise on the Law of Eminent Domain in the United States.* Chicago: Callaghan & Co., 1888.

Love, W. DeLoss. *The Navigation of the Connecticut River.* Worcester, Mass.: Press of Charles Hamilton, 1903.

Lowenthal, Larry. *The Titanic Railroad: The Southern New England: The Story of New England's Last Great Railroad War.* Brimfield, Mass.: Marker Press, 1998.

Martin, John Frederick. *Profits in the Wilderness: Entrepreneurship and the Founding of New England Towns in the Seventeenth Century.* Williamsburg, Va.: Institute of Early American History and Culture, 1991.

McGowan, Christopher. *Rail, Steam and Speed: The Rocket and the Birth of Steam Locomotion.* New York: Columbia University Press, 2004.

Mitchell, Isabel S. *Roads and Road Making in Colonial Connecticut.* New Haven: Yale University for the Tercentenary Commission of the State of Connecticut, 1933.

Mittelmann, Michael. "Dr. Gurdon Wadsworth Russell's Account of the 1853 Railroad Accident at Norwalk, Connecticut." *Connecticut Medicine,* May 2000, 291–97.

Moeller, Roger W. "Ten Thousand Years of Indian Lifeways in Connecticut." In *Connecticut History and Culture.* Hartford: Connecticut Historical Commission, 1985.

Morrison, John H. *History of American Steam Navigation.* New York: Stephen Daye Press, 1958.

Morse, Jarvis Means. *A Neglected Period of Connecticut's History, 1818–1850.* New York: Octagon Books, 1978.

"New London c. 1812." In *Voices of the New Republic: Connecticut Towns 1800–1832.* Vol. 1. New Haven: Connecticut Academy of Arts and Sciences, 2003: 361–65.

Niven, John. *Connecticut for the Union: The Role of the State in the Civil War.* New Haven: Yale University Press, 1965.

Nye, David E. *Electrifying America: Social Meanings of a New Technology.* Cambridge, Mass.: MIT Press, 1990.

Oberg, Michael Leroy. *Uncas: First of the Mohegans.* Ithaca: Cornell University Press, 2003.

Osborn, Norris Galpin. *A History of Connecticut in Monographic Form.* New York: States History, 1925.

Parks, Roger N. *Roads and Travel in New England, 1790–1840.* Sturbridge, Mass.: Old Sturbridge Village, 1967.

Petroski, Henry. "Harnessing Steam." In *Remaking the World: Adventures in Engineering.* New York: Knopf, 1997: 117–25.

Prager, Frank D., ed. *The Autobiography of John Fitch.* Philadelphia: American Philosophical Society, 1976.

Private Laws of the State of Connecticut.

Public Statutes of the State of Connecticut.

Records of the Colony and Plantation of New Haven. 2 vols.

Records of the Colony of Connecticut. 1636–1776. 15 vols.

Records of the State of Connecticut. 1776–1818. 19 vols.

Remarks by Mellen to Stockholders at Annual Meeting, October 25, 1911.

Robbins, Peggy. "On the Boston Post Road." *American History Illustrated* 13.2 (May 1978): 20–31.

Roberts, Christopher. *The Middlesex Canal: 1793–1860.* Cambridge, Mass.: Harvard University Press, 1938.

Rosenberry, Lois. *Migrations from Connecticut Prior to 1800.* New Haven: Yale University for the Tercentenary Commission of the State of Connecticut, 1934.

Saladino, Gaspare John. "The Economic Revolution in Late Eighteenth Century Connecticut." Ph.D. diss., University of Wisconsin, 1964.

Salisbury, Neal. *Manitou and Providence: Indians, Europeans, and the Making of New England, 1500–1643.* New York: Oxford University Press, 1982.

Scharchburg, Richard P. *Carriages without Horses: J. Frank Duryea and the Birth of the American Automobile Industry.* Warrensdale, Pa.: Society of Automotive Engineers, 1993.

Shank, William H. *Historic Bridges of Pennsylvania.* Rev. ed. York, Pa.: American Canal and Transportation Center, 1980.

Shaw, Ronald E. *Canals for a Nation: The Canal Era in the United States: 1790–1860.*Lexington: University Press of Kentucky, 1990.

Silliman, Benjamin. *Remarks Made on a Short Tour between Hartford and Quebec in the Autumn of 1819.* 2nd ed. New Haven: S. Converse, 1824.

Smith, Harvey, and Tim Clark. "Wild Animals in Connecticut's Changing Landscape." In *Voices of the New Republic: Connecticut Towns 1800–1832.* Vol. 2. New Haven: Connecticut Academy of Arts and Sciences, 2003, 197–214.

Spencer, Frank, Jr. *The Journey of Benjamin Wadsworth in 1694.* Sharon, Conn.: Sharon Historical Society, 1988.

Spiess, Mathias. *Connecticut circa 1625: Its Indian Trails, Villages and Sachemdoms.* Connecticut Chapter of the Colonial Dames of America, 1934.

Staples, Henry Lee, and Alpheus Thomas Mason. *The Fall of a Railroad Empire: Brandeis and the New Haven Merger Battle.* Syracuse, N.Y.: Syracuse University Press, 1947.

Stevens, John R. *The Derby Horse Railway and the World's First Electric Freight Locomotive.* New Haven: New Haven Colony Historical Society, 1987.

Stone, Arthur F. *The Vermont of Today.* New York: Lewis Historical, 1929.

Sutcliffe, Andrea. *Steam: The Untold Story of America's First Great Invention.* New York: Palgrave Macmillan, 2004.

Taylor, Philip Elbert. "The Turnpike Era in New England." Ph.D. diss., Yale University, 1934.

Taylor, Robert J. *Colonial Connecticut: A History.* Millwood, N.Y.: KTO Press, 1979.

Taylor, William Leonard. *A Productive Monopoly: The Effect of Railroad Control on New England Coastal Steamship Lines, 1870–1916.* Providence: Brown University Press, 1970.

Temin, Peter, ed. *Engines of Enterprise: An Economic History of New England.* Cambridge, Mass.: Harvard University Press, 2000.

Town, Ithiel. "Ithiel Town's Bridge." *Essays in Arts and Sciences,* March 1982, 207–14.

Trolley Trips through New England and the Hudson Valley. Hartford: Trolley Press, 1913.

Trout, Amy L. *The Story of the Farmington Canal.* New Haven: New Haven Colony Historical Society, 1995.

Trumbull, Hammond J. *The Memorial History of Hartford County, Connecticut, 1633–1884.* 2 vols. Boston: Edward L. Osgood, 1886.

Turnbull, Archibald Douglas. *John Stevens: An American Record.* New York: Century, 1928.

Turner, Gregg M., and Melancthon W. Jacobus. *Connecticut Railroads: An Illustrated History.* Hartford: Connecticut Historical Society, 1986.

u.s. Department of Commerce. Bureau of the Census. *Historical Statistics of the United States: Colonial Times to 1970.* Pt. 2. Washington, D.C.: Government Printing Office, 1975.

u.s. Department of the Interior. National Park Service. *Washington–Rochambeau Revolutionary Route, Resource Study and Environmental Assessment.* 2006.

u.s. House of Representatives. "Answer to the Remonstrance of the Agent of the Connecticut River Company." Report 221. 21st Congress, 1st Session, April 20, 1830.

——. "Petition of the Farmington, and Hampshire and Hampden, Canals." Report 221. 21st Congress, 1st Session, February 22, 1830.

——. "A Report of a Survey of the Connecticut River." Doc.154. 19th Congress, 1st Session, April 12, 1826.

——. "Statement of the Connecticut River Company, in relation to the petition of the Farmington and Hampshire and Hampden Canal Companies." Report 341. 21st Congress, 1st Session, April 2, 1830.

——. "Surveys, With a View to making Roads and Canals." Report 102. 19th Congress, 2nd Session, March 2, 1827.

——. "Veto of the Internal Improvement Bill." 14th Congress, 2nd Session, March 1817.

U.S. Senate. "Roads and Canals." Report 250. 10th Congress, 1st Session, April 6, 1808.

Urofsky, Melvin I. *Louis D. Brandeis: A Life.* New York: Pantheon Books, 2009.

Van Dusen, Albert E. *Connecticut: A Fully Illustrated History of the State from the Seventeenth Century to the Present.* New York: Random House, 1961.

Warmsley, Arthur J. *Connecticut Post Offices and Postmarks.* Hartford: Connecticut Printers, 1977.

Warren, H. A. "Clearing the Trail for Civilization." *Connecticut Magazine* 8.1 (1903): 193–200.

——. "Thoroughfares in Early Republic Controlled by Corporations." *Connecticut Magazine* 8.4 (1903): 721–29.

Weaver, Glenn, and J. Bard McNulty. *An Evolving Concern: Technology, Safety and the Hartford Steam Boiler Inspection and Insurance Company: 1866–1991.* Hartford: Hartford Steam Boiler and Insurance Company, 1991.

Weller, John L. *The New Haven Railroad: Its Rise and Fall.* New York: Hastings House, 1969.

Whittlesey, Charles Wilcoxon. *Crossing and Re-crossing the Connecticut River; A Description of the River from Its Mouth to Its Source, with a History of Its Ferries and Bridges.* New Haven: Tuttle, Morehouse & Taylor, 1938.

Withington, Sidney. *The First Twenty Years of Railroads in Connecticut.* Tercentenary Commission of the State of Connecticut, 1935.

——. "Marking Time in 1883." In *Sixty-Seventh Annual Report.* Connecticut Society of Civil Engineers, 1951, 120–33.

——. "The Strange Case of Robert Schuyler." *Bulletin of the Railway and Locomotive Historical Society,* October 1935. 32–46.

Wood, Frederic J. *The Turnpikes of New England: A New Edition of the 1919 Classic.* Pepperell, Mass.: Branch Line Press, 1997.

Woolacott, Evan, ed. *The Gavel and the Book: Simsbury Town Meetings 1670–1986.* Simsbury, Conn.: Simsbury Historical Society, 1987.

Wright, George E. *Crossing the Connecticut: An Account of the Various Public Crossings of the Connecticut River at Hartford since the Earliest Times.* Hartford: Smith-Linsley, 1908.

Connecticut, 42, 70, 187; New York to
  Boston, 42, 67–68, 77–78, 187–88
steamboats: above Hartford, 92, 107–
  114; accounts of travel by, 86, 91, 94,
  95; advent of, 85–89; charters, 92,
  94; design of, 95, 159–61; and Fulton-
  Livingston monopoly, 90–94; after
  Gibbons v. Ogden, 94–99; on Long
  Island Sound, 90–93, 94–95, 158–61,
  170; New York to Boston, 158–62;
  regulation of, 93, 97–99, 229n31;
  relationship with railroads, 125–26,
  146–47, 158–62
Stevens, John, 88, 89, 90
Sullivan, John Langdon, 91–92, 104, 108

Talcott Mountain Turnpike, 55, 72
technological revolution: American System of Manufactures, 81, 152; and
  mass distribution, 121, 154; and mass
  production, 80–81, 84, 152, 174, 188;
  system building, 150, 154, 156–57, 171
technology: electricity, 156, 165, 189;
  gasoline engine, 189, 191; steam
  power, 78, 83, 85, 95, 121, 164, 189;
  telephone, 156; telegraph, 125, 152,
  155; water power, 80, 82, 83

Titanic, 181, 236n54
toll roads. *See* turnpikes
Town, Ithiel, 56–57, 58
transportation policy, federal, 49, 99–
  100, 109; Gallatin Report, 100; General Survey Act, 109
transportation policy, state, 52, 102, 104,
  187, 190
travel accounts. *See individual modes*
travel time, 77–78, 187–88
trolleys. *See* electric street railways
turnpikes: accounts of travel by, 50, 76–
  77; chartering of, 52–53; Connecticut's first, 50–52; construction of, 53–
  55; decline of, 71–74; English influence on, 49; impact of, 76–78, 187;
  regulation of, 62–64, 74–76, 227n33

United States, 93, 94
U.S. Patent Board, 88, 94

Vermont, 113
Victory, 97

Walcott, Jonathan, 58
Whitney, Eli, 80, 81, 152
Winthrop, Governor John, 14, 27, 28

Garnet Books

Early Connecticut Silver, 1700–1840
by Peter Bohan and Philip Hammerslough
Introduction and Notes by Erin Eisenbarth

The Connecticut River:
A Photographic Journey through the
Heart of New England
by Al Braden

Connecticut's Fife & Drum Tradition
by James Clark

The Old Leather Man:
Historical Accounts of a Connecticut and
New York Legend
by Daniel DeLuca

Post Roads & Iron Horses:
Transportation in Connecticut from
Colonial Times to the Age of Steam
by Richard DeLuca

Dr. Mel's Connecticut Climate Book
by Dr. Mel Goldstein

Westover School:
Giving Girls a Place of Their Own
by Laurie Lisle

Crowbar Governor:
The Life and Times of Morgan Gardner Bulkeley
by Kevin Murphy

Water for Hartford:
The Story of the Hartford Water Works and
the Metropolitan District Commission
by Kevin Murphy

Henry Austin:
In Every Variety of Architectural Style
by James F. O'Gorman

Making Freedom:
The Extraordinary Life of Venture Smith
by Chandler B. Saint and George Krimsky

Welcome to Wesleyan:
Campus Buildings
by Leslie Starr

Gervase Wheeler:
A British Architect in America
by Renée Tribert and James F. O'Gorman

Connecticut in the American Civil War:
Slavery, Sacrifice, and Survival
by Matthew Warshauer

Stories in Stone:
How Geology Influenced Connecticut History
and Culture
by Jelle Zeilinga de Boer

About the Author

Richard DeLuca is a writer and historian who
early in his career worked as a transportation
planner in Connecticut. His articles have
appeared in the journals *Connecticut History* and
California History, and he is the author of *We,
the People: Bay Area Activism in the 1960s.* DeLuca
is a member of the Association for the Study of
Connecticut History and is on the editorial board
of *Connecticut History.* He lives in Cheshire, Connecticut.

About the Driftless Connecticut Series

The Driftless Connecticut Series is a publication award program established in 2010 to recognize excellent books with a Connecticut focus or written by a Connecticut author. To be eligible, the book must have a Connecticut topic or setting or an author must have been born in Connecticut or have been a legal resident of Connecticut for at least three years.

The Driftless Connecticut Series is funded by the Beatrice Fox Auerbach Foundation Fund at the Hartford Foundation for Public Giving. For more information and a complete list of books in the Driftless Connecticut Series, please visit us online at http://www.wesleyan.edu/wespress/driftless.